Routledge Revivals

Education and Enmity

First published in 1973 Professor Akenson's book traces the series of religious and political controversies which have battered the state schools of Northern Ireland. After the government's admirably intentioned, but muddled, attempt to create a non-sectarian school system in the early 1920s, the educational system was progressively manipulated by sectarianism. The way in which the author describes how children are schooled reveals a great deal about the attitudes and values of the parental generation and also helps to explain the actions of later generations.

T0299991

Education and Enmity

The Control of Schooling in Northern Ireland
1920-50

Donald Harman Akenson

Routledge
Taylor & Francis Group

First published in 1973
by David and Charles Ltd

This edition first published in 2012 by Routledge
2 Park Square, Milton Park, Abingdon, Oxon, OX14 4RN

Simultaneously published in the USA and Canada
by Routledge
711 Third Avenue, New York, NY 10017

Routledge is an imprint of the Taylor & Francis Group, an informa business

A Library of Congress record exists under ISBN: 0715360434

ISBN 13: 978-0-415-51947-2 (hbk)
ISBN 13: 978-0-203-12264-8 (ebk)
ISBN 13: 978-0-415-51990-8 (pbk)

Education and Enmity

The Control of Schooling in Northern Ireland
1920-50

DONALD HARMAN AKENSON

A publication of the Institute of Irish Studies
The Queen's University, Belfast

DAVID & CHARLES : NEWTON ABBOT
BARNES & NOBLE BOOKS : NEW YORK
(a division of Harper & Row Publishers, Inc.)

This edition first published in 1973
in Great Britain by
David & Charles (Holdings) Limited
Newton Abbot Devon
in the U.S.A. by
Harper & Row Publishers Inc
Barnes & Noble Import Division

0 7153 6043 4 (*Great Britain*)
06 490135 1 (*United States*)

Printed in Great Britain by
W J Holman Limited Dawlish

To
J. U. M.

Contents

I

Introduction

This is not a book about Northern Ireland's recent street battles. It is about an extremely complex, fascinating, and bewildering culture, one which has a historical richness and an integrity that long antedate the flood of 'analytic' periodical articles and instant-history books about the region's troubles. Unhappily, almost no serious attention has been devoted to Northern Ireland by historians, although there have been significant works by social scientists and members of the bar.

The way in which people school their children is culturally diagnostic and one can learn a great deal about Northern Ireland's social and political configurations by studying the history of the region's educational system. Furthermore, the way in which children are schooled not only reveals a great deal about the attitudes and values of the parental generation, but helps to explain the later actions of the children's generation. Although this study deals primarily with the provision and manipulation of Northern Ireland's educational system by successive groups of adults, the last chapter speculates, tentatively, about the effects of the system upon successive waves of school children. I am aware only too acutely that this book will have to be rewritten—by another author—in thirty to fifty years when the government of Northern Ireland finally allows access to its education files for the first half of this century. It is, then, only a beginning.

I have drawn a line at the year 1950 for the sections of this book which treat education in Northern Ireland from a historical viewpoint. The date is a convenient one and seems to me to mark approximately the point where one crosses the line from matters of past history to questions of present policy. In the last chapter I have ventured to discuss live policy issues. I hope this will not be taken as arrogance but as an honest concern with educational problems which are difficult, but not insoluble. Probably, however, I shall be double-damned, by some of my fellow historians for dealing with the present and by some Ulstermen for meddling in their affairs.

The reader may be surprised to find that scant attention is paid to educational events in the south of Ireland after 1920, but interesting as those events may be in their own right, they had almost no impact on northern developments. The relevant comparisons are with events in England, for these comparisons are causal; the Ulster Unionist government has consistently modelled its social policy on English precedents.

Also, in explaining the reason why Northern Ireland's school system assumed its singular outlines, I have given considerably more attention to the actions of Protestants than to those of Roman Catholics. The reason for this is simple: the Protestants have been the dominant group in Northern Ireland and therefore have had a much greater influence on governmental procedures.

The vocabulary used in this study should not be taken as indicative of any particular religious or political viewpoint. 'Catholic' and 'Roman Catholic' are used as synonyms, without intending to derogate the Protestant Churches' claim to be part of the universal Catholic Church. Also, the Protestant Churches are often referred to as if they were a single group; this is for the sake of convenience and not a denial of the significance of the theological differences which distinguish the various Protestant groups. Further, the words 'church', 'denomination', and 'faith' are not used in their precise sociological sense but as synonyms. In referring to clergy I have shortened their ecclesiastical titles; no disrespect is intended.

When referring to events after 1920, 'Ulster' and 'Northern Ireland' mean the same thing; I am fully aware that the historical province of Ulster is not coterminous with the region presently under the control of the government of Northern Ireland. No judgement is implied in these pages on whether or not the government of Northern Ireland has a moral right to exist. The empirical fact that it has existed and continues to exist is all that matters for the purposes of this book. I have used 'the south' and 'Southern Ireland' as identical in meaning to the official titles which the twenty-six-county government has assumed since 1922.

The librarians and staffs of the following institutions were especially helpful: Armagh Public Library; Belfast City Library; Belfast Town Clerk's Office; Douglas Library, Queen's University, Kingston, Ontario; Durham County Record Office; Linen Hall Library, Belfast; National Library of Ireland; Presbyterian Historical Society of Ireland; Public Record Office of Northern Ireland; the library of the Queen's University of Belfast; Sterling Memorial Library, Yale University; the library of Trinity College, Dublin.

Special appreciation is due to Lady Mairi Bury for granting access to the Londonderry papers in her possession at Mount Stewart, Newtownards.

I gratefully acknowledge the assistance of Professors J. C. Beckett, E. Estyn Evans, E. R. R. Green, J. V. Kelleher, and J. V. Rice; of Drs H. G. Calwell, George I. Dent, R. J. Lawrence, David W. Miller, and T. O'Raifeartaigh; and of Messrs J. J. Campbell, Alistair Cooke, A. A. Dickson, John Gamble, T. J. McElligott, Sean McMenamin, Nicholas Wheeler Robinson, and James Scott. For clerical and editorial help I thank Mary E. R. Akenson.

*　　*　　*

The educational structure which Northern Ireland inherited from the United Kingdom can be simply described. First, and most important, the overwhelming majority of Irish schools were under denominational control even though they were financed chiefly by the state. The primary school system (the so-called 'national school system') was in theory non-denominational, but in practice control of all but a few schools was vested in the parish clergy. Among the academic secondary schools (usually termed 'intermediate schools') the Catholic institutions were entirely under clerical control, the Protestant foundations usually being governed by a mixed board of clergy and laymen. There was also a scattering of schools conducted by laymen for private profit. In neither the primary nor the academic secondary network was there provision for local civic support of the schools through the rates, or any statutory provision for the participation of the local citizenry in controlling the schools. Only the technical schools, institutions operating under an act of 1899, were under lay control and in receipt of regular financial support from local taxation as well as from the central exchequer.

Secondly, the government of Northern Ireland inherited an educational machine which had serious mechanical difficulties. In fact, it is possible to argue that Ulster did not succeed to *a* mechanism of education but to three separate, self-enclosed systems: national education, intermediate education, and technical education. Like a great, untracked locomotive, each of these educational engines went its own way with little effort at overall guidance and coordination being made by the central government.

Of the specific flaws in the national school mechanism— that is in the primary schools—a particular vexing one was the predominance of small schools. The leading professional educators were disturbed that early in the twentieth century more than sixty per cent of the primary schools were single-teacher schools having fewer than fifty pupils in average daily attendance.[1] The one-teacher schools were usually ill-equipped and the hard-pressed teacher had to deal with children of six or seven ages simultaneously. In 1904 the commissioners of national education, at the behest of their chief civil servant, William Starkie, began a campaign to amalgamate small schools, but here they ran foul of the Catholic bishops and clergy. Catholic canon law delegated the moral supervision of each child to his parish priest and this supervision, the church leaders believed, could be most efficiently conducted if the children of a given parish were educated in a primary school under the direct control of the priest of their parish. Hence, amalgamation of several parish schools was undesirable because it would blur the lines of pastoral responsibility. Further, pastoral considerations aside, control of the local parish school implied certain secular prerogatives and patronage rights and it was a rare parish priest who was willing to give up the unfettered exercise of those powers. In addition, some clerics opposed the amalgamation of boys' and girls' schools on the grounds that the mixing of young boys and girls in the same school was morally dangerous. In the test of wills between the educationists and the Catholic authorities, the religious forces prevailed.[2] Whereas in 1904, on the eve of the amalgamation campaign, the average number in daily attendance in each Irish national school was fifty-six, the corresponding figure for 1919 had risen only to sixty-one.[3]

A slightly more tractable problem was the low proportion of children who attended school regularly. In the decade before the new states were established the average attendance in Irish primary schools was approximately seventy per cent of the number of children on the rolls, instead of the eighty-five to ninety per cent which it was reasonable to expect. At the heart of the problem was the Irish compulsory attendance act of 1892 which applied only to urban areas—a fatal flaw in an agrarian country. Moreover, the most important municipal corporations (eg, Dublin, Cork, Limerick and Waterford) refused to cooperate in enforcing the act, partly because the Catholic hierarchy was opposed to compulsory attendance as an infringement of parental rights, and partly because the government steadfastly refused to give financial aid to the Christian Brothers' schools.[4]

The most difficult problem concerning chiefly (but not solely) the primary schools was the lack of local involvement by the citizenry in educational affairs. From its earliest years the national system had effectively excluded parents and the majority of the local citizens from a voice in the management of the schools. Further, the citizenry were not required to aid the schools through the local rates; indeed, they could not have done so legally even if they had so desired. This was an especially thorny problem as related to Ulster because the cross-perceptions of four groups were involved: the educational professionals, the English Liberals, the Ulster Protestants, and the Roman Catholic authorities. The educational professionals, by and large, were convinced that the existing arrangements (or lack thereof) deprived the child of parental involvement in his schooling which could have been educationally beneficial. The English Liberal Party, a group especially important in any Irish matter, saw the problem through a lens originally shaped to suit the English situation, namely the principle that public educational institutions should be controlled by local civic authorities and underwritten in considerable measure by local rates. The third group, the leaders of Ulster Protestantism, were deeply concerned about the lack of local involvement in the control and financing of primary education. Crucially for the future of Northern Ireland, the fourth group, the authorities of the Roman Catholic Church, failed to perceive that the problem was significant. They viewed the educational system as a moral rather than as a strictly educational responsibility, and believed that the system of clerical control over each primary school was a moral necessity. In 1907 and in 1919-20 the Catholic authorities were able to block four separate bills which would have introduced a strong element of lay control into education. Obviously the matter of control was an explosive one which would have to be dealt with immediately by the new Ulster government.[5]

Turning to the intermediate educational system—that is, to the academic secondary schools—one finds that they too were often too small for efficiency: in 1904 no less than 110 of the 275 intermediate schools in operation had fewer than fifty pupils.[6] The overwhelming majority of the schools were conducted under religious auspices and the fractionalism of the Irish religious situation made merging schools difficult. A much more serious aberration in the intermediate education mechanism was the method through which the government distributed grants to each school according to the performance of that school's pupils on annual written examinations. From an administrative viewpoint this mercenary mechanism was simple enough, but it had the great disadvantage of turning many schools into mere cramming establishments. Departures from the set syllabus were discouraged because such intellectual excursions cost the school managers money, through diminished examination scores, even though the departures may have been educationally beneficial to the children. During the first two decades of the twentieth century the commissioners of intermediate education softened some of the harsh edges of the examination system by introducing bonus and incremental grants which were paid according to school inspections. Nevertheless, the system taken over by the Northern Ireland government was rigid and examination-bound.[7]

The curricular rigidity of the intermediate schools was compounded by serious staffing difficulties. Although male clerical teachers and nuns (who comprised about one fifth of the teaching force) were usually well educated and competent, the lay staff were not. Less than twelve per cent of the male Catholic lay teachers and eight per cent of the Catholic lay women were university graduates. Parallel figures for Protestants were better—fifty-six per cent and thirty per cent respectively—but hardly impressive, especially in view of the propensity of Protestant graduates to use school teaching as an interim occupation before moving on to some more desirable profession.[8] The reasons why the intermediate schools were unable to attract suitable lay personnel were the low pay, the insecure tenure and, among Catholic schools, the near impossibility of anyone not in holy orders becoming principal of a school. Intermediate school teachers were little better than educational serfs and persons of ability and background generally avoided such posts.[9]

Of course, most of the creaking and grinding in the intermediate education apparatus could have been smoothed into silence if enough financial lubricant had been applied. Curricular rigidity, the proliferation of small schools and the unsatisfactory position of the teacher all could have been reduced if the commissioners of national education had possessed adequate resources. Unfortunately, a combination of rapid inflation and growing intermediate school enrolment during the first two decades of the twentieth century meant that the real income of the intermediate education commissioners was decreasing, not increasing. In their report for the year 1920 the commissioners reported that 'the whole edifice of secondary education in Ireland is toppling to destruction', and that 'if something is not done immediately to place Irish secondary education in the position of financial equality with that of Great Britain, it is impossible to see how the complete disruption of the system can be avoided'.[10]

In sharp contrast to the state of the intermediate schools the technical school system was in good order. The system, founded in 1899, differed from all Irish precedents in being controlled by laymen and in being non-denominational. The state authorities in charge of technical education encouraged local civic agencies in the planning and management of each technical school and in almost every case the school received some aid from local taxation. Not surprisingly the clerical authorities were suspicious of these secular institutions, but they could do little to impede their development: the department of agriculture and technical instruction had been created with strong Nationalist support and local civic leaders had heartily embraced the system. In any case, the technical schools were not a serious rival to either the national schools (because the technical schools took pupils after they had received their primary education) or to the intermediate schools (because the vocationally-oriented technical schools catered to a different clientele than did the academic intermediate schools).[11]

Whereas the intermediate schools were tied to a nation-wide examination system, the technical schools received grants on a capitation basis with each school's programme being framed to fit local needs. Whether or not the technical school system was a model to be copied or an embarrassingly successful experiment to be ignored was something the new Ulster government would have to decide.

Although several ad hoc attempts were made at coordinating the systems of national, intermediate and technical education, in most matters each organisation went its own way without reference to the other. Thus, there was a gap between the attainments of those who left the national schools at fourteen, the normal leaving age, and the standards demanded for those entering the technical schools. On the other hand, as far as the intermediate schools were concerned, those students who stayed on at the national schools until fourteen began their intermediate education at too late an age! In mid-1919, to eliminate these problems the government, with the support of the Ulster Unionists, introduced a bill to form a single ministry of education which would control and coordinate policy for all three types of schooling. In addition, the bill provided for the establishment of local education committees which would have the power to control technical education and to provide rate aid to national and intermediate as well as to the technical schools. Although careful provisions were made to protect the existing managerial rights of the clergy in the national and intermediate schools, the Catholic bishops and clergy strenuously opposed both the 1919 bill and its

B

successor of 1920. The measures were crushed.[12]

All of the flaws and idiosyncrasies of the Irish school systems should be kept in mind when evaluating the educational activities of the newly created government of Northern Ireland. The problems it faced in the field of education were great. But so, too, were the opportunities.

2

Life in a Northern Climate

Precisely how the government of Northern Ireland would attack its inherited educational problems depended upon the religious and social configurations of Ulster and upon the constitutional structure of the new state. Hence, at this point we must pan our camera in a full circle, taking in the chief features of Ulster life in the years 1920-50. Inevitably, all our shots will be tinged in some degree with religious matters, for religion is the bedrock reality upon which the political, social, and constitutional structure of Northern Ireland rests.

Turning first to politics, no one should be surprised to learn that in the years 1920-50 Ulster politics followed denominational lines. Protestants almost always voted Unionist and Catholics almost always voted Nationalist. The split was more than merely political; it involved two radically divergent constitutional positions. The Protestant, Unionist, position was that the one inviolable principle of government was that the union with Great Britain must be maintained. The Catholic, Nationalist, position was less clear, ranging from active hostility to the union to grudging, unenthusiastic acceptance of it as a constitutional reality that had to be lived with. Thus, a religious division became coextensive with a political division, which in turn became intermeshed with a clash in constitutional beliefs.

Ulster politics were static. The condition was a natural derivative of the interpenetration of politics and religion and of the fact that the religious composition of the Northern Ireland population had changed little since the Northern Ireland government was formed.[1] The Unionist Party was in power from the formation of the Ulster government and was never seriously challenged for control of the Stormont government. The question of the union crowded matters of ideology out of Ulster politics. The Unionist policy was stated succinctly by Sir James Craig: 'It is necessary to keep on repeating that Ulster is British and is as much an integral part of the United Kingdom as Yorkshire or Lancashire.'[2] Not only did constitutional questions override ideological considerations in Ulster politics but constitutional matters greatly overshadowed social class considerations. Protestant working men voted overwhelmingly for the Unionist Party and Catholic workers for the Nationalist. The frozen nature of Ulster politics is indicated by there having been only five prime ministers of Northern Ireland between 1922 and 1970.[3]

In contrast to the Unionist Party, for a long time after the establishment of the northern government the other major party, the Nationalist, did not act purposively or efficiently. Partly this was because of the widely held belief that the Ulster government would not survive long and that in any case involvement in the Ulster political system would violate Nationalist principles. In the election of 1921 six Nationalists were returned to the Northern Ireland parliament along with six Sinn Fein candidates. All twelve refused to take their seats. In 1925 ten Nationalists and two Sinn Fein nominees were elected and some of the Nationalists took their seats.

In the 1929 election eleven Nationalists and no Republicans were returned and from that point on the Nationalists, who had formed a rudimentary party organisation in 1928, dominated the anti-Unionist ranks, although one or two independent anti-Unionists were usually chosen at each election.[4]

The Nationalists as a political group were faced with two handicaps. First, they had no hope of obtaining control of the government. This meant that it was difficult to maintain party discipline, because a Nationalist MP had little to lose by stepping out of line. Secondly, the issue of whether or not the Nationalists should implicitly recognise the Northern Ireland government by taking seats in the Ulster parliament long divided the Nationalist cadre. An act of 1934 made abstentionism impossible, but in the preceding decade the question had devitalised the party. Even when Nationalist Party members took their seats they refused to become an official opposition, for in the politics of the British Isles, an official opposition is a loyal opposition.[5]

The structure of government to which these political differences relate was found in the government of Ireland act of 1920.[6] In theory this act provided for the establishment of home rule parliaments in both Northern and Southern Ireland, with powers roughly equal in each case to those allocated to the Irish parliament under the 1914 home rule act. The act also provided for the creation of a 'council of Ireland', an institution that was intended ostensibly to bring about the eventual unification of the country; at any future date the council could be transformed into a united Irish parliament through the passage of affirming acts by the parliaments of Northern and of Southern Ireland. Most of these provisions rang hollow; the United Kingdom government knew that the only provision which would be carried into effect was the creation of a parliament of Northern Ireland. The Nationalists in the south were beyond the stage when they would accept home rule, and in no case would they implicitly recognise the partition of their country by participating in a system whereby Northern Ireland obtained a separate parliament. The third of May 1921 was the date set for the establishment of both the northern and southern parliaments, but only the northern parliament was formed under the act, the southern representatives continuing to sit as members of the republican Dail Eireann.[7]

The basic principle underlying the Northern Ireland constitution was the principle of devolution.[8] Northern Ireland was not a sovereign state. The powers of the government of Northern Ireland were devolved upon it by a superior governmental unit, the parliament of the United Kingdom. This meant that the government of Northern Ireland had powers and responsibilities only in matters specifically defined and delegated by the Westminster government. The merits of devolution in the case of Ulster were two-fold. First, from the viewpoint of the British government, many routine matters relating to Northern Ireland were taken from the halls of Westminster, thus leaving the United Kingdom parliament more time for other topics. Secondly, from the Ulster viewpoint, matters of local importance received greater attention and more careful scrutiny in the northern parliament than they would have received in the imperial parliament. Potentially, the greatest disadvantage of the scheme of devolution is that the smaller a subsidiary governmental unit becomes, the greater the chance for its affairs to be dominated by a special interest group—a drawback which many would argue was operative in Northern Ireland.

The division of powers between the London and the Stormont governments was between matters of local concern and those of concern to regions other than Ulster. Reserved for the Westminster government were all decisions having to do with taxation, the Crown, foreign and commonwealth affairs, foreign trade, titles, the armed services, the postal service, radio, coinage and copyrights. The parliament of Northern Ireland was permitted to legislate on all other questions of local concern, with the limitation that these laws were not to have extra-territorial effects.

The formal governmental relations (other than financial relations) between Northern Ireland and the United Kingdom were three-fold. First, the Crown appointed the governor of Northern Ireland who represented the Crown at Stormont. The governor summoned, prorogued, and dissolved the Stormont parliament, and affixed the royal assent to bills passed by the legislature. The office was symbolic, not functional. Secondly, the northern prime minister dealt with the home secretary of the United Kingdom (under whose jurisdiction Northern Ireland fell) on matters needing administrative coordination. Thirdly, the United Kingdom parliament legislated on a large number of matters affecting the entire United Kingdom, including Ulster. Under the 1920 act Northern Ireland's interests in these matters were represented at Westminster by thirteen Ulster MPs (twelve after the abolition of university seats in 1949), elected under the same electoral rules which prevailed in Great Britain.

The Ulster parliament was modelled on the United Kingdom parliament, being bicameral. The government of Ireland act of 1920 provided that elections for the fifty-two seats in the Northern Ireland House of Commons were to be conducted on the basis of proportional representation, involving the single transferable vote. This was an attempt to protect the rights of minorities. The procedure was abolished by the Ulster government in 1929 on the grounds that the proportional representation system tended to create a multiplicity of parties. The abolition of proportional representation strengthened the position of the two main parties, the official Unionists and the Nationalists, and weakened that of all others.

The government of Ireland act of 1920 required that the upper house of parliament, the Senate, be elected indirectly. It consisted of twenty-four persons (plus the lords mayor of Belfast and Londonderry *ex officio*) who were elected by the members of the Northern Ireland House of Commons. The twenty-four elected members held office for eight years, half the group retiring every fourth year. The Senate had the power to delay legislation for two parliamentary sessions, but this right was more theoretical than real: the members of the upper house were chosen by the men who controlled the lower house and conflict between the two chambers was rare.[9]

The Ulster cabinet was a regional replica of the United Kingdom cabinet. The first Northern Ireland cabinet had six members. Four of these were department heads: education, finance, home affairs, and labour. In addition, one man served simultaneously as minister of agriculture and minister of commerce, and the prime minister served without departmental affiliation. The attorney general and parliamentary secretaries were not included in the Ulster cabinet. With the exception of the leader of the Senate (a post which for many years was held simultaneously with the ministryship of education), cabinet members were usually members of the Commons. When one notes that at minimum there were five members of the Commons in the cabinet, plus eight parliamentary secretaries (one for the 'department of the prime minister', one for each administrative department excepting finance which had three), plus the attorney general, all of whom received official salaries, it becomes clear that a considerable proportion of the membership of the House of Commons of Northern Ireland had financial ties with the government. In relation to the size of the Commons there was always a good deal of ministerial patronage at the disposal of the dominant political party.

Northern Ireland's local government scheme was similar to that of England. The government of Ireland act of 1920 made no innovations in the local government system, which rested on the local government (Ireland) act of 1898. There were in the mid-1930s, to take a representative point in time, six administrative counties, two county boroughs (Londonderry and Belfast), two boroughs, thirty urban districts, and thirty-two rural districts—seventy-two units of local government in all, each headed by an elected council. The important points about local governmental operations in all but the most recent past are first, that there was plural voting for the elected councils; secondly, universal suffrage was not granted in local elections, one had to be a rate payer; and thirdly, the constituency boundaries for local government elections were bent to maximise the power of the dominant political party.

Perhaps above all else Ulster has been a religious region. A responsible estimate made in the early 1960s suggested that at the time, a full decade after mid-century, church attendance in Northern Ireland was probably higher than in England at the beginning of the century.[10] Of course, involvement in religious affairs is a matter of social custom as well as genuine devotion, but that is beside the point; the key point is that inhabitants of Northern Ireland have expended a large portion of their energies on religious affairs and have defined their identities in terms of religious categories. Any analysis of the history of Northern Ireland in the present century which underestimates religious factors is possible only through a massive distortion of the available evidence.

The best place to begin a discussion of the religious situation in Northern Ireland is with the population data given on the following page: [11]

The revealing trends are in total population and in the Roman Catholic population. Despite the fact that Northern Ireland has the highest rate of natural population increase in the British Isles the population has grown little since 1926; and despite the fact that the Roman Catholics in Northern Ireland have the highest rate of natural increase of any religious denomination their percentage of the population has grown only slightly. Massive emigration obviously has taken place and this emigration has involved Catholics more than Protestants. The result has been that the population of Northern Ireland has been a very stable one in terms of religious composition and that demographic alterations have not impinged significantly upon political developments. The Roman Catholics have remained the largest single denomination but within a predominantly Protestant populace.

Northern Irish social life has consisted of two separate social

RELIGIOUS COMPOSITION OF NORTHERN IRELAND
1926–61

Year	Total population	Catholics	Catholic proportion of total population	Presbyterian	Church of Ireland	Methodist	Brethren	Baptist	Unitarian	Congregationalist	Others (or not stated)
1926	1,256,561	420,428	33.5	393,374	338,724	49,554	13,401	7,390	8,206	7,897	17,587
1937	1,279,745	428,290	33.5	390,931	345,474	55,135	16,881	9,376	7,908	6,756	18,994
1951	1,370,921	471,460	34.4	410,215	353,245	66,639	17,845	11,870	9,346	6,273	24,028
1961	1,425,042	497,547	34.9	413,113	344,800	71,865	16,847	13,765	9,822	5,606	51,677

systems, Protestant and Roman Catholic (each Protestant denomination has formed its own sub-system but for the sake of our discussion these are here ignored). In each case the churches have provided a social nexus where one meets friends without any danger of having to face those of another faith. Religion in its own right has been very important in Northern Irish life and regular attendance at Sunday services has characterised both faiths. Most local churches have sponsored a variety of social activities as well as religious services. The majority of clubs and societies in Northern Ireland, including those organised outside a specific church setting, have been predominantly denominational. The Ulster community has been, in an apt phrase, 'a dual community' in which almost every association has existed in duplicate.[12]

In many instances the separatist mentality on the part of both Protestant and Catholic communities has produced a pattern of 'ecological segregation'. One has only to sample the property advertisements during the 1920s, thirties, and forties in the Belfast *Newsletter* (a Protestant paper) or the *Irish News* (a Catholic paper) to realise that both groups have often been extremely sensitive about property transfer and would often offer to sell only to their co-religionists. In some rural areas only the 'right people' have been permitted to buy property. Both religious groups have employed their own auctioneers, men expected to know all the people over a wide area. In the case of the highest bid coming from the wrong party the auctioneer states that the minimum selling price has not been met and asks for bids by post.[13] Obviously such practices can not have been universal since a good deal of property has changed denominational hands; in such matters it is most accurate to speak of a system of inhibitions, not absolute prohibitions, upon property transfer between the two religious groups.

Segregation patterns have been much more precise in the towns than in the countryside. Thorough investigations of patterns in Belfast, Derry, and Lurgan have made it clear that 'natural areas' have existed within Ulster towns and cities, each given over almost exclusively to Protestants or Catholics. Parallel sets of shops, services, and recreational facilities have developed in each of these areas with the result that opportunities for personal friendships between persons of different groups have been minimised. This is not to say that residential segregation has been complete or that there have been no contacts across denominational lines; especially among the professional classes segregational patterns have often been transcended. But the majority of adherents to the Protestant and Catholic faiths have chosen to live amongst their co-religionists.[14]

Even when territorially integrated, Protestants and Catholics have shown remarkably different social attitudes and activities. It is not a cliché but an empirical fact of Ulster social life that Protestants have tended to have a sabbatarian streak and have usually avoided frivolous amusements on Sunday. Catholics, on the other hand, have usually used Sunday as a day for recreation once mass has been attended. Even sports have been differentiated. Rugby, cricket, and girls' field hockey have long been identified as predominantly Protestant games, while the various Gaelic games have been almost exclusively Catholic. Tennis and golf have been ecumenical sports, though they have been limited to the middle classes wherein religious mixing is most likely anyway.[15]

These differences in social style have been accentuated by economic differences. Studies for earlier periods and for the entire region are lacking, but Dr Emrys Jones's thorough study of the Belfast census data of 1951 demonstrated conclusively that Roman Catholics were more apt to be in the lower socio-economic levels than were Protestants.[16] Similar conclusions for Derry have been drawn from the census data of 1926 and 1937.[17] Definitive studies for rural areas are unavailable, but one complete sample of two rural communities produced the same conclusion as the Derry and Belfast data: Protestants have been over-represented in the middle and upper classes.[18]

Similarly, the Protestants have been more highly educated than the Catholics. In the late 1950s approximately three-quarters of the grammar school and university population of Northern Ireland was Protestant.[19]

One of the most important results of the Northern Ireland system of voluntary religious segregation, compounded by social, educational, and economic differences, is that Catholic–Protestant marriages have been rare. Indeed, one social scientist has concluded that 'intermarriage is so rare that they can be considered as two endogamous societies'.[20] Both communities disapprove strongly of marriages outside the faith, but in the Catholic case the views have been stated more explicitly and more offensively. During the nineteenth century the Irish custom in mixed marriages was that the boys would be brought up to follow their father's religion, the girls their mother's.[21] But during the latter half of the nineteenth century the hierarchy of the Irish Catholic Church became self-assertive, this at the very time the Papacy was becoming increasingly dominated by a siege mentality. The Vatican's condemnation of Anglican holy orders in 1896 was but a prelude to the notorious *Ne Temere* decree of August 1907, which became effective in April 1908. The decree placed the matrimonial legislation of the Catholic Church on a new basis. Previously in certain countries, notably Ireland, Holland, Belgium, and Germany, mixed marriages made outside the Catholic Church were officially recognised, even though seriously discountenanced. The *Ne Temere* decree was of universal application and required that to be valid under canon law all mixed marriages had to be celebrated by a Catholic priest. Further, the non-Catholic party was required to sign a contract which in Ireland contained four points: (1) that there would be no interference with the religious practices of the Catholic partner; (2) that the Catholic party would endeavour in every reasonable way to bring the non-Catholic to the faith; (3) that all children were to be baptised Catholics and educated in Catholic schools; and (4) that the couple

would not either before or after the Catholic marriage ceremony present themselves for a similar ceremony before the
minister of any other religion.[22]

Given that we are dealing with nearly endogamous communities, it is not surprising to discover that significantly
different marital and familial patterns predominate among
Catholics and Protestants. For example, the Protestant rate of
marriage has been considerably higher than the Catholic rate.
The figures below give the married percentage of men and
women of both denominations in Northern Ireland according
to the 1937 census:[23]

	Ages 20-25	*Ages 25-30*
Catholic men	8%	28%
Presbyterian men	10	35
Church of Ireland men	13	40
Catholic women	19	40
Presbyterian women	22	47
Church of Ireland women	29	53

The reason why Protestants have married younger and have
less often remained unmarried is partially attributable to the
economic distinctions between the faiths mentioned earlier:
a Protestant couple is apt to be better off financially and thus
able to afford marriage sooner.

There are important differences in the theology of marriage
of the two communions which reinforce the economic differences. The Catholic Church has held that the ordained end
of sexual relations is procreation and has remained unam-
biguously opposed to all but the 'natural methods' of family
limitation. This ethic has given rise among Catholics to the
popular belief that establishing a large family is a virtue, and
that something is wrong in a marriage with only one or two
offspring. Protestant inhibitions about family limitation and
the use of birth control devices had effectively disappeared by
1930 when the Lambeth conference of that year revised earlier
statements and approved the use of scientific methods to
prevent conception.[24]

Thus, the average Roman Catholic young person, earning less than his Protestant counterpart, has realised that within his community marriage implies the production of offspring and, soon, the expense of a large family. In contrast, a typical Protestant couple have been allowed to marry with the knowledge that it is theologically and socially permissible to postpone child-bearing for a time and that limiting the number in their family is equally acceptable. Thus we find that in 1937 the general fertility rate in Northern Ireland, expressed in terms of children under three years of age per 1,000 women between the ages of fifteen and forty-five, was 267 for Catholics, 230 for Anglicans, and 197 for Presbyterians.[25] The high fertility of the Roman Catholics has more than offset their tendencies to remain single or to contract late marriages.

Two errors should be avoided when discussing Northern Ireland's dual social system. First, one should not assume that relationships among Protestant denominations have always been simple and smooth. In particular there appears to have been a longstanding tension between liberal Protestants and fundamentalist Protestants. The Presbyterians, Anglicans, Methodists, and non-subscribing Presbyterians, who have tended to take a liberal interpretation of the scriptures, have often been at odds with the more fundamentalistic sects, such as the Brethren, Baptists, Reformed Presbyterians, and Pentecostals. Also, the Church of Ireland's insistence on the necessity of episcopal ordination of ministers has caused some ill-feeling with the other liberal groups.[26]

It is equally erroneous to assume that the Protestant and Catholic social systems are completely self-enclosed and totally dissimilar and that all relations between Catholics and Protestants are hostile or brittle. Despite the differences between Protestant and Catholic social practices, members of both groups are also members of a larger, regional social system. Whatever his convictions about the unity of Ireland, the northern Catholic has assumed regional characteristics which have differentiated him from his southern counterpart. Professor Eoin MacNeill's view was that the northern Catholic was 'hardly less grave, sedate, unresponsive, taciturn, laconic, keen at a bargain, tenacious of his own, critical towards others, than the typical Ulster Presbyterian'.[27]

Especially in the rural areas of Northern Ireland there have existed forces which have limited the friction between members of the two systems. In mixed rural areas the desire to maintain peaceful relations has been shown by the practice of never refusing to give help to a member of the opposite group when it is asked. It is possible to be rude or unhelpful to someone of one's own group, but not to one's opposite number. This form of social over-compensation has been reinforced by a mythology common to both sides stating that it is the leaders of the opponents' group (the Pope, the prime minister, etc) who are sending people astray and that most of the other side are basically good people. This mythology has allowed each group to continue to denounce vitriolically the other's religious system while asking and giving help to members of the other set. Further, one of the unstated rules of social life in small towns and in the Ulster countryside has been that hostility-provoking behaviour is avoided. Proselytising, potentially the most threatening of all activities, is not attempted. Also, to some extent the pervasive and clear-cut nature of Northern Ireland's dual social system has served as a protection against overt hostilities. The party badges worn by so many Ulstermen make it possible for even a stranger to avoid giving offence, for a quick glance at a lapel pin usually tells one instantly to what camp the man belongs.[28]

When two communities are as self-contained as the Protestants and the Catholics of Northern Ireland have been, it is almost inevitable that members of each will discriminate for their co-religionists and against their opposite number whenever possible. Obviously the side with the greater political and economic power will be the more effective in favouring its own against the others. In practice, religious discrimination in Northern Ireland in the years 1920-50 was chiefly a matter of Protestant discrimination against Roman Catholics because Protestants controlled most of the instruments of power. Emphatically, this does not mean that the Protestants were any more intolerant or self-seeking than the Catholics, only that they were more effective. This section will discuss first electoral discrimination; secondly, inequities in housing allocations; thirdly, discrimination in employment; and finally, the civil law as a minority grievance.

In discussing discrimination in electoral matters it is essential to distinguish between the three levels of government: United Kingdom, provincial, and local. Although there were minor inequities on the first two, these were not so great as to constitute a Catholic grievance.[29] Where gross discrimination in Ulster politics occurred was at the local level and there the Protestants made an all-out effort to maintain control, without much ethical consideration of the methods involved. The local government (Ireland) act of 1919 had prescribed a proportional representation system for all local government elections in Ireland and this practice initially was adopted in the Northern Ireland local elections. The Unionist Party, however, had consistently opposed the introduction and implementation of the proportional representation system and in 1922 proportional representation was abolished in local elections and a simple majority system introduced. This change in electoral methods was coupled with scandalous gerrymandering in marginal areas, with the result that in the city of Derry and in County Tyrone, Nationalist majorities were transformed into minorities.[30] (To these notorious cases one might add the Armagh, Omagh, and Dungannon town councils, the Fermanagh county council, and the Dungannon urban district council.) To give only two numerical examples of gerrymandering in marginal areas: before the revision of the electoral system Catholic representatives held twenty-six of the thirty-nine seats on the Omagh urban district council, but under the new system they held only eighteen;[31] before Derry was gerry-

C

mandered, Catholics returned twenty-one of the then forty city council members, afterwards Protestants controlled the city council even though they comprised less than forty per cent of the voters.[32] This cynical manipulation of the instruments of local government by the Protestants has important implications for the development of educational institutions in Northern Ireland, because it confirmed the Catholic clergy's fear of any educational ties with local government agencies.[33]

Further discrediting the local government system, the Northern Ireland government maintained an archaic requirement that to vote in local elections a person (or his spouse) had to be in occupation of property of at least five pounds' annual value. In other words, only occupiers of houses could vote and lodgers, sub-tenants, servants, and adult children living with their parents were excluded. The result was that in the mid-1930s approximately forty per cent of the total number of persons eligible to vote in elections for the Westminster and the Stormont parliaments were unable to vote in local government elections.[34] Given the relatively poor economic position of the Roman Catholics one can safely infer that the great majority of those excluded from voting in local elections were Catholics.

Inseparably tied to the anti-Catholic discrimination in local elections was discrimination in the allocation of local government-provided housing. Any political party can be expected to reward its followers, but the Protestant handling of housing was more than merely a patronage exercise. As indicated above, to vote in local government elections in Northern Ireland one had to be the occupier of a residence. Thus, if a Protestant-controlled local government built houses and filled them with Catholics, it would have increased the Catholic vote and undercut the Protestants' political position. Therefore the Protestants in the local government areas they controlled (and the Nationalists in the areas under their control) discriminated against the religious opposition for political as well as religious reasons.[35] This situation was especially dys-functional socially because the Catholics, being less well off and having larger families, were usually in greater need of public housing assistance than were Protestants.[36]

Mention of the fact that Catholics as a group have been less well off than the Protestants raises the matter of discrimi-nation in employment. Comprehensive statistics on the private sector are not available, although discrimination by both groups undoubtedly has been severe. But there is abundant evidence that religious discrimination in appointments by local government bodies is a practice of long standing. For example, in 1922 the Belfast corporation employed 714 paid officials, of whom 681 were Protestants. The total annual salaries of the Protestants amounted to £17,223, the Catholic total was £637.[37] Now, to recent times: in 1968 only thirty per cent of the Londonderry corporation's administrative, clerical, and technical employees was Catholic and only one of the ten best paid posts was held by a Catholic. In 1968 no senior post under the Fermanagh county council was held by a Catholic. (The reader will note that in each of the latter two cases the local government body was a Protestant body whose hold on power was the result of gerrymandering.) In order to be fair, however, it should be added that the 1968 figures for Newry, a Catholic-controlled council, revealed that few Protestants were employed.[38] Again, as in the case of private enterprise, both sides have discriminated viciously, the only difference being that the Protestants have had more oppor-tunity to do so.

Discrimination in appointment to the Northern Ireland civil service seems to have been less obvious, but nonetheless real. In 1927, of the 229 highest appointees in the service 215 were Protestant. Certainly it might be argued that the 1920s were an atypical and unsettled period and that Catholics had not applied for positions, but actually the pattern was a continuing one: in 1959, 694 of the 740 highest appointees (a group equivalent in grade to the 1927 cohort) were Protestant.

In each case the percentage of Protestants was ninety-four per cent.[39] Even when one makes allowances for the higher Protestant educational attainments (in the late 1950s about three quarters of the students in selective secondary schools and universities were Protestants),[40] the high Protestant percentage is a matter for suspicion. The attitude of one major cabinet member was made clear when Sir E. M. Archdale, the minister for agriculture in the first Northern Ireland cabinet, said on 31 March 1925: 'I have 109 officials, and as far as I know there are four Roman Catholics, three of whom were civil servants turned over to me whom I had to take when we began.'[41] Certainly not all departments and not all ministers were as crude or overt in their policies as was Archdale.[42] The ministry of education seems to have been extremely scrupulous about its appointments, but the overall conclusion dictated by the statistics is quite clear: throughout its existence the government of Northern Ireland has favoured Protestants over Catholics in positions of high civil responsibility.[43]

All the matters mentioned thus far—franchise rights, gerrymandering, housing allocation, employment practices—may be called discrimination without any hesitation. In a final matter, namely the manner in which certain segments of the Northern Ireland system of justice has operated, the issue is less clear. Northern Ireland has been covered by a set of summary civil laws, usually known as the 'special powers acts', a rigorous code for the maintenance of civil order. It is usually forgotten that the precedent for this code was the United Kingdom's defence of the realm act of 1914, whose provisions were reapplied to Northern Ireland by the United Kingdom parliament in the restoration of order in Ireland act, 1920. In 1922 the Northern Ireland government framed its own version of these regulations in its first special powers act designed to quell the civil war in the north. Under the act, which had to be reaffirmed annually, *habeas corpus* procedures became a dead letter, home searches without warrants were permitted, summary jurisdiction for many offences was given to magistrates and the death penalty was introduced for the possession and use of explosives. The special powers act of 1922 was made perpetual rather than annual in 1933. To it have been added through the years the summary jurisdiction and criminal justice act of 1935, aimed at controlling inebriates and insurgents alike, the public order act of 1951, which provides a tight control of party and religious processions, and the flags and emblems act, 1954, which prohibits any interference with the display of the United Kingdom flag and prohibits the display of any other flag that might engender a breach of the peace.[44]

Behind the issue of the special powers acts lay an almost intractable problem. When Northern Ireland was formed the great majority of Roman Catholics considered the government illegitimate and a significant minority promoted violence against it. Thus, the Ulster government was faced with the problem of how to deal with a large minority which from the governmental point of view was potentially treasonous. If one assumes for a moment the government's perspective, measures taken to assure the constitutional stability were relatively moderate as compared with the actions of European and American governments when faced with similar problems. But once the serious threat to the government had passed in the early 1920s the chief problem was to convince the Catholics of the impartiality of the government's system of justice. However, one cannot with any credibility treat a Catholic citizen as a potential traitor and simultaneously convince him that the law-enforcement system is impartial.

Thus, in the case of the special powers act we have a classic instance of the toxins of the Northern Ireland dual social system. The two religious groups have held incompatible, hostile perceptions of each other, views which become self-fulfilling predictions. The Protestants have viewed the Catholics as traitors, the Catholics have seen the Protestants as oppressors. In the Protestant view the special powers acts were objectionable only to those who are contemplating rebellion or disloyalty, so the Catholics in opposing the special powers acts have affirmed their guilt. And the Catholics in denouncing the Protestants who invoke the special powers acts as oppressors have only stiffened the Protestants' resolve to keep the acts on the statute books.

Just how difficult it has been to escape from the nightmarish hatreds of Northern Ireland's dual social system is illustrated by the fact that in Ulster two laudable concepts, the protection of civil liberties and the protection of civil rights, have long been incompatible. That the civil rights of Catholics have been abridged and that the Catholics were justified in seeking redress is too obvious to need amplification. What is often forgotten, however, is that for decades the Protestants have been viewing the world from a perspective that made abrogation of Catholic civil rights a necessity. Long before Ireland was partitioned the northern Protestant became convinced that Protestant civil liberties would suffer if a Catholic government came to power. This conclusion was reinforced by the actions of the southern government after partition. Heavy literary and artistic censorship, the ban on the distribution of birth control devices and related information in the south, and the refusal to consider the possibility of divorce in the case of unsuccessful marriage came to be viewed by Protestants as infringements of civil liberties. In particular, the 1937 Free State constitution seemed to confirm the northern Protestant fears, for it enshrined Catholic teachings about family and social life and gave recognition to the special place of the Catholic Church in Irish society.[45] Thus, a situation existed whereby the Protestants in Northern Ireland believed that to protect their own civil liberties they had to abridge the Catholics' civil rights. When the ideals of civil rights and civil liberties come into conflict it is scarcely an exaggeration to conclude that one is viewing a tragedy.

3

The Londonderry Reforms, 1921-3

In May 1921 the parliament of Northern Ireland was legally
established under the terms of the government of Ireland act,
1920. As expected, the Unionist Party dominated the elections
held late in May, capturing forty of the fifty-two House of
Commons seats.[1] The man who headed the new government
was Sir James Craig. Sir Edward Carson, who had led the
Ulster Unionists from 1910 onwards, had withdrawn enigmati-
cally from the Unionist leadership in 1921 and subsequently
accepted a lordship of appeal in ordinary.[2] Craig was a competent but far from brilliant politician and administrator. He
was a strong Protestant and a stronger Unionist, but not a
blind fanatic. Craig's background was almost perfect for an
Ulster Unionist politician: he was born in Belfast, educated
in Edinburgh, and had been a stockbroker, a military officer,
and had held minor posts in the United Kingdom parliament.
During the years 1921-3 Craig was involved in the demanding
task of restoring civil order in Northern Ireland as well as
conducting complicated negotiations with the southern
republicans and the United Kingdom government.

Before the House of Commons first met, on 7 June 1921,
Craig named his cabinet:[3] minister of agriculture and minister

of commerce, Edward M. Archdale; minister of education, the Marquess of Londonderry; minister of finance, Hugh M. Pollock; minister of home affairs, Sir Richard Dawson Bates; minister of labour, John M. Andrews. Of the cabinet members, Edward Archdale seems to have had the most narrowly Protestant viewpoint. As mentioned in Chapter 2 he complained publicly about the number of Catholic civil servants the agriculture department had inherited from the United Kingdom government. Educated at the Naval School in Portsmouth, England, he served for a time as the grand master of the Irish Orange lodges. In contrast, Hugh M. Pollock was a man of high abilities and considerable tolerance. He appears to have been the most influential member of the cabinet and later was to serve as deputy prime minister. In education debates he often intervened in defence of governmental policies. Judged by his parliamentary performance Sir Richard Dawson Bates was a political lightweight but he was nothing if not zealous in attempting to repress civil dissidents. John Andrews, a prosperous landowner and company director, a faithful unspectacular party man, was destined to become prime minister of Northern Ireland in 1940 in succession to Craig and then to be the victim of a right-wing palace revolution.[4]

To this styleless band was added the electric presence of Charles Stewart Henry Vane-Tempest-Stewart, seventh Marquess of Londonderry, the minister of education. Educated at Eton and Sandhurst, for a time an officer in the Royal Horse Guards, he had entered the United Kingdom parliament in 1906 and had held the under-secretaryship for air in 1920-21. The marquess sat in the Senate and seems at times to have served almost as a one-man House of Lords. As leader of the Unionist Party in the Senate, Londonderry enjoyed a pre-eminent position in that house. Why should such an elegant English aristocrat involve himself in the tawdry politics of Northern Ireland? Certainly not for economic reasons, for most of his family's income stemmed from Durham coal mines. In part, Londonderry became involved for reasons of principle. He was deeply committed to maintenance of the union of Great Britain and Ireland which his ancestor Castlereagh had been instrumental in creating.[5]

To the officials of the ministry of education Londonderry loomed as one of the kingdom's last imposing noble figures. He would appear in the morning meticulously groomed; his face almost shone, as if he had been shaved twice and then polished with pumice by his valet. One observer noted: 'he apes his ancestor the great Lord Castlereagh, wears a high black stock over his collar and a very tightly fitting frock coat, and doesn't look as if he belongs to this century at all.'[6] On the day of a hunt, he appeared in his riding gear, whip in hand. On those days the wiser civil servant spoke to him only from the periphery of the room because he had the unconscious habit of emphasising the points he made with his riding crop. The most honourable marquess treated the civil servants as if they were part of his domestic staff, but far from being rebellious, the officials were unswervingly loyal to him, even adulatory. He was a consummate actor and would often practise his stories (including mimicry of his fellow cabinet members) on his education department staff. Doubtless much of his department's loyalty stemmed from his being genuinely philanthropic. A joke among the civil servants was that the telegraphic address of the ministry, which was 'Education, Belfast', should be changed to 'Sympathetic Belfast', to reflect his lordship's benevolence.[7]

Yet operating as an eighteenth-century nobleman in the early twentieth century had its drawbacks. Londonderry, the gifted amateur himself, tried too many things and was fully master of none. He had to oversee the family coal mines in Durham, plus lands in England and in Ireland, in addition to serving as leader of the Northern Ireland Senate and minister of education, and as a spokesman for Ulster in the House of Lords. This meant that he was often absent from Belfast for long periods of time and that many educational decisions were left to senior officials. Moreover, it is clear that Lord Londonderry was not altogether at home in the world of political democracy. Without conscious irony he once wrote to a friend that 'if you asked me which form of government I like best, I would at once say a benevolent dictatorship, next a very wise privy council; and as neither of these is possible in this country, I am prepared to make the very best I can of what is called democracy'.[8]

The difficulties facing Lord Londonderry in establishing a ministry of education in Northern Ireland should not be underestimated. The region was at war, there were severe educational deficiencies, and there existed no trained cadre of educational administrators in Belfast because previously the central administration had been located in Dublin. The ministry of education was established on 7 June 1921,[9] but it was some time before control of the educational services was actually transferred from the Dublin authorities to the northern ministry. This delay in acquiring operative powers stemmed from the refusal of the southern government to cooperate fully in working the government of Ireland act, 1920. As late as September 1921 Londonderry still did not have any idea when the actual transfer of authority would take place,[10] and only in early November was 1 February 1922 finally set as the transfer date.[11] Even after the southern government had grudgingly agreed to allow the bifurcation of Ireland's educational services, according to Ulster authorities there were difficulties in securing the transfer of personnel to the north and avoidable delays in the transfer of necessary files and documents.[12]

In meeting these problems Lord Londonderry had two pieces of good fortune. The first of these was that the structure of his ministry placed him in a strong position administratively. The establishment in Ulster of a single unified ministry of education solved at the outset of the new regime the problem of coordinating the various levels of educational activities which had so bedevilled the former all-Ireland authorities. Under Londonderry's aegis were placed all the activities of the former commissioners of national education and of the former intermediate school commissioners, plus control over technical education which had previously been exercised by the department of agriculture and technical instruction. The establishment of a unified ministry not only strengthened Londonderry's hand administratively but placed his ministry in a favourable relationship with Unionist politicians and Protestant educators, both of whom were strongly in favour of such a unified arrangement.[13]

Secondly, Londonderry was fortunate in assembling a talented band of associates—in particular, McKeown, McQuibban, and Wyse. Robert McKeown was a prominent Belfast businessman, MP for north Belfast, and parliamentary secretary to the ministry of education. His responsibilities as parliamentary secretary were heavy. Since Lord Londonderry was in the Senate, it fell to McKeown to represent the education ministry in everyday Commons debates (as a cabinet member Lord Londonderry had the right to speak in the Commons, but he exercised this privilege only sparingly), to present the education estimates, and to answer parliamentary questions. Further, because Lord Londonderry was often involved in non-education business connected with his role of leader of the Senate, McKeown's post was especially important. The permanent head of the ministry's civil servants was Lewis McQuibban. McQuibban was a former Scottish civil servant with considerable experience in drafting educational legislation.[14] Andrew N. Bonaparte Wyse was transferred from the Dublin government, a coup for Lord Londonderry because Wyse in all probability was the most able and widely experienced Irish civil servant in educational affairs. A Roman Catholic, Wyse first served the Ulster government on an important committee constituted in 1921 to plan the reform of the Northern Ireland educational system. Thereafter he was placed in charge of Northern Ireland's elementary school network. Eventually he became the permanent secretary of the Northern Ireland education ministry.[15]

Even after full legal control of the educational services in

Northern Ireland was transferred from the Dublin administration to the Ulster ministry, the problems encountered by
Lord Londonderry and his associates were vexing. The most
irritating difficulty was obtaining recognition of the ministry's
authority from the managers and teachers of the Catholic
elementary schools. On 25 January 1922 all school managers
and teachers were informed that as of 1 February 1922 the
final educational authority in Ulster would no longer be the
commissioners of national education but the Northern Ireland
ministry of education.[16] Soon thereafter, Catholic school managers and school teachers began discussing publicly whether
or not to recognise the northern ministry. This debate was
especially important in the areas near the border where the
Catholics were a majority of the population and were therefore most reluctant to yield control of education to the Unionist regime in Belfast. Thus, for example, a well-publicised and
widely reported meeting of Catholic teachers in Strabane in
late February called upon the provisional government of the
Irish Free State to continue to administer the schools throughout Ireland and pledged themselves not to accept salaries
from the northern government. They also called upon the
southern government to reimburse them for the financial losses
incurred through their non-cooperation with the northern
ministry of education.[17] Similar resolutions were passed in the
same week by a large number of Catholic teachers meeting at
Omagh.[18] Altogether, 270 Roman Catholic elementary schools,
representing about one third of all Catholic elementary
schools, refused to cooperate with the Ulster government.[19]

At this point in time it is hard to tell whether the clergy or
the teachers were more important in instigating and maintaining the non-recognition campaign. The clerical managers
tended to be more discreet in their statements than did the
teachers, but not necessarily less important; given the absolute
control by the clergy over local primary schools, it is certain
that the non-recognition policy could not have been effected
without their tacit approval. Significantly, Joseph MacRory,

Roman Catholic Bishop of Down and Connor, the most prominent spokesman of the northern bishops in governmental and
educational affairs, stated in his lenten pastoral for 1922 that
'in regard to the recognition or non-recognition of the Ulster
education authority [the ministry of education] I have issued
no instruction whether public or private, to either managers
or teachers. I think it is better to leave the matter to themselves as for the present at any rate it is a political rather than
a religious issue.'[20]

The long-term results of the refusal of a significant proportion of the Catholic clergy and teachers to work with the
northern government can only have been detrimental to the
Church's educational interests. At the very moment when the
Ulster government was establishing the new educational
system, the Church's already weak bargaining position was
being destroyed by the non-cooperation policy. For a time the
teachers and managers were able to maintain a precarious
independence of the Belfast authorities with the aid of doles
sent from Dublin, but when in the autumn of 1922 the Dublin
authorities announced that their payments would cease the
non-cooperation campaign collapsed.[21] With the cessation of
the non-recognition campaign in late October 1922, the
teachers and managers sought aid from the Ulster ministry
and offered to comply with its regulations. After a period of
negotiation it was agreed that the ministry would again make
grants to the schools, but that as a precondition the manager
and teaching staff had to sign a declaration that they would in
the future carry out the rules and regulations of the ministry.
No payment was made to the teachers for the period of non-
cooperation, but for salary, pension, and promotion purposes
the teachers were not penalised.[22]

In assuming control of the intermediate schools, the officials
of the new ministry of education were keenly aware of the
failings of a system of education based heavily upon external
examinations, but without legislation it was impossible to
change the grant regulations. Therefore, the ministry decided

to continue the old examination system until a reforming statute could be passed. But here the ministry encountered difficulty. In late November 1921 Lewis McQuibban, the permanent secretary of the Ulster ministry of education, requested that the commissioners of intermediate education in Dublin administer the annual examinations for the year 1921-2. This was a sensible and economic course for the northern ministry since the intermediate education commissioners had years of experience in setting and marking these examinations. The intermediate education commissioners agreed to conduct the examinations in Northern Ireland[23] but early in 1922 Lord Londonderry decided against allowing the Dublin-based commissioners to set the examinations for the north. The reason was, in the words of the parliamentary secretary of the ministry of education, Robert McKeown, that 'the provisional government wished to give undue prominence to the Irish language in the intermediate examinations. This could not be accepted by our administration. . .'.[24] Hence, the civil servants of the northern ministry had to set and mark large numbers of examinations at quite short notice.

Then, just as in the case of the primary schools, the ministry's officials were faced with the refusal of a considerable number of Catholic schools to recognise their authority. Whereas all the Protestant intermediate schools in Northern Ireland recognised the northern ministry and presented their students for the examinations set by the Ulster ministry, some twenty-three Catholic intermediate schools either refused to recognise the authority of the northern ministry or did not present candidates for the intermediate examinations conducted in June 1922. These twenty-three intermediate schools, twelve for boys, ten for girls, and one coeducational, enrolled 1,469 students and comprised the great majority of Catholic intermediate education institutes.[25] To serve these Catholic schools the Dublin government set up twenty-two examination centres in Northern Ireland, and 738 candidates sat for their examinations.[26]

The boycotting of the Ulster government's intermediate education examinations was of a piece with the policy of non-cooperation amongst primary school managers and teachers, and similar in motive to the refusal of the Nationalist MPs to take their seats in the northern parliament. As with the non-cooperation movement in the primary schools, the boycott of the intermediate examinations was essentially political in nature, not religious. (In both primary and intermediate education the northern government was operating under the same procedures which the previous national commissioners and intermediate commissioners had followed, so no question of religious hardship could be raised legitimately.) By taking this political stand against recognition of the Ulster ministry of education—and hence against the recognition of the northern government—the Catholic school managers were placing themselves in a dangerous position. Their political activities would make it very difficult in the future for them to defend their religious interests. The intermediate school boycott was futile, for the Ulster ministry simply refused to make any grants to the non-cooperating schools[27] and in the autumn of 1922 all of the Catholic intermediate schools accepted the authority of the Ulster ministry.[28]

In contrast to the systems of primary and intermediate education, the technical education system was taken over by the northern ministry with a minimum of difficulty. At the time of transfer there were in the north technical education committees operating in each of the six counties, in the two county boroughs, and there were fourteen schemes conducted by urban district councils, plus one school operating under convent management. Only two committees, Armagh and Newry, both in Catholic areas, refused to cooperate and in those two instances the local technical education committees had to be replaced by governmental commissioners.[29] Because the system of technical instruction was the most efficient of the educational schemes inherited from Dublin Castle, few changes had to be made, and the Ulster ministry of education simply conducted technical education on the existing lines.

After Lord Londonderry and his staff were firmly in control
of the existing educational machinery they were free to frame
reform legislation. However, long before Londonderry and the
ministry officials began focusing their attention on reforms, a
consensus was emerging among interested parties about the
direction reforms should take. The influences upon the formation of the Londonderry act of 1923 were four-fold: initiative
and expectations stemming from the thwarted attempts to
improve Irish education in 1919 and 1920; impetus and ideas
generated by the 'Belfast coordination conference' of 1921;
pressures for emulating the English education acts of 1902
and 1918; and, most important, the report in mid-1922 of the
'Lynn committee' of educational inquiry.

In 1919 and 1920, it will be recalled, the Ulster Unionist
MPs in the Westminster parliament wholeheartedly supported
two reform measures. The first had called for the establishment of a single ministry of education, and rate aid for primary, intermediate, and technical education, and the second
for rate aid to the Belfast primary schools, which were in a
deplorable condition, and for local involvement in the control
of those schools.[30] Unfortunately for the development of
education throughout Ireland, the hierarchy of the Roman
Catholic Church had opposed these reforms and the Irish
Nationalist MPs blocked the measures. Thus, even before the
parliament of Northern Ireland was convened, one finds
knowledgeable commentators predicting that Ulster 'which
lost the education bill through southern opposition, is not
likely to lose the chance of shattering the present scheme of
things and remoulding it nearer its heart's desire. Legislation
on the lines of the Belfast education bill may therefore be
expected in the northern parliament. . .'.[31] Lord Londonderry
emphasised the primacy of the government's commitment to
education change when, in moving the third reading of the
eventual reform bill, he stated, 'this bill was introduced in

accordance with an undertaking of the government that it would be one of the first measures which they would propose in this parliament'.[32] Thus, the new Ulster government, responding to the sentiments of the political majority, was committed to establishing a coordinated regional educational system involving rate aid and introducing at least partial local control of education.[33]

Ever since the nineteenth century educational experts had recognised the need for a single ministry of education and for local involvement in school affairs, including financial support through the local rates. The necessity of such reforms had been painstakingly documented by the viceregal commissions of 1918 and 1919. That the leading professional educators in Northern Ireland strongly favoured such reforms was made clear during the spring of 1921 by the activities of the 'Belfast coordination conference' chaired by R. M. Jones, headmaster of the Royal Belfast Academical Institution. The conference, which was composed of representatives of the various teachers' associations, primary, secondary, and technical, commenced sitting in April 1921 and endeavoured to be fully representative by distributing questionnaires on major issues to all Ulster teachers. Its report, published in June 1921, recommended the establishment of a single ministry of education responsible to parliament; creation of local education authorities on English lines; instigation of a requirement that county councils and borough councils levy rates to aid education; and introduction of a policy whereby the ministry of education and the local education authorities would be jointly responsible for the building and enlargement of schools.[34] Obviously, these recommendations by the educators could only reinforce the predisposition of the Ulster government to move quickly to reform the educational system. To note that the Belfast conference represented chiefly the viewpoint of Protestant educators would be an accurate observation, but not an argument against its having been influential.

Underlying the readiness of Ulster Unionists to introduce

D

local control of state educational institutions was their desire
to keep in step with the English. R. J. McKeown was striking
a responsive chord when he told a Unionist gathering that the
goal of the education ministry was to give the boys and girls of
Ulster all the advantages possessed by children in other parts
of the United Kingdom.[35] A single board of education for
England had been formed in 1899 and the 'Balfour act' of
1902 (2 Edw. 7, C. 42) had established approximately three
hundred local education authorities responsible for the development of primary and secondary schools. These local education authorities, which were in essence subcommittees of
county councils, county borough councils, and urban district
councils, gave rate-aid to the local schools and in return they
assumed, in addition to continuing control of the state-
provided schools, control of the secular instruction in denominational schools and the right to representation upon the
board of governors of the denominational schools. The 'Fisher
act' of 1918 (8 and 9 Geo. 5, C. 39) affirmed these arrangements. It is far from irrelevant that the sixth Marquess of
Londonderry, father of Northern Ireland's first minister of
education, had been president of the English board of education from 1902-5, the very years in which the principle of
local control of all schools, both state and denominational,
was being brought into practice.

This modelling of Ulster efforts on British and especially
upon English precedents is worth marking, for the achievement of parity with England came to dominate the social
policy of the Ulster government, not only in educational
matters but also in such things as unemployment benefits,
pensions, and other social welfare programmes. Thus, after
1921 the actions of the Ulster government in most matters,
and especially in education, diverge sharply from their southern counterparts. Hence, while comparisons between Northern Ireland and the Irish Free State in education matters
might be interesting, such comparisons do not, from the
Northern Ireland standpoint, illuminate any causal links.

Since 1921 the operative comparison for Northern Ireland education has been with English developments.

The most detailed articulation of reform ideas came from the 'Lynn committee'. This body was appointed in September 1921 and it issued an interim report in late June 1922 which formed the basis of Lord Londonderry's reform legislation. The chairman, Robert J. Lynn (he was knighted in 1924), was an Orangeman,[36] the Unionist MP for West Belfast, and the editor of the *Northern Whig*, a vigorously Unionist paper. Lynn was not altogether open-minded or tactful in matters involving the cultural patterns of the Roman Catholics. For example, while his committee was still drafting its final report, he rose in the Commons to state his opinion of the value of teaching Irish in the school. It is, he said, 'purely a sentimental thing. None of these people who take up Irish ever know anything about it. They can spell their own names badly in Irish, but that is all. I do not think it is worth spending any money on.'[37]

The members of the Lynn committee elected R. M. Jones, headmaster of the Royal Belfast Academical Institution, as vice-chairman.[38] In addition to Jones, six Old Instonians sat on the thirty-two member committee,[39] thus guaranteeing that the interests of academic secondary schools would be well protected. Jones, it will be recalled, had served as chairman of the Belfast coordination conference and his appointment to the Lynn committee served the dual purpose of representing the secondary schools and ensuring continuity with the opinions of the educators who had formulated the Belfast conference report. The primary schools had several representatives on the committee, the most important of them being A. N. Bonaparte Wyse. Because of his high rank in the service of the former commissioners of national education in Dublin, Wyse possessed an unrivalled knowledge of the primary school system. His influence was guaranteed by his appointment to the sub-committee on procedure, a group which, the minute books of the Lynn committee make clear, did the lion's share of the committee's work. In contrast to the primary schools and the academic secondary schools, the technical schools were poorly represented, having only two seats on the Lynn committee. Technical school teachers and principals and local technical instruction committees protested,[40] but Lord Londonderry refused to increase their representation.

Strikingly, there were no representatives of the Roman Catholic Church on the Lynn committee. Invitations had been sent by Lord Londonderry to the Catholic authorities, but they were in every case refused.[41] The only Catholic on the committee was a layman, A. N. Bonaparte Wyse, who, as one education journal noted, 'does not belong to Ulster and whom the Roman Catholics of Ulster would not regard as representing them'.[42] In October 1921 the Catholic clerical primary school managers met in Dublin and issued a clear warning to the northern reformers that 'in view of pending changes in Irish education, we wish to reassert the great fundamental principle that the only satisfactory system of education for Catholics is one wherein Catholic children are taught in Catholic schools by Catholic teachers under Catholic auspices'.[43] In other words, they opposed any alteration in the existing system.

In all probability the refusal of the Roman Catholic authorities to join the Lynn committee was the single most important determinant of the educational history of Northern Ireland from 1920 to the present day. By refusing to sit they surrendered their last shred of influence at the very time when the basic character of Ulster's educational development was being determined. From the recommendations made by the Lynn committee emerged the principles of the 1923 Londonderry act, and that act was the foundation of all later developments. The refusal of the Catholic religious authorities to exert their influence upon the Lynn committee and subsequently upon the Londonderry act was especially unfortunate because, despite the civil war which was raging in Northern Ireland, the Unionist government was making a determined effort to govern in a non-sectarian manner, an attempt which was abandoned in the mid-1920s.[44] Although the Lynn committee claimed to have kept in mind Catholic interests,[45] its recommendations were inevitably framed according to Protestant educational assumptions.[46]

The major groups which held the floor were the Presbyterians,[47] Anglicans,[48] the Northern Ireland association of technical instruction committees,[49] the association of urban district councils of Northern Ireland,[50] and the Belfast teachers' association.[51] Each of these groups assumed that the secondary school structure would not be significantly changed. The technical education committees and the urban district councils pressed for the maintenance of the status quo in technical education and were not opposed by the religious groups in this demand. Thus, the real question became what changes should be made in the elementary schools? Both the Presbyterian and Church of Ireland representatives pressed for local rate aid to the elementary schools and for some increase in local control, with strong safeguards for denominational interests in general and religious instruction in particular. Although none of the other groups opposed rate aid or the extension of local control, the teachers were somewhat suspicious of local government bodies and wanted a strong ministry of education to keep its eye on the local agencies.

From the strands of testimony presented to the committee and from the opinions and expertise of its members the Lynn committee framed an interim report, submitted to Lord Londonderry in late June 1922. This interim report was to serve as the basis of Lord Londonderry's educational reform act. As was to be expected the report focused chiefly upon the primary schools. The Lynn committee accepted the principle that the amount of control over a school assumed by the appropriate local government body should be in direct proportion to the total amount of local and central government aid which the school received. Specifically, the Lynn committee recommended that three classes of primary schools be established.

Each county borough council, urban district council and rural district council would be asked to form a local committee for primary education. The relations between the committees and the individual elementary schools in their respective areas would fall under one of three heads, depending on the class of school involved. Class I schools would be elementary schools built by local rates in combination with ministry of education grants and existing schools handed over by their previous managers to the local primary education committees. Class II elementary schools would be those schools for which special school management committees were formed, composed of two representatives of the local primary school committee and four representatives of the school patrons. Class III schools were to be those schools whose managers wished to remain entirely independent of local governmental authorities. All of the schools in each of the three categories were to continue to have their teachers' salaries paid in full by the ministry of education, as in the past, but there the equality ended. In the case of Class I schools the local committee for primary education was to pay all costs of furnishing, heating, maintaining, and repairing the schools from the local rates. Class II schools were to have half the cost of maintaining, repairing, and furnishing paid for by the local primary education committee from the local rates. Class III schools were to receive no aid from local rates but were to be eligible for the customary grants towards heating and cleaning made directly by the ministry of education. In the crucial matter of capital expenses, both for new buildings and for expansion of old, Class I schools were to have two thirds of such expenses borne by the central government and one third raised on the local rates. In Class II schools the ministry of education was to provide two thirds, the local rate one sixth, and the remainder was to be raised by the school patrons. As for Class III schools, the ministry of education could, at its discretion, lend money to the school managers but the entire amount had to be repaid by the managers.[52]

Because these proposals were, with slight modifications, eventually included in the Londonderry act and were thereby to determine the structural outline of Northern Ireland's elementary school system from 1923 to the present day, it is important to make two clarifying comments. First, it is clear from the minute book of the Lynn committee that committee members realised early in their deliberations that the Catholics would have nothing to do with the local primary school committees; any contemporary familiar with the Catholic reaction to the education bills of 1919 and 1920, or aware of the policy statement of the Catholic school managers opposing all reforms in Ulster primary education, could hardly have thought otherwise. Secondly, however, one should not infer from the preceding point that the Lynn committee in recommending a scheme of local aid and local control of elementary schools was moving aggressively against the Catholics. Quite the opposite was true. The Lynn committee, while firmly convinced of the need to increase educational resources through rate aid and to increase citizen involvement in control of the schools, was willing to recommend that those who did not accept this position nevertheless would continue to have the bulk of their educational expense underwritten by governmental funds: all primary teachers' salaries were to be a charge on the ministry of education. It is incontestable that the Catholic schools under the Lynn-inspired system were to be relatively deprived in relation to schools receiving local aid (and deprived in absolute terms by the loss of the grants towards school construction they had received under the old regime); but this misses the crucial point that under the Lynn committee guidelines, the Catholics *did* participate in the state system. The minimum any recognised primary school received from the ministry of education was full payment of its teachers' salaries, a grant which covered about three quarters of the expenses of operating an elementary school.[53] Thus, the Ulster educationalists were willing to continue to pay hundreds of thousands of pounds each year to underwrite a minority school system which was based on educational premises with which the government disagreed.

In contrast to the Lynn committee's structural recommendations, which were clearly stated, the committee's one page of discussion of religious education was ambiguous and thoroughly confusing. Lynn himself boasted with ill-founded pride that 'I think there is no chapter in the interim report so short as the chapter dealing with religious education... We tried to make that chapter as simple as possible, and we tried to make it as non-controversial as possible.'[54] The committee prefaced its recommendations about religious instruction on false history. Specifically, they stated that the original intention of the Irish primary school system should be maintained, that is the affording to children of all faiths combined literary and moral instruction within each school, and separate denominational instruction at distinct hours specified in advance. This was nonsense, for the Irish primary schools had been religiously segregated and *de facto* denominational in curricular matters since the middle of the nineteenth century. In reality, when the Lynn committee recommended that the existing rules regarding religious instruction be modified only in detail it was not suggesting that ecumenical education be pursued, but that denominational schooling be continued. No mention whatsoever was made of Class III schools. They were to continue to operate under existing rules. The old rules were to hold as well for Class II schools, it being explicitly stated that the clergy or others to whom the parents and guardians of the children did not object had the right of access to the school to give 'scriptural and denominational' instruction at fixed times. Most important—but highly confusing—were the suggestions for Class I schools, the schools operated by local authorities and fully subsidised by ministry and local funds:[55]

> In schools of Class I such religious instructions as is approved by the parents or guardians of the children should be given for a period of, as a rule, at least half-an-hour in each school

day, or its equivalent within each week.

The churches should prescribe the programme of religious instruction for their own children either separately or in agreement amongst themselves. It is hoped that a common scripture programme will be agreed upon for the religious instruction of children belonging to all Protestant denominations.

Neither 'religious instruction' (specific denominational instruction or general moral teaching?) nor 'in each school day' (within the hours of compulsory attendance or as a non-compulsory addition to those hours?) was adequately defined. However, the later actions of the Protestant denominations which were involved in shaping this recommendation indicate that what was here desired was (1) that in the religious instruction time-slot, during which attendance on the part of the children was *not* compulsory, (2) the teachers would be *required* to give (3) a programme of 'simple Bible instruction' agreed upon by the various Protestant denominations, or (4) if the school manager preferred, *allowed*, but not required, to give religious instruction peculiar to a specific denomination.[56]

Unhappily, in formulating these religious recommendations the Lynn committee had departed from the path of equity and generosity which had characterised its earlier structural formulations. Emphatically, it was these partisan religious arrangements and not the recommendations for the involvement of local authorities in controlling primary schools which made the Lynn report a biased document. Given the fact, well known to the committee, that the Roman Catholic primary schools would not become Class I schools, the recommendation that Class I schools be allowed to provide a programme of Protestant Bible instruction was actually a recommendation for a double standard: Catholic denominational schools (Class III schools) were to receive less than complete governmental financial support while Protestant schools (Class I schools) were to be underwritten fully by local and central government funds. Certainly it could be argued

that the Class I schools were not under clerical management
and that they were not denominational in the strict sense
because they usually would be attended by children of more
than one Protestant denomination, but such arguments are
sophistic. The plain fact was that the Lynn report favoured
granting similar religious rights to two distinct classes of
schools, but proposed to finance fully only the Protestant
schools.

This partisan blight could, however, be cauterised by Lord
Londonderry and then the Lynn committee's organisational
recommendations could be introduced in an even-handed
manner. To Lord Londonderry's great credit he rewrote the
Lynn religious recommendation so that his 1923 educational
act prescribed rate aid to primary schools and local control
of those schools which were supported wholly by public funds
without being unfair to the Roman Catholic minority. And
in response the Protestant religious authorities were to spend
the remainder of the 1920s fighting for the inclusion of the
Lynn committee's partisan stipulations in Northern Ireland's
educational code.

Having received the Lynn committee's interim report in
late June 1922, Lord Londonderry now had to direct the
drafting of a major education act. Both Londonderry's private
papers and the proceedings in the Stormont parliament give
the distinct impression that he was given full control of the
shaping and passage of the reform act. A first draft was ready
by 20 October 1922 and this draft was discussed by the Northern Ireland cabinet in December 1922 and January 1923 and
also referred to members and officials of the English board of
education for their advice.[57] A final draft bill, drawn up
by Sir Arthur Queckett, the Northern Ireland legislative
draughtsman, was sent to the prime minister on 8 February
1923.[58] The bill was introduced in mid-March and was on
the statute books by mid-October.

In discussing the structural changes in the Ulster educational system effected by the Londonderry act of 1923, it is wise to begin with the least important changes: alterations in terminology.[59] Primary schools, which previously had been denominated officially as 'national schools', were renamed 'public elementary schools'. Further, the term 'secondary school' was introduced to refer to an academic post-primary school giving at least a five years' course of instruction. Although the term 'intermediate school' remained in official existence, redefined to mean a school giving a three or four year academic post-primary course, it became general usage to refer to all academic post-primary schools as secondary schools, and that usage is adopted in the discussion which follows.

In substantive matters, Lord Londonderry accepted the Lynn committee's recommendation that local school committees be created whose chief duty would be to deal with primary education. But whereas the Lynn committee had recommended that the local education committees be established as subcommittees of the existing urban district, rural district, and county borough councils, the Londonderry act introduced a complicated set of arrangements involving the establishment of entirely new governmental units. Each county and county borough council was to be a 'local education authority' responsible primarily for financial and rating matters. A subcommittee was to act as educational adviser to each council. Actually, the real educational powers resided in 'regional education committees', it being expected that there would be two or more formed in each county. These regional education committees possessed the actual supervisory power over the schools in their areas. The county boroughs of Belfast and Londonderry had subcommittees of the county council which dealt both with most financial matters and exercised jurisdiction over local primary schools.[60]

Two comments are in order about this extraordinary system. First, the Londonderry act's departures from the Lynn committee recommendations were not improvements. Whereas the Lynn committee's idea had been to minimise complications by constituting existing units of local government as educational agencies, the Londonderry plan added an entire new tier of governmental agencies, the regional education committees. Moreover, the relationship between the local education authority of the county councils, with its financial power, and the regional committees, which dealt with policy and administration, was unclear and apt to produce tensions. It is impossible to understand why these departures were made from the Lynn plan, although the opinion of a well-informed senator, James Leslie, bears notice. Leslie was convinced that the germ of the proposal for the regional education committees was to be found in the dissent to the Lynn report of Mr Adam Duffin.[61] Duffin had argued that rural district councils were often ineffective and that the recognition of urban and rural district councils as primary education authorities would produce too many education committees. Hence, while agreeing with the Lynn committee's majority that the counties were too large to be practical administrative units, Duffin had argued for the creation of some new unit midway between the county councils and the rural and urban district councils.[62] Whatever the virtues of the regional committee plan, simplicity was not among them.

Secondly, the rhetoric with which Lord Londonderry clothed the establishment of the various educational committees bears notice chiefly because it was so far removed from reality. Londonderry continually emphasised that his reforms were replacing the old centralised system of Irish education with the democratic system of education for Ulster.[63] Obviously 'centralised' and 'democratic' are false antonyms. Moreover, the educational reforms over which Londonderry presided always had included the establishment of a single ministry of education where previously three separate school systems had existed. That the establishment of a single ministry was necessary for the efficient coordination of the various types of education does not vitiate the fact that Londonderry's reforms were predicated upon an increase, not a decrease, in educational centralisation.

When dealing with individual schools the Londonderry act followed closely the Lynn committee's recommendations. Three classes of schools were established.[64] The first class consisted of two categories, 'provided schools' and 'transferred schools'. The former were schools built by the local education authority, the latter were institutions transferred to civic management by their former managers. In transferred and provided schools the teachers' salaries were paid by the ministry of education and all heating, cleaning, maintenance, and capital expansion items were covered by a combination of central and local government funds. Both transferred and provided schools were completely under the control of local school management committees, which were in turn subordinate to regional education committees or to the county borough education committees.

The second class of schools were those schools whose managers accepted the establishment of a special management committee, four of whose members were named by the manager or trustees, and two by the regional education authority. These schools (which are hereafter called by their universally accepted label 'four-and-two schools') received complete payment of teachers' salaries, one half of all heating, lighting, cleaning and equipment repair and general upkeep expenses from the local rates, plus a capital expenditure grant from the local education authority 'if they think fit'. These schools were also eligible for a capital grant from the ministry of education, awarded at the ministry's discretion.

The third class of schools were those whose managers elected to remain completely independent of local control. These schools continued to receive full payment of teachers' salaries from ministry of education funds, but no money whatsoever for capital expenditures. In the usual case they did receive from the local rates one half of the cost of heating, lighting and cleaning the schools. Confusingly, both the four-and-two schools and those under completely independent management were called 'voluntary schools'.[65]

Continuing our examination of the structural provisions of Lord Londonderry's act, we find that the arrangements for technical instruction added another layer of complications. One would have thought that to avoid administrative confusion technical education should have come under the control of the same regional education committees which were established to oversee the primary schools, with the education committee of county councils serving as financial supervisor as in the case of primary education. It will be recalled, however, that under the old technical instruction act the urban district councils had functioned efficiently as overseers and financiers of technical education and that there was strong sentiment that they should be allowed to continue controlling technical education in their respective areas. Therefore, a peculiar scheme of dual control arose.

For the purposes of technical instruction the urban district councils were allowed to continue as education authorities and to strike a rate for technical education in their respective areas. Schools which had been established by county councils, however, were allocated to the control of a regional education committee and financed by the education rate struck by the county. Thus, in urban areas the technical education authorities were independent of the regional education committees and county authorities, but in rural areas the regional committees assumed control both of primary and technical instruction. In order to avoid double taxation the citizens of those urban areas which struck their own technical education rate were exempt from that portion of the county rate which went to support technical education in the country areas. While recognising that it was politically expedient to allow the urban district councils to continue their activities in the field of technical education, Lord Londonderry hoped that ultimately they would merge themselves into the administrative machinery established to govern primary education.[66]

Under the Londonderry act it was lawful for the managers of secondary schools to transfer them to the control of the regional education committees, or, in Belfast and Londonderry, to the borough's education committee. Also, the local education authorities could, with the financial support of the county rating authorities, construct new schools.[67] These provisions allowed the educational administrators to dream of a time when the regional education committees would have power over primary, technical, and secondary schools. These were unrealistic dreams, however, for in actual fact only a handful of secondary schools were under the supervision of local authorities.

The most important change in the legislation concerning academic secondary schools was the repeal of all the legislation of the old intermediate schools board which made certain grants dependent upon the results of students' annual examinations, and which added six or seven additional categories of grants, payable according to various idiosyncratic formulas. Examinations continued to exist but for the purpose of awarding school leaving certificates, not for allocating funds to secondary school managers. Grants now depended upon each school's being satisfactorily conducted according to ministry regulations as adjudged by a ministry of education inspector and upon the school's paying salaries as prescribed by the ministry to its lay teachers. At the same time as the old grants system was being scrapped, a new regulation was introduced precluding schools conducted for private profit from receiving state grants.[68]

In direct imitation of England's Fisher act of 1918, Northern Ireland's 1923 education act made it permissible for local education authorities to establish nursery schools, vacation schools, and 'central schools' (the central schools were post-primary schools for children who attended neither academic secondary education nor technical schools.[69] These provisions were destined to remain unfulfilled, for the economic problems of the 1920s and 1930s prevented the development of new types of schooling.

Perhaps the least controversial change in the primary education system was the Londonderry act's replacing the previous farcical arrangements for compulsory education with an effective scheme covering children between the ages marred by one major loophole: local education authorities of six and fourteen. Nevertheless, the Londonderry act was could permit children to begin work in certain occupations at age twelve, with the weak proviso that 'any such child shall attend school on school days other than those on which the child is so employed.'[70]

Primary education, it must be emphasised, was not made free, but fees in existing primary schools were fixed at the low level determined by the Irish education act of 1892. Contingent upon there being an adequate supply of free places, fees in new primary schools provided by local education authorities were permissible, the exact scale to be fixed only with the approval of the ministry of education.[71]

When one turns to the Londonderry act's provisions for religious instruction one is dealing with a topic destined to engender great bitterness in Northern Ireland. To his credit, Lord Londonderry refused to accept the Lynn committee's recommendations about religious education, for they would simply have created two denominational systems, separate but unequal. Londonderry wished to be fair to the Catholics. Also, in some vague and undefined way he was an ecumenist. He opposed the segregation of children according to religious faith and spoke rosily of schools where children of different faiths studied and played together. His bill, he believed, provided opportunities but not compulsion for denominational integration.[72]

But Lord Londonderry was not a secularist. 'The state is non-sectarian, but not secular....' summarised his philosophy.[73] As for the primary school, 'We are determined,' he stated, 'that moral instruction shall be associated with secular instruction...'[74] Thus, his statute declared, 'for the purposes of this act, the expression "elementary education" means an education, both literary and moral...',[75] a phrase which harkened back to Lord Stanley's letter of 1831 which had created the Irish system of primary education.

In framing his legislation, the ministry of education had been guided by section 5 of the government of Ireland act, 1920. Under section 5 it was *ultra vires* of the parliament of Northern Ireland to 'make a law so as either directly or indirectly to establish or endow any religion...'. Those portions of any law which contravened this stricture were void. Because of this clause in the government of Ireland act, the government deliberately refrained from making any positive provision for religious instruction in schools.[76]

Sections 26 through 28 in Lord Londonderry's original bill contained the religious education proposals. Section 27 provided that arrangements for religious instruction in schools under denominational managers and under four-and-two committees should be determined by the managers, which is to say that in those schools *de facto* denominationalism should continue as under the former commissioners of national education.[77] Section 28 provided elementary safeguards applicable to all elementary schools, such as the requirement that every school be open to children of all religious faiths and that no child in any school could be forced to undergo religious instruction against his parents' wishes. Neither section 27 nor 28 was controversial, but section 26 was another matter entirely. In the original bill it read as follows:

> It shall be the duty of the education authority, if it is so desired by parents for their children attending any public elementary school, being a provided or transferred school, to afford opportunities for catechetical or other religious instruction according to the tenets of the religious denominations of those parents (in this Act referred to as 'religious instruction'), and such clergyman or other persons as shall be approved by

E

those parents shall have access to the children in the school
for the purpose of giving them their religious instruction, at
times to be arranged in accordance with the regulations of the
Ministry: provided that the education authority shall not provide religious instruction in any such public elementary school
as aforesaid.[78]

Clearly, Lord Londonderry was trying to navigate between
two dangerous shoals. On the one side he was striving to avoid
clashing with the judicial committee of the United Kingdom
privy council which could declare portions of his act invalid
if they ran counter to the religious endowments clause of
the government of Ireland act; hence a phrase was included
prohibiting the local education authorities from providing
denominational religious instruction in the schools they controlled. On the other side Londonderry was trying to avoid
the politically fatal charge that the new category of schools,
those controlled by the local civic authorities, would be secular or Godless institutions. In the actual event Londonderry
was to escape difficulties with the United Kingdom legal
authorities but to run foul of the Protestant denominations.

Throughout the ensuing difficulties Lord Londonderry was
able to maintain the principle that 'religious instruction in
a denominational sense during the hours of compulsory attendance there will not be . . .',[79] but this meant that he could
not satisfy his Protestant critics that sufficient attention was
being paid to religious matters. During the spring of 1923
the Protestant Churches became increasingly vocal on the
religious instruction clause of the Londonderry bill. In particular they wanted it to be clearly stated that religious teaching would be provided in all primary schools under control
of the local authorities, and that teachers would be permitted
to give the religious instruction. Many Protestant clerical
leaders wanted the religious teaching to be given during
compulsory school hours.[80] The agitation reached a peak in
April 1923 when a committee representative of the Protestant denominations was appointed to negotiate with the

ministry of education. Sometime during April or early May[81] it appeared that a compromise was arranged. According to a later report of Hugh M. Pollock, minister of finance, who represented the government in the final negotiations, section 26 was redrafted to meet the Churches' objection. Pollock personally submitted the draft to the heads of the 'Protestant Churches' (meaning, in all probability, the heads of the Anglican, Presbyterian, and Methodist Churches) in an interview at the general assembly buildings in Belfast. Each of the representatives accepted the clause and the archbishop of Armagh, Charles Frederick D'Arcy, said that it was admirable, that it was excellent, and that it satisfied the demands of the Churches.[82] Robert McKeown, parliamentary secretary of the ministry, introduced a redrafted clause 26 with the colourless explanation that 'we understand fears have been expressed that the wording of the bill would preclude, in provided or transferred schools, religious instruction which, while non-catechetical, might include the reading of the scriptures. The amendment now proposed will, it is believed, remove all doubt on this point.'[83]

Section 26, as finally engrossed upon the statute books, provided a less than lucid statement of the rules governing religious teaching:

> 26.   It shall be the duty of the education authority to afford opportunities for catechetical instruction according to the tenets of the religious denomination of the parents of children attending any public elementary school, being a provided or transferred school, and for other religious instruction to which those parents do not object (in this Act referred to as 'religious instruction'); and those clergymen or other persons (including teachers at the school) to whom those parents do not object shall have access to the children in the school for the purpose of giving them there religious instruction, or of inspecting and examining the religious instruction there given, at times to be arranged in accordance with regulations of the Ministry: provided that the education authority shall not provide religious instruction in any such public elementary school as aforesaid.

What this meant was that neither the teaching of the tenets of individual denominations nor the teaching of tenets agreed upon by the Protestant denominations ('other religious instruction to which these parents do not object' referred to plans to develop a pan-Protestant doctrinal syllabus) could be paid for by public money or conducted during compulsory school hours.

But what did Lord Londonderry mean when he talked about moral instruction being given in all schools as part of the required curriculum? In public he was studiously vague. In parliament he invariably spoke of 'moral' and of 'ethical' instruction without defining the terms. Later he was to write that under the 1923 act 'the curriculum will contain instructions in Christian ethics and moral principles, the holding of which is the common basis of all the creeds and the foundation of good citizenship.'[84]

Only in private did Lord Londonderry fully define his views. His clearest statement was penned to the Protestant bishop of Down, Connor and Dromore:

> Religious instruction in the sense in which the term is used in the Bill will only be given outside the hours of compulsory attendance. This involves no change from previous practice. Under the rules of the Commissioners [of national education] which have been adopted by the ministry, four hours of secular instruction alone constitutes an attendance. The phrase 'school hours' within which religious instruction was given under the rules of the commissioners simply meant that opportunity should be afforded at the schools for such instruction in exactly the same way as the Bill provides.
>
> And now let me come to that other type of instruction which I shall call for the sake of clearness, not *religious* but *moral* instruction... Such teaching must by necessity be absolutely undenominational... It thus cannot include reading from pages of the Bible itself.[85]

Had the Protestant clergy generally known about the exclusion of Bible teaching from moral instruction it is hard to believe that they would have allowed the bill to pass as quietly as they did.[86] Soon after its passage they were to become aware of Londonderry's intention and a bitter controversy was to ensue.

Yet another of the Londonderry act's sections was destined to rankle Protestant clerics. The clergymen were disturbed by rules for the appointment of teachers in schools controlled by the local education authorities, especially in the transferred schools. As in the case of the religious instruction controversy, the Protestant clerics were not to awaken fully to their alleged grievances until after the act was on the statute books. The pivotal provisions were embodied in section 66 (3) which in final form stated:

> The power of appointing teachers for any provided or transferred school shall be exercised by the education authority and shall not be delegated by them to a school committee appointed under this Act, nor shall the education authority have power to require that the teachers appointed for or holding office in any provided or transferred school shall be teachers who belong to or profess the tenets of, or who do not belong to or profess the tenets of, any particular church or religious denomination.

(In contrast to these provisions the four-and-two school committees were to maintain the right to appoint teachers without prohibition on the introduction of denominational considerations, and the managers of schools which remained totally independent of the local authorities were to have unfettered right of appointment; these two sorts of schools, it must be recalled, received less financial aid from governmental sources than did the local authority schools.)

The opposition which emerged to the provision of section 66 (3) was chiefly clerical. It was threefold. First, in giving the power of appointment of teachers in transferred and provided primary schools to the regional educational committees (to which they devolved from the county education authorities by section 7 of the act) rather than to the local school committees the Londonderry act undercut localism. Protest against this trend was voiced in June 1923 by the general assembly of the Presbyterian Church: 'the assembly express its disapproval of the provisions of the education act which deprive the parents of the children and others intimately associated with schools of any direct power in the appointment of teachers...'[87] It is obvious that the 'others intimately associated with schools' were the clergy who quite naturally did not wish to have their influence in local education appointments reduced.

Secondly, the concerned Protestants were worried about the possibility that in certain areas the regional committees would be under Catholic control. 'In the judgement of the [Presbyterian general] assembly the safeguards provided in the act are entirely inadequate to secure the appointment of secular teachers in schools now under Protestant management in predominantly Roman Catholic areas should they be transferred to the management of regional committees.'[88] More graphically, Dr Hugh Morrison, an MP for Queen's University, stated:

> If you have a Regional Committee, you may have this extra-ordinary position in Ulster: the Roman Catholic schools will not be transferred. That is the position. And if the Roman Catholic schools are not transferred you will have in some Roman Catholic districts in Ulster Roman Catholics controlling the Regional Committee. They will appoint the teachers to the Protestant schools. That is a thing I do not think the Roman Catholic Church wants, and it certainly is a thing that the Protestant Church will not submit to.[89]

Thirdly, it will be recalled that in the revising of the religious instruction clause the Protestant Churches had pressed successfully for the specific statement that teachers were permitted to give religious instruction. This was important because the school teachers, rather than the Protestant clergymen, actually bore the brunt of the teaching of religion. Hence, the Protestant clergy very strongly objected to the appointment of teachers being made irrespective of the religious beliefs or unbeliefs of the candidates. Obviously if a person of the wrong religious persuasion or of an agnostic or atheistic bent were appointed the traditional arrangements for religious teaching would be destroyed. Hence one finds an assembly of the Church of Ireland school managers from the entire six counties resolving 'that strict regard should be had, in making an appointment, to the effect that the vacancy should be filled by a teacher who is of the same religious denomination as the owners or trustees of the school'.[90] The threat of non-cooperation with the ministry of education's new scheme for local control of education was clear in the resolution of the Armagh Anglican diocesan board of education which declared, with the archbishop of Armagh in the chair, that the Londonderry measure did not provide sufficient safeguard 'against unfair appointments, in which teachers who on religious or other grounds are unsuitable, might be appointed and therefore cannot recommend managers to transfer schools until this defect has been remedied'.[91]

Yet Lord Londonderry remained firm. Why? One reason was that he was anxious to abolish the old managerial system from which so many of Ulster's educational ills stemmed. If he gave way to the churches he was convinced that he would be perpetrating the old managerial system.[92] Further, Londonderry was idealistic enough to maintain that the appointment of a teacher should be made solely upon the basis of his educational and moral qualifications without taking into account the colour of his religious beliefs. But apart from any educational grounds, section 5 of the government of Ireland act, 1920, prohibited the imposition of religious tests upon candidates for posts in the public service.[93]

In holding firm on two crucial issues, the exclusion of Bible reading from compulsory school hours and the prohibition of religious tests in appointments to those primary schools wholly underwritten by governmental funds, Lord Londonderry had charted and navigated an idealistic course. He had also laid open his ministry to several years of virulent attack by the Protestant clergy.

4

The Protestant Clergy Attack, 1923-5

Having successfully drafted and placed on the statute books a major piece of educational reform legislation, Lord Londonderry and the officials of the ministry of education could reasonably have expected a respite from controversy during which they could have brought their act into operation. The timetable for making the act operational was quite swift considering the legislation's complexity. The provisions of the Londonderry act relating to the powers and duties of the ministry of education became effective on 1 October 1923, the provisions concerning the county boroughs became effective on 1 April 1924, and those involving the county and regional education committees on 1 October 1924. The first regional education committee in Northern Ireland (Omagh, County Tyrone) met early in January 1925. On 1 April 1926 the remaining miscellaneous provisions of the Londonderry act were brought into operation.[1]

But the ministry of education, swift as it may have been, could not outrace the educational controversialists. Even before the statute had received the royal assent, a cadre of

Protestant clergymen had begun an agitation against the Londonderry act. In order to understand succeeding events, one must realise that Lord Londonderry and the ministry of education were in a difficult position in facing the Protestant agitation. The clergymen had three grievances, two of which were bound in social paradoxes endemic to Ulster life, and the third was too vague to permit effective rebuttal. The first area of conflict concerned moral and ethical instruction. Under the 1923 act such instruction was required in all public elementary schools, but the controversialists' attention was focused only on the provided and transferred schools. Because moral instruction was not defined in Lord Londonderry's act (whether by intention or inadvertence is unclear) the act became enmeshed in one of the unhappy paradigms which have governed Ulster's educational history:

1 Northern Ireland's populace refused to accept secular education.
2 Hence, moral education was compulsory in all schools.
3 To the Ulster Protestant clergy moral education necessarily included Bible instruction.
4 But to require Bible instruction, while prohibiting the commentary of the Church fathers, was to enforce the teaching of Protestantism, since the Catholic Church held that the Scriptures had to be interpreted in the light of the Church's traditions.
5 Hence, to require Bible instruction during school hours was to implicitly establish and endow the Protestant faith.
6 But such endowment was prohibited by the government of Ireland act, 1920.

Further, Lord Londonderry and his ministry were in an uncomfortable position vis-à-vis the regulations for the selection of teachers in provided and transferred schools:

1 In deference to the opinion of the Ulster populace the Londonderry act made it a duty of local education authorities to give opportunities for denominational religious

instruction in the transferred and provided primary schools, but outside the hours of compulsory attendance.

2   The Protestant clergymen either could not or would not give that instruction themselves.

3   Thus, the Londonderry act specifically stated that the teachers were permitted to give denominational instruction as they had done in the past.

4   But the ministry of education believed that the teachers employed in the provided and transferred schools were public servants under the terms of the government of Ireland act, 1920, and religious considerations could not be taken into account when appointing public servants.

5   Therefore, there was no legal way in which the regional education committees could guarantee that a teacher suitable and willing to give denominational religious instruction would be appointed in provided and transferred schools.

Obviously the ministry's manoeuvring room was dangerously cramped. In these constricted circumstances, the ministry had to deal with yet a third difficult clerical complaint, namely that the 1923 act was a secularising act. This Protestant clerical complaint was so nebulous as to be nearly impossible to deal with. The closest to specificity on this point the clerical agitators came was to point out that the definition of elementary education promulgated in the Londonderry act did not mention religious education but referred only to reading and writing in the English language and to the acquisition of arithmetical skills.

Throughout the campaign to amend the 1923 education act, the clergy were in the vanguard and certain Presbyterian clergymen at the very forefront. The tone the Presbyterian cleric attacks would take was indicated by the speech to the general assembly given by the Reverend Dr Strahan, former moderator of the general assembly, who had been the Presbyterian Church's chief representative on the Lynn committee. Strahan compared the Londonderry act to a beautiful ring 'gemmed' with precious jewels, but possessing also a secret source of poison that might be deadly to the life of the community. He denounced Lord Londonderry for stating that the Bible must be considered a denominational book.[2]

The man destined to become the chief Presbyterian organiser was not Strahan, however, but the Reverend William Corkey. Corkey had become convener of elementary education for the general assembly's board of education in 1917, which meant that he was in the most influential position in the Presbyterian Church in matters of primary education. The general assembly's board of education served as an executive committee in educational matters, reporting annually to the full assembly. Thus, Corkey acquired great powers in day-to-day matters, while being given the chance each year to take the stage at the assembly to deliver his annual report. He was also the manager of nine elementary schools in the Shankill road district.[3] A man of great organising ability, Corkey also was a man of passion. He was capable of immense bitterness and of vicious invective. His actions were to reveal that he was, at minimum, a zealot in matters of religious education. His opponents might have depicted him as a monomaniac; a historian can, perhaps, best describe him as being, in educational matters, the Henry Cooke of the twentieth century.[4]

In 1923, soon after the general assembly of the Presbyterian Church had met, a joint meeting of the representatives of the clergy of the Church of Ireland and the Presbyterian Church met and drafted a letter to Sir James Craig demanding that a bill to amend the Londonderry act be introduced at an early date. This letter of 31 July 1923 was also signed by the Methodist's representative, who, although unable to attend the drafting session, agreed with the other Protestant Churches' demands. The signers of the letter to Craig included some of the most influential clergy of the three denominations: among them were the archbishop of Armagh, the bishops of Derry, of Clogher, and of Down, Connor and Dromore, the moderator of the Presbyterian Church in Ireland, and an ex-moderator, plus the president of the Methodist Conference in Ireland.[5]

Having received no satisfaction from Craig, the Presbyterian and Church of Ireland leaders met in midsummer to redefine their demands. They strongly recommended that the trustees of primary schools should not transfer them to the control of regional education committees until satisfactory modifications had been made in the Londonderry act. With Charles D'Arcy, archbishop of Armagh, in the chair, the group resolved that in each transferred school the power of appointing teachers and controlling day-to-day management should be granted to a six-member committee, composed of two representatives of the parents, two representatives of the managers and trustees, and two persons nominated by the regional education authority. In the normal case the principal teacher of a transferred school should be, the Protestant clerics stated, of the denomination of those who transferred the school, and the other teachers should be distributed denominationally in proportion to the denominational allegiance of the children attending the school.[6] Early in 1924 these demands were elaborated by a Protestant conference which this time included the Methodist representatives. To the cry of 'Protestant teachers to teach Protestant children' was added the demand that Protestant children in provided and transferred schools be taught the Bible for at least half an hour each school day.[7]

During the early phases of the Protestant clerical agitation the government's tactics were to remain calm and hope that the movement would not gather momentum. The cabinet was well aware that the movement at this point was chiefly clerical in composition and therefore, mistakenly, underestimated its importance.[8] Also, the government's response was based on the assumption that the Protestant clergy's worries were largely imaginary. For example, being pragmatic men themselves, the politicians thought that the clergy would realise that it was impossible for anyone applying for a teaching position to do so without his denomination being known: his school background would indicate his religious affiliation. Therefore, it was implied, the regional education committees could silently take religion into account when making appointments without violating the letter of the law.[9] But at this point the government made a miscalculation, for the clergy were not pragmatists who would be satisfied with *de facto* arrangements but legalists who demanded that every permissible practice be spelled out on the statute books.

Pragmatic suggestions having failed, the ministry of education went to the opposite extreme and tried to sweep away the issue with a tide of words. The ministry issued regulations under section 26 of the Londonderry act, specifying the rules for religious instruction. The Protestant clergy had been demanding that religious instruction find a place on the timetable of each school. By this they meant (even though they rarely articulated the point clearly) that they wanted the Bible to be taught during those hours when teachers were required to teach. Recognising the ambiguous nature of the Protestant clerics' demands the ministry issued a set of regulations, dated 11 March 1924 and published on 17 March, which stated that religious instruction should be part of the timetable of each school. This was a rhetorical gambit for, although they were using the words of the Protestant clerical agitators, they were infusing them with a totally different meaning. Religious instruction, although given a place on the timetable, meant denominational religious instruction which no teacher was required to give. Further, the reading of the Scriptures was considered to be religious instruction in the denominational sense.[10] The clergy were not fooled by this ploy and, indeed, important laymen were offended by the regulations: five of the thirty sitting members of the Ulster parliament voted against approving them.[11]

Tempers were becoming short. 'Yes, I have had great difficulty with the Protestant Churches in the north of Ireland,' Lord Londonderry wrote to a friend, 'and I am not through with it yet, but I am saying to them "take it, or leave it." '[12] When, in a letter dated 21 March, Londonderry tried to convince the Protestant clergymen that religious instruction would be provided adequately under the new regulations the clergy firmly reiterated their conviction that only an amending act would set matters right.[13] The agitators' spokesman in the Commons, Dr Hugh Morrison, a member for the Queen's University, denounced Londonderry's 'revolutionary attitude': 'I do not think there is a parallel case in recent history, except it be that of Sir Robert Peel at the head of a Conservative government repealing the corn laws or of Benjamin Disraeli introducing a franchise bill.'[14]

The Protestant clerical opponents of the Londonderry act had two weapons. First, they could neutralise the offensive portions of the act by refusing to transfer their schools to the regional education committees. This refusal required school managers to make considerable financial sacrifice but left the schools free to operate as denominational institutions. So effective was the campaign against transfer that of the approximately 2,000 public elementary schools operating in 1925, only ten were schools which had been transferred by the former managers to the local educational authorities.[15]

But non-cooperation was essentially a passive strategy. To bring about an amendment the clerical agitators realised that they had to go on the attack and that they had to enlist large numbers of laymen in their campaign. Here the clergy's task was not an easy one because many Ulster Protestant laymen were predisposed to distrust their clergy when the clergymen entered the field of politics. Thus, for example, at a special meeting of the Banbridge urban council to discuss educational matters it was decided that enough had been heard from the clergy and that it was time the laity investigated matters; whereupon it was resolved that the Londonderry act was basically sound and beneficial and that the clergy were being unjust in implying that the laymen in charge of the regional education committees would be any less zealous for the Gospel than the clergy![16] A similar tone ran through the speeches of Alderman James Duff, probably the most influential civic representative in Belfast education affairs. Duff declared that 'any clergyman who says that under the new education act the Bible is thrown out of the schools is a man who has no right to wear the cloth and supposed to be a spiritual leader of the people'.[17]

Further to impede the clerics in raising a mass campaign was the attitude of the teachers, most of whom favoured the Londonderry provisions and resented the implied slurs upon their religious devotion, as well as the clergy's continued meddling in educational issues. Simply put, the teachers were on one side of the controversy, the clergy on the other.[18] The Irish national teachers' organisation, being predominantly Catholic, did not speak out forcibly, but the Protestant teachers made their views known. In April 1924 the Ulster national teachers' union passed a vote of confidence in the Londonderry act. In moving the vote Isaac McLoughlin, a leading figure in teachers' union circles, denounced 'discontented divines who were misleading people who could not think for themselves'.[19]

Despite these obstacles the clerical opponents of the Londonderry act decided to agitate the laity. The initial steps in gaining the adhesion of the laity came at the general assembly of the Presbyterian Church in Ireland in June 1924, when the moderator, the Reverend R. W. Hamilton, and the convener of primary education, the Reverend William Corkey, used the occasion to speak out at length about the imminent danger in which the 'secularising act' placed the Presbyterian schools. The keynote for future agitation was sounded by a cleric's motion that the presbyteries and kirk sessions should prepare resolutions about education with the intention of influencing politicians when elections were called.[20] The whole performance was so smoothly orchestrated that Corkey was able to have the proceedings and resolution printed and distributed amongst the Presbyterian community in Northern Ireland as an official statement of the general assembly's position.[21]

During the latter part of 1924 three Protestant clergymen came together to form the nucleus of a highly effective pressure group. They were the Reverend William Corkey for the Presbyterians, the Reverend James Quinn, a Belfast Anglican clergyman of views similar to Corkey's, and the Reverend W. H. Smyth, who represented the Methodists. In December these men rallied the Protestant school managers and eventually the 'United Education Committee of the Protestant Churches' was formed. Not surprisingly, the three honorary secretaries were the Reverends Smyth, Quinn, and Corkey. Using this front Corkey and colleagues published a pamphlet (*The Case Against the Education Act* by the Reverend W. S. Kerr, an Anglican clergyman) and, more important, were able to inveigle the representatives of the Belfast Orange lodges and of various Unionist associations to promise to send delegates to a strategy meeting to be held in late February 1925.[22]

Lord Londonderry, sensing that the agitation was gaining strength, tried to back-pedal. He argued in late January in a speech given at a lord mayor's luncheon in Belfast that the problems came from the clerics' having made 'a perfectly honest misreading of the act...'. In particular, he argued that the employment provision of his education act simply meant that no one was to be excluded on the basis of religion from making an application or from being considered for a teaching vacancy in an elementary school under public control. But, he said, the act did not operate at every stage to prevent the appointing authority from taking cognisance of an applicant's religious beliefs. In fact, in making the actual appointment, as distinct from advertising for the appointment, the ministry expected the appointing authority to take everything into account with a view to selecting the best candidate, not only from the view of academic qualifications but also of character and of acceptability to the parents of the children in the school.[23] That Londonderry was here advocating procedures which violated both his own education act and the

government of Ireland act, 1920, is obvious. All he earned
from his opponents for being untrue to his original principles
was a long vile letter from the three chief agitators which all
but accused him of conscious duplicity.[24]

So crude was this attack upon Lord Londonderry by the
three clerical secretaries of the United Education Committee
of the Protestant Churches that the Protestant archbishop of
Armagh felt compelled to write to the press expressing regret
at the letter and stating that it was neither just nor generous.[25] The lord primate's refusal to be associated with the
actions of the joint secretaries of the United Education Committee of the Protestant Churches allows one to emphasise
two points about the agitation. The first is that as the Protestant committee leaders assumed more and more extreme
postures, it became increasingly clear that a significant portion
of the Protestant clergy did not subscribe fully to their statements. The moderate clergymen, led now by the archbishop
of Armagh, held that the actual arrangements made by the
ministry of education secured for the Protestants, in the
words of Archbishop D'Arcy, 'practically all that we desire'.[26]
The fact that the clerical agitators did not have the complete
adhesion of their clerical colleagues underscores a second
observation: that the clerical lobbyists were extremely effective. Eventually they were able to force a surrender by the
Unionist government, an accomplishment out of all propor-
tions to their actual numbers.

The secret of the United Education Committee's success
was that it chose a nodal moment in Ulster political life in
which to enlarge its campaign to include Orange leaders and
Unionist politicians. In 1925 the Ulster government was
waiting anxiously for the report of the boundary commission,
determined not to surrender any Ulster territory, but apprehensive about whether or not it could withstand combined
pressures from the Irish Free State and Great Britain if major
changes in the boundary were recommended by the commission. Sir James Craig realised that a show of strength before

F

the boundary report was published would improve the government's position. He intended, therefore, to hold a general election on the pledge that 'not an inch' of Northern Ireland's territory would be abandoned. Certainly no opposition group could capture power from Craig, but dissidents within his own party could destroy his hopes of presenting a perfectly united front to the Dublin and London governments.

As late as 20 February 1925 Craig still had not realised how dangerous the clerical campaigners could be to his position: on that day he spoke about education to an Orange meeting near Aughnacloy, County Tyrone, and he gave no hint of any intention to introduce an amending bill.[27] But soon the leaders of the Protestant committee moved to convince him of their significance. On 27 February 1925 the United Education Committee of the Protestant Churches had met with the leaders of the Belfast County Grand Orange Lodge and prominent Unionist politicians. Together they decided to hold a six-county educational conference early in March whose purpose would be to pressure the government into amending the Londonderry act. Knowing that an election was pending the United Education Committee printed and distributed a leaflet, bearing the time-honoured rallying cry 'Protestants Awake' in large red type, and reading, in part, as follows:

> The recent Education Act secured many valuable reforms but in the case of transferred and provided schools, are you aware:
> 1 That the Education Authority is forbidden to provide Religious Instruction (Clause 26)?
> 2 That the Committee appointing teachers is expressly forbidden to pay any regard to the religious views of any applicant (Clause 66)?
> 3 That therefore, the door is thrown open for a Bolshevist or an Atheist or a Roman Catholic to become a teacher in a Protestant school?
> 4 That the object of the National Education Board, viz. combined secular and separate religious instruction for all denominations (though recommended by the Lynn Committee) has been set aside for a system which is secularist

in its terms and tendencies?
The Act of Parliament which makes these things possible
should be amended without delay.[28]

The mass meeting held on 5 March in the assembly hall of
the Presbyterian Church in Ireland was an unmistakable
political threat to Sir James Craig. The meeting was chaired
by the moderator of the Presbyterian Church, the podium
was studded with leading clergymen, and most important,
Sir Joseph Davison, grand master of the County Grand
Orange Lodge, Belfast, was in the forefront. Sir Joseph
claimed to represent 20,000 Belfast Orangemen and, in addition, his influence among Orangemen throughout Ulster
was considerable. A 'campaign fund' was begun with a goal
of £20,000. By the time the meeting was adjourned it was
obvious that the Protestant clergymen had been able to
garner a great deal of lay support and that they now had the
financial resources to bring massive pressure to bear on MPs
and parliamentary candidates.[29]

In the face of this electoral threat Sir James Craig surrendered with almost dazzling swiftness. The next day, 6
March, he invited the organisers of the education campaign
to consult with him. Soon after it was announced that an
education amending bill would be introduced and that 'education peace' reigned.[30] This was a rapid development indeed:
on 3 March Lord Londonderry had held a press conference
in which he made clear what was then the official government
position, that there would be no change in his 1923 act.[31]

Nearly a year earlier, with considerable prescience, Lord
Londonderry had written to a friend about his dealings with
the Protestant Churches, stating that 'if they like something
better than what I propose, they must get someone else to
give it to them'.[32] This is exactly what happened, for after
holding his press conference on 3 March Londonderry had
gone off to England. He was not present at the negotiations
with the representatives of the United Education Committee
and of the Orange Order. The government's representatives

were Sir James Craig, Richard Best (the attorney-general), and Herbert Dixon, the government chief whip. Londonderry was apprised of the negotiations by telegraph.[33]

The political strategy of the Protestant clerics had been shrewd: they had gone over the head of the minister of education and by threatening the prime minister with political embarrassment they forced him to modify the policy of the minister of education. Having made his decision, Craig proceeded rapidly. When parliament opened on 10 March the speech from the throne announced a dissolution. The election was held on 21 April, Craig was resoundingly victorious, and the strength of his position was visibly demonstrated to the Dublin and London governments.[34]

What were the terms of settlement? Seemingly they were defined in an amending act which was passed with extraordinary speed, receiving the royal assent on 13 March 1925. The act had only three operative provisions. The first added to the list of topics upon which the school management committees of transferred and provided schools might advise the regional education committee, 'if the education authority so desire', 'the appointment of teachers by the education authority'. The second was the deletion of the proviso in section 26 prohibiting the local education authorities from providing religious instruction. Thirdly, the proviso in section 66(3) which forbade the education authority's taking cognisance of a candidate's religion in the appointment of teaching posts was repealed.[35]

The meaning of the amending act seemed simple enough, but in point of fact such was not the case. In explaining the act in parliament Lord Londonderry made the assertion that although the amending act removed the prohibition on the provision of religious education by the local education authorities in provided and transferred schools, the schools were still restricted by the prohibition imposed by the government of Ireland act. He added that although the clauses prohibiting religious discrimination in the choosing of candidates for teaching posts was removed, those who appointed teachers were still restricted by the government of Ireland act.[36] Londonderry seemed to be saying that the amending act changed nothing. But if this was true why had the Protestant clerics accepted the act?

An equally peculiar interpretation, seemingly having as little to do with the actual amending act as did Londonderry's, was that of the Protestant clerical leaders. The Reverend Mr Corkey's interpretation was that the amending act meant that hereafter when Protestant schools were transferred to local control there could be inserted into the deeds of transfer two conditions: (1) that Bible instruction would be given each day by the teaching staff of the school and (2) that in the case of a vacancy in the teaching staff appointed by a regional education committee, the teacher selected would be chosen from a list of three persons nominated by the local school committee.[37] This interpretation was as far from the actual words of the amending act as was that of the minister of education. Nothing was said in the amending act about title deeds, about daily Bible instruction, or about lists of three candidates.

There are only two reasonable explanations of the conflicting interpretations of the amending act held by the minister of education and by his chief Protestant opponent. One is the unlikely, but possible, occurrence that both men had individually and independently reached his own misinterpretation. Much more probable is the suggestion that Sir James Craig in negotiating the settlement had gained the electoral silence of the Protestant agitators and the continued allegiance of his minister of education by promising them both what they wanted. This would not have been difficult because Lord Londonderry's absence in London precluded a face-to-face meeting of the minister of education and his Protestant clerical opponents, and thus opened the possibility of Craig's providing a different interpretation for each side. This explanation, of course, is speculative, but not unrealistic.

Whatever illusions either man and his associates had about the 'settlement' were dashed as the results of an inquiry by the Protestant committee on 24 April 1925 asking the ministry if it were prepared to approve the following conditions in the deeds of transfer of former voluntary schools: (1) that religious instruction was to be given by the teaching staff on a programme approved by the persons or body transferring the school, and (2) that if someone offensive religiously to the transferring body were appointed as a teacher the transferors had the right to resume control of the school. The ministry replied that under the government of Ireland act neither of the two conditions would be legal.[38]

There followed in late June a set of negotiations between Lord Londonderry and the United Education Committee of the Protestant Church which was finally to produce a truce. These negotiations lasted from 22 to 26 June 1925 and included, in addition to the main treatings, dealings between Lord Londonderry and representatives of the teachers' unions.[39] The terms of the 'concordat' between the parties were embodied in a letter of 4 July 1925, addressed by the permanent secretary of the ministry to all local education authorities. The compromise may be summarised as follows: first, in the future local education authorities were empowered to require that a 'programme of simple Bible instruction' be given in provided or transferred schools in the period set apart on the timetable for religious instruction. Secondly, this simple Bible instruction, although given during the hours set apart for religious instruction, was not to include denominational dogmas or catechetical points. In other words, it was tacitly understood that the simple Bible reading was to be Protestant in nature but not distinctive of any Protestant denomination. Thirdly, the daily period specified on the timetable for the Bible instruction was not to be included within the hours of compulsory attendance by the children. Given this point, the fourth part of the agreement was crucial: nevertheless, teachers *were* to be compelled to give such simple Bible instruction as part of their required educational duties. The fifth point was that the teachers were not compelled to give denominational instruction if the school managers chose to use the religious time slot for specific denominational teaching instead of general Protestant instruction.[40] By 1930, 430 former voluntary schools (all Protestant) had been transferred under these terms to local civic control.[41]

The chronicle of the amending act of 1925 is a tawdry and often tediously complicated tale, but it is important both because of the nature of the final concordat, and because of what the story indicates about the social and political character of Northern Ireland in the 1920s. As far as the result of the Protestant agitation is concerned, there can be no doubt that Lord Londonderry surrendered and permitted the introduction of a pernicious double standard in Ulster education. The concordat's permitting regional education committees to require that teachers give Bible instruction actually meant that the teachers could be required to give Protestant religious instruction. (That this instruction was not to be distinctive of any specific Protestant denomination does not obviate the fact that simple Bible reading was distinctly Protestant, being acceptable to all the Protestant denominations, but not to the Roman Catholics.) Recalling that the entire salary of the primary school teachers was paid by the ministry of education and, further, that all educational expenses of transferred and provided schools were paid by local and central government authorities, it is quite clear that the new arrangement involved an endowment of the Protestant faiths.

Despite this fact the attorney-general of Northern Ireland certified the legality of the 1925 act and raised no objections to the interpretation of the act articulated in the ministry-Protestant committee concordat.[42] This is hardly surprising since the attorney-general was dependent upon the government's good will for his office. What is significant is that the legal authorities of the United Kingdom took no cognisance of the actions of the Ulster government even though there was good reason to believe that the actions of the Northern Ireland government violated the terms of the government of Ireland act of 1920. This is indicative of a decision upon the part of the United Kingdom government to give the Ulster government its head and to become enmeshed in Ulster affairs as little as possible.

The London government's policy of limiting involvement in Northern Ireland affairs to a minimum was a precondition for the increasingly sectarian bent of the Belfast government which dates from the mid-1920s. Educational developments serve as a reliable index of that process.

Perhaps most important for future developments in the educational sphere, the course of the campaign against the Londonderry act revealed clearly the political strength and sophistication of many of the Protestant clergy. Before partition, the Protestant Ulsterman had often denounced the Catholic 'priest in politics', but no band of Catholic priests in the former united Ireland had engaged in politics with the energy and the efficacy of the Protestant clerics who led the United Education Committee of the Protestant Churches.

5

Progress and Controversy, 1925-30

When discussing education in Northern Ireland in the 1920s it is easy to become hypnotised by the oscillations of the religious controversies and to forget that many educational developments had little or nothing to do with religious problems. Thus, before turning to the renewed religious strife which flared in the last years of the decade it is well to discuss the improvement in the educational system which occurred under the Londonderry act of 1923.

In the field of primary education the most important developments were the improvement in school attendance and the rehabilitation of the Belfast school system. In 1925 the regional education committees were formed, one of their chief duties being to enforce school attendance.[1] Average daily attendance in Northern Ireland's elementary schools improved from 77.5 per cent in 1923 to 85.4 per cent in 1930 (see Appendix, Table IV). This improvement, while significant, should not be overrated. No education committee took advantage of the option open under the Londonderry act of requiring that children start school at the age of five or five and a half instead of six.[2] Further, the Londonderry act's dependence upon regional committees resulted in uneven enforcement. The Ulster teachers' union charged that not only were certain local education authorities lax, but that some physicians indiscriminately issued medical excuses and that magistrates were often foolishly lenient in assigning penalties upon parental offenders. The union claimed that under the new arrangements it was in the interest of the school attendance officers to show a high percentage in attendance, and the officers sought to have a child's name struck off the roll as soon as possible after his attendance became irregular.[3] When, in 1929, the English government decided to attempt to raise the school-leaving age to fifteen (in the actual course of events the age was not raised until after World War II) pressures were brought to bear upon the Ulster government to do likewise. John Hanna Robb, parliamentary secretary to the ministry of education, squelched these forces by pointing to the practical difficulties in keeping children in school to fourteen in rural areas, much less fifteen, and by arguing, less convincingly, that most pupils would not get any appreciable educational benefit from another year of schooling![4] Lord Craigavon (Sir James Craig had been created a viscount in 1927) later elaborated, explaining that the heavy dependence of Northern Ireland's economy on agriculture made the extension of compulsion impractical because many farmers depended upon the labour of their young sons. In any case, the government could not afford the costs of expanding its school system to include all fifteen year olds.[5]

The elementary schools in Belfast were in a deplorable state when the Northern Ireland ministry of education assumed power. The Belfast schools had been neglected under the old system controlled from Dublin. The commissioners of national education had relied upon voluntary efforts for initiating school construction, a policy which operated satisfactorily in rural areas but which was patently unsatisfactory in Belfast, a thriving industrial centre. The Lynn committee estimated that in Belfast, which had 60,000 elementary school places, 12,000 children of school-going age were without school accommodation.[6] When, in 1924, the Belfast education committee conducted its own child census, it discovered that the solution to the problem was more difficult than it first appeared. The committee discovered that over 9,000 places in the schools were occupied by children under or over the statutory attendance ages (six to fourteen). Six thousand of these children were aged three to six. Although it was possible to solve most of the Belfast accommodation problem by excluding from the schools the 9,000 children who were outside the compulsory attendance ages, this was socially undesirable: the education authority wished to encourage the older children to stay on to improve themselves as much as possible, and the younger children were usually the offspring of mothers engaged in the Belfast linen trade. In the absence of day nurseries the education authority had little choice but to shelter the younger children during school hours.[7] In any case the solution to the problem of the under-supply of school places was complicated because, given Northern Ireland's dual school system, it was necessary for the authority to initiate the building of the proper number of schools for Protestant children, while encouraging the Roman Catholic authorities (who no longer received governmental building grants) to provide schools for the Catholics.

Nevertheless, the greatest defect in the elementary education structure of Belfast was qualitative rather than quantitative. In 1924, of the 194 elementary schools only six could be classed as satisfactory physically, twelve more could be made satisfactory, and, according to the Belfast education committee, 'the great majority of the remainder would not be tolerated in any other part of the United Kingdom. There are about forty of these schools which are a direct menace to the health and physical development of the children and it is almost doubtful whether the children attending them would not be better in the street.'[8]

Although the Belfast corporation had never been noted either for its efficiency or for its incorruptibility, the Belfast education committee operated smoothly and without major scandal. One facet of the committee's activities was to take over the management of former voluntary schools. By March 1930, seventy-four of the 184 elementary school buildings in Belfast had been transferred to the Belfast education authority. All of these were Protestant schools.[9] According to the inspectors of the ministry of education in Belfast the transfer of a school to the Belfast education committee meant an immediate improvement in the building's equipment, heating, and cleaning.[10]

By the end of the 1927-8 academic year the committee had completed building two large new primary schools;[11] the next year two more were finished, a third was nearing completion, contracts had been drawn for two more, and several additional sites in the city had been acquired for future construction.[12] Although Belfast's educational problems had by no means disappeared, by the end of the decade they were well on the way to being solved.

If marked improvements were shown in school attendance and in school accommodation in Belfast, the ministry of education was only partially successful in a third matter, the amalgamation of primary schools in rural areas. The ministry's policy was to require the amalgamation of neighbouring, but previously separate, schools for boys and girls, or for infants and senior pupils, when the average attendance of one of these schools fell below fifty. In enforcing this policy the commissioners were careful to protect the rights of teachers, the amalgamations taking place only when the teacher of one of the schools either retired or resigned.[13] (It goes almost without saying that amalgamations occurred only within the unwritten rules of Ulster's dual social system; Catholic and Protestant elementary schools were not amalgamated.) Admittedly, some progress was made: whereas in 1922 there were ninety-seven children on the rolls of an average elementary school, the average in 1930 was 106 (see Appendix, Table III). Nevertheless, the ministry's work was difficult. The natural parochialism of rural communities militated strongly against amalgamation. 'Opposition to the amalgamation of small schools is strong and determined in most of the rural areas, where every parent's desire seems to be to have a school almost at his door,' stated the ministry of education's annual report for 1929-30. 'And at present many of these rural parents are deaf to reason on the subject. They assert that small schools are just as good—some say better than large schools. They oppose amalgamation on the ground of health, on the ground of the danger to pedestrians on the roads in modern times, and on grounds far less reasonable and sensible even than these.'[14] Thus, despite the ministry's efforts, in 1930, 810 of the 1,893 public elementary schools in Northern Ireland had an average daily attendance under fifty (see Appendix, Table V).

Turning to the field of secondary education, one finds that the ministry of education's efforts were as successful as its attempts were modest. The most important change, the abolition of the payment by results system, took place rapidly and without difficulty. Related to the abolition of payment by results was the decision to cease making grants to secondary schools operated by private individuals for their own profit. In the past when secondary school grants were allocated in terms of pence-for-examination scores, it had made no difference where the child had obtained his coaching; now that the ministry of education was granting funds only to schools which established an approved educational environment (irrespective of how children did on annual examinations), it was reasonable to take the grants away from the profit-making institutions unless they met quite stringent government regulations. The most important of the new requirements were that the entire income of these schools from all sources had to be devoted to educational purposes and that a governing body of reputable persons had to be established to see that the headmaster and teachers acted responsibly in conducting the schools. Surprisingly, the private schools did not fold. Instead most of them accepted the ministry's regulations and continued to function independently of local control but now under close supervision by the ministry of education.[15]

During the 1920s a new system of scholarships to secondary schools was introduced. Before the Ulster ministry of education was created the main provision for scholarships had consisted of entrance scholarships offered by the headmasters of some of the schools and of a scattering of prizes awarded by the intermediate education board according to the results of its annual examinations. Thus, the Lynn committee noted the paucity of educational opportunities for poorer children and recommended the creation of a governmental scholarship scheme. Under the terms of the 1923 education act each county and county borough framed a scholarship system. Most awards were of £20 annual value and granted by competitive examination. This system, while comprehensive in the sense that it covered all of Northern Ireland, was hardly lavish. By the end of December 1929, 516 pupils in Northern Ireland had been awarded scholarships to make possible their attending secondary schools.[16] When compared to the total enrolment of approximately 11,600 in academic secondary schools in the year 1929-30 (see Appendix, Table VII), the narrowness of the Ulster government's scholarship programme becomes apparent.

Under the Londonderry act, it will be recalled, it was permissible for managers of secondary schools to transfer them to the control of the regional or county borough committees and also possible for the regional and borough committees to establish secondary schools on their own initiative. These provisions, however, were more in the nature of wishful thinking on the part of the officials of the ministry of education than actual operative regulations. Few secondary school managers were tempted to cede control of their schools. When, in the academic year 1926-7, the Fermanagh Protestant Board actually transferred control of the Enniskillen High School for Girls to the Fermanagh regional education committee[17] this inspired the parliamentary secretary to the ministry of education to announce proudly to the Commons: 'one education authority has actually embarked upon the management of a secondary school of its own. Long may it flourish!'[18] His enthusiasm was not contagious, for by 1947 only nine secondary schools were under the management of local educational authorities.[19]

Early in 1926 Lord Londonderry wrote to Sir James Craig resigning as minister of education. The chief reason he gave was that he was a large employer of labour and because of the crisis in the coal industry he must now devote his time and energy to that situation.[20] There is no question but that he was being truthful when he gave this reason, for he was making similar statements revealing his concern with the Durham coal industry in his private correspondence as well,[21] but this reason was not the complete explanation for his resignation; as detailed in Chapter 4 he had been soundly beaten by the Protestant clergy on education matters, and, at a crucial point in the negotiations, Sir James Craig had made pivotal decisions while Londonderry was absent in London. It is hard to believe that these occurrences did not influence Londonderry's decision to resign. Further, Sir James Craig's official biographer points out that when the joint British–Irish Free State–government of Northern Ireland agreement of 3 December 1925 was signed in London, Lord Londonderry, who was in London at the time, was not asked to sign it and a senior civil servant was. Londonderry, a man of considerable pride, had taken offence at this gaucherie on Craig's part.[22] The snub, coming on top of his difficulties at the education ministry, and the very real need to protect his Durham interests, probably account for his quitting the Ulster stage.

Some measure of Londonderry's stature within the Craig government is indicated by the fact that in choosing his replacement Craig tried to find someone who was as close as possible to Londonderry in background and outlook. The man chosen was James Edward Caulfield, eighth Viscount Charlemont, appointed on 13 January 1926.[23] Not only did Charlemont take Londonderry's former cabinet post but he assumed his former position as leader of the Senate as well. Those who worked for Charlemont found that he had an attractive impish streak and an ability to remain buoyant amidst the squalls that beset his ministry.[24] Perhaps most important, unlike his predecessor he was able to deal with the Protestant clergy without losing his temper or becoming discouraged. 'I have had a long conversation with Lord Londonderry...' he merrily informed his permanent secretary before receiving a delegation of Protestant clergymen, 'and I have come to the conclusion that he doesn't really *like* the clergy in their collective capacity!'[25]

Although less dramatic than the appointment of another peer to be minister of education, the elevation in 1927 of A. N. Bonaparte Wyse to be permanent secretary was in the long run more important, for Wyse directed the daily administration with unfaltering skill and guided the policy decisions of successive ministers with subtlety and tact. His appointment was noteworthy because he was a Roman Catholic and a southerner. Moreover, after having been spirited away from the southern government by Lord Londonderry, Wyse had continued to maintain his permanent residence in Blackrock, Dublin, where he was a near neighbour of Eamon de Valera. Each week he commuted home to the south. Wyse entered the northern education service as a member of the Lynn committee and then proceeded to take charge of elementary education in the Ulster ministry, much the most important sub-department. Born in Limerick in 1870, Wyse counted in his family background Sir Thomas Wyse, the most famous Irish educationist of the nineteenth century. He was especially proud of his descent from Lucien Bonaparte, brother of Napoleon I. (Acquaintances noted a remarkable physical resemblance to his forebear, a perception borne out by photographs.) He attended Downside and received a University of London BA in French and an MA in classics. After teaching for three years at an English grammar school in 1895 he was appointed an inspector of national schools for Cork and the vicinity. Because of his linguistic ability he was sent to France and Belgium for the Belmore commission, his report being published in the appendix to the main document. Significantly for his later work, he served from 1898 to 1903 as an inspector for national schools in the Ballymena area, County Antrim. In 1905 he entered the central education office, Dublin, and in 1915 was promoted to the Roman Catholic secretaryship to the commissioners, the post of secretary being the second highest rank in the national education service. It was generally expected that he would succeed to the highest rank in the Dublin organisation, but Lord Londonderry lured him to Belfast. In this case Lord Londonderry's judgement was perfect, for Wyse turned out to be the most able of civil servants, cultured (he read Greek for a time each morning, doing his cultural devotions rather as a clergyman does his religious meditations), tactful with ministers, and absolutely fair with his subordinates. That damage than it did from the buffeting of the Protestant the Northern Ireland education system did not suffer more clergymen can in large part be ascribed to Wyse's administrative acumen.[26]

Once again the Protestant clergy attacked. The 1925 education amending act and its associated regulations had allowed regional and county borough education committees to require that teachers in their employ teach the Bible for half an hour daily, but it did not compel the committees to impose such a regulation. Thus, when managers of Protestant primary schools transferred their institutions to local control they usually insisted on the inclusion of a clause binding the regional education committee to see that the Bible was taught for half an hour daily. Some transferors sought to have an additional clause inserted whereby the school would revert back to the original managers if the Bible instruction agreement were broken by the local education authorities. Most education committees were able to develop workable agreements with the Protestant school managers, but in some areas difficulties arose. The actions of the Armagh regional education committee and the clerical response thereto triggered a new religious agitation.

The first sign of trouble in Armagh came in early October 1927 when the Armagh diocesan synod of the Church of Ireland resolved that its board of education, when dealing with the Armagh regional education committee, should safeguard the property and interests of the church with special care.[27] The next spring resolutions of the Lurgan clerical union directed the attention of the Northern Ireland government to the fact that the Armagh regional education committee was refusing to insert in the deeds of schools it accepted for transfer a clause requiring daily Bible instruction.[28] The ministry of education responded with a stiff letter to the secretary of the Armagh regional education committee, reminding the committee that a truce in the education war had been agreed upon in 1925: 'It was of course a necessary condition for the success of this agreed policy that education committees would be willing on their side to bind themselves in the transfer deeds to insist on the teaching of Bible instruction in the schools, and it was evident that a refusal on the part of any authority to do so would revive the agitation against the act in an acute form...'[29]

The Armagh regional committee responded by pointing out that Bible instruction was carried out in all schools under its control and that a clause in the contract of each teacher required him or her to provide Bible instruction as part of his classroom duties. The provision of simple Bible instruction was better guaranteed by such a clause in the teacher's contract than by a clause in the deed of transfer. Further, the committee noted that it had already accepted, or was in the process of accepting for transfer, a total of fifty-six schools, and that in only four cases had the transfer actually fallen through by reason of the committee's refusal to include a Bible instruction clause in the transfer deed.[30] These arguments brought from the ministry a reply which simply restated its anxieties: 'The minister has no desire to dictate to the committee what action it should take in cases of transfer, but he feels compelled to reiterate his opinion that the action of your committee in this matter ... is unfortunate and calculated to imperil the harmonious and successful working of the new legislation.'[31] When, in counter response, the committee made it clear that it had no intentions of accepting any clause which required the contingent reversion of all transferred property or allowing the transferors of schools to have a veto right over the nature of any Bible instruction programme,[32] it was obvious that a stalemate had been reached.

At this point the Armagh issue ceased to be of any significance in itself, for it had initiated a train of events which resulted in another clerical agitation throughout Ulster and eventually another amendment to the Londonderry act. The new campaign took form in the months of March through May 1928. In those months each of the presbyteries of the Presbyterian Church in Ireland, at the instigation, it appears, of the Reverend William Corkey, passed a resolution pressing for further amendment of the education laws. In June 1928 Corkey, as convener of primary education for the Presbyterian Church, led the general assembly in framing resolutions demanding further amendments of the Londonderry act.[33]

The new campaign centred on a triad of themes. The first was that some means had to be found to guarantee that in Protestant schools which were transferred to regional or county borough education committees the committees could not abandon the Bible instruction programme at some date in the future. The general assembly urged that the Londonderry act be modified so as to state that in every provided or transferred school, where the parents of not less than ten pupils in attendance signified such desire in writing, Bible instruction would have to be given.[34] This was a shrewd tactical move for it outflanked the opposition of groups such as the Armagh regional education committee, which were opposed to perpetual Bible clauses in transfer deeds, while guaranteeing at the same time that Protestant children would always be able to obtain Bible instruction in provided and transferred schools; it was noted at the time that one prolific fundamentalist couple could compel the local authorities to provide Bible instruction!

A second theme, which had neither a basis in fact nor any precise policy implications, befogged much of the Protestant thinking: this was the complaint that the primary educational system gave preferential treatment to Roman Catholics. The thought behind this extraordinary argument was that the Protestant Churches were being asked to hand over school property whose estimated worth exceeded £500,000 to local committees which might one day be controlled by secularists or by Roman Catholics. The Roman Catholics of course were not handing over any of their schools, ergo, the educational system was unfair to Protestants.[35] The absurdity of this argument is obvious because the Protestants were just as free as were the Catholics to continue to maintain complete control of their own schools as long as they were willing to pay the same price as the Catholics, namely foregoing the luxury of having all their educational expenses underwritten by local and central government funds.[36]

The third theme was that ministers of religion regularly should be appointed to sit on regional education committees. This demand had been articulated clearly in October 1927 by a delegation from the Presbyterian Church's board of education which waited upon the minister of education,[37] but it was later disguised so as to make it more palatable to laymen: it was rephrased to say that the ministry of education should have the power to appoint a certain proportion of members of each regional and county borough education committee. The intention remained, however, to introduce Protestant clergymen into membership on each local education committee.

Although the themes of the new agitation were somewhat different from those in 1924-5, the personnel were the same. In

July 1928 the United Education Committee of the Protestant Churches joined with the Grand Orange Lodge of Ireland in demanding reforms from Lord Charlemont. No one acquainted with the earlier agitation will be surprised that the names of the three honorary secretaries of the United Education Committee were the Reverend Messrs Corkey, Quinn, and Smyth.[38]

In December 1928 the clerical committee realised that an opportune moment had come to begin to press their attack with vigour. It became known that in imitation of English practice the Ulster government was likely to introduce derating in agricultural areas (that is, to reduce the taxation on rural property) thereby reducing to insignificance the local contributions to the cost of education. Since local contributions represented well under five per cent of the total cost of education already, any further reduction would necessarily weaken the local authorities' claim to control education. Naturally a weakening of local civic control would open the way to greater clerical control.[39]

After a certain amount of difficulty in formulating their precise demands,[40] a joint delegation from the United Education Committee of the Protestant Churches and representatives of the Grand Orange Lodge of Ireland confronted Lords Craigavon and Charlemont on 21 February 1929. The government promised nothing but Craigavon argued that the best method of procedure would be for the United Education Committee of the Protestant Churches to appoint a small subcommittee to negotiate an agreed settlement with the ministry of education. If that were done, Craigavon stated, he would undertake to introduce the necessary amending legislation.[41]

Undeniably the agitation for educational reform was chiefly clerical in origin. That the clergymen were the energisers and extremists within the movement was clearly indicated in mid-March 1929 when a split between the clerics and the Orange Order became visible. At first both sides tried to minimise the fissure, stating that it had been decided that it was in the interests of both the Orange Order and the United Education Committee to decide separately what steps needed to be taken and to proceed accordingly.[42] The surface amiability was dissipated, however, by G. C. Young, grand master of County Antrim, who stated that it was clear to the Orange leaders that the clergymen were less concerned with improving the education act than with getting Lord Craigavon and his government into the greatest difficulty they possibly could.[43]

Just as they had done in 1924-5, the primary school teachers of Ulster opposed the clergy. The Ulster teachers' union, which represented most of the Protestant elementary teachers, was especially opposed to replacing elected representatives on regional and county borough education committees with persons (almost certainly clergymen) whose appointment rested solely on their attachment to a particular religious denomination. The clerical demands were described as undemocratic and it was widely believed among the teachers that the clergy had hoodwinked the Orangemen.[44]

Almost simultaneously with the teachers' attack on the clerical agitators, the heads of the association of Northern Ireland education committees met with Lords Craigavon and Charlemont and strongly opposed displacing of elected representatives on the education committees with appointed clergymen.[45] The Protestant committee replied that education was a different kind of public service than the paving of roads or the building of houses; the implied conclusion was that whereas the former duties could be entrusted to laymen, clergymen must necessarily be involved in controlling character formation.[46]

The clerical leaders knew that a general election was imminent so although increasingly deserted by their Orange allies and attacked by lay opponents, they kept harrying the ministry of education. Their rhetoric and strategy were neatly encapsulated in the statement of the United Committee that 'it is only the feeling that the Protestant cause was in grave peril that has compelled them to lay their case before the public on the eve of the general election'.[47] Once again, the clerical agitators had chosen a point in time when they would have maximum political leverage, and once again they sounded the Protestantism-in-danger cry. They published a detailed statement of their demands in mid-March,[48] and when Lord Charlemont attempted to reply dismissed his statements 'as calculated to mislead the public and confuse the issue'.[49]

Viscount Charlemont realised that the Orange Order and the United Education Committee of the Protestant Churches were far from united, the former wanting assurances of the continuation of Bible instruction in transferred primary schools, the latter wishing, in addition, the appointment of clergymen to each education committee. Therefore, on 10 April he tried further to split the opposition by promising that legislation would be introduced to meet the first demand but making no promise about the second.[50] This strategy worked handsomely for on 23 April the leaders of the Orange Order met with Charlemont and announced that they found his proposal satisfactory.[51]

Meanwhile, on 16 April, Lord Craigavon had called a general election for 22 May.[52] In its only reference to education Craigavon's election manifesto stated that the government intended to provide adequate safeguards to secure that Bible instruction should continue in transferred schools and that those schools should be conducted in accordance with the principles of the parents of the children who attended them.[53] No mention was made of the appointment of clergymen to regional and county borough education committees and it is reasonable to conclude that the prime minister was here engaging in the same tactics as his minister of education, in playing to the Orange Order and ignoring the Protestant clerics. Craigavon took much the same tack at Holywood on 23 April, pledging to secure Bible reading and the appointment of teachers in harmony with the children's religion, but making no statement on other issues.[54] At this point the Protestant clerics chose to cease fighting the government.

Unfortunately it is impossible to tell if the Protestant clerics ceased fighting because they had won or because they had lost. Two points are clear: first, they were *not* at this time given a promise that clergymen would be appointed to regional and county borough education committees, and secondly, in the amending act that was passed more than a year later they *did* obtain governmental concessions that satisfied them on this point. Now the chief agitator and sole memorialist of the clerical movement, William Corkey, writing almost three decades after the event, implied that the Protestant clergy retired from the fray victorious, but this seems questionable. Corkey reports (accurately) Craigavon's Holywood speech in which the prime minister refused to make any specific promises on the appointment of clergy to regional committees[55] but the commitment from the government implying the appointment of Protestant clergymen to the education committees which is cited by Corkey was not given until early July *after* the general election took place.[56] Therefore, instead of accepting Corkey's suggestion that the Protestant clergymen won the appointments concession from the government and then retired victorious, one should substitute as more plausible the following: that the government shrewdly played upon the Orange–clerical divisions, and satisfied the Orangemen's demands. When the clergy saw this happening they quickly joined the government's claque, with the hope (correctly as it turned out) that the government would be generous to those who had supported it. Thus, although the clergy received eventually everything they had demanded, the appointment of clerics to regional education committees was a boon granted to supplicants, not a prize won by conquerors.[57]

The events leading to the 1930 education act were different in one signal regard from those which led to the 1925 act: in the later 1920s the Roman Catholic Church ceased its sojourn in the political wilderness and began exerting its influence to shape the educational system of Northern Ireland. This is an appropriate point, therefore, to review the Catholic position in educational matters.

The most clear-cut statement of the contemporary Roman Catholic position in educational matters is found in the code of canon law. Under canon 1374 Roman Catholic students were prohibited from attending non-Catholic schools, including 'neutral' or 'mixed' schools.[58] Neutral schools in this respect mean what would usually be called secular institutions and mixed schools referred not to Catholic schools in which non-Catholics were admitted, but to schools under non-Catholic sponsorship which admitted pupils of any religion or of no religion at all. Only the bishop of the diocese (not the parents of the child) was competent to grant exception to this rule,[59] but because there was a complete network of Roman Catholic elementary schools in Ireland, such exceptions can only have been extremely rare. Catholic children were forbidden to attend the schools controlled by the regional and county borough education committees.

Canon 1373 stipulated that religious training was to be given in every elementary school. As elaborated by the Irish Catholic bishops, education was defined as the training of the whole man in all the physical, mental, moral, natural, and supernatural powers with which God had endowed him. The end of education, according to the bishops, was to contribute to the ultimate end of human existence, namely the salvation of man's immortal soul.[60] Obviously, within such a theological framework there was no room for secular or for non-Catholic education.

In order to safeguard the education of Catholic children the bishop of each diocese was given, under canons 1381 and 1382, the right to inspect religious instruction of Catholic youths in schools of all kinds. The bishops also had the right to approve teachers and the books used in religious instruction and to cause the removal of unsatisfactory texts and unacceptable teachers.[61] In practice, the requirements of the code of canon law and the evolution of the Irish primary school system during the nineteenth and early twentieth centuries combined to dictate that the Catholic Church would accept only a denominational school system.

There was nothing in the nature of Roman Catholic educational policies to preclude the Church's pressing its case through political means. But however pure the Catholic case may have been theologically, the Church's position was extremely weak politically, because Catholic clerical leaders had refused to cooperate with the Northern Ireland ministry of education during its formative period, and Catholic lay leaders had refused to recognise or cooperate with the civil government. The 1920s were years during which the Catholic leaders gradually accustomed themselves to the harsh facts of reality. Both lay leaders and clerical authorities finally comprehended that the Ulster government was going to survive and that if they wished to protect the interests of the Catholic people they perforce had to abandon their isolation and begin to operate in the political arena.

The key event in the Catholics' relief from their self-imposed exile came in 1925 when Joseph Devlin and one associate took their seats in the Ulster parliament. By 1928 Devlin had a party of ten in the Commons and was using the legislature as a forum to articulate Catholic grievances. In the field of primary education, Devlin argued that under the new Ulster government the Catholics were worse off than under the old national system. Whereas previously they had received a two-thirds grant for the building and expansion of schools, under the new regime schools controlled by private managers received no state aid for such expenses.[62]

Among the clergy one sign of the new realism was the attachment during the academic year 1926-7 of the Christian Brothers' elementary schools to the ministry of education, an arrangement which gained their managers approximately £10,000 annually.[63] But the real awakening among the religious authorities did not come until early 1929 when the Protestant clerics were pressing for modification of the elementary education system. This time, instead of sitting passively by as they had in the past, the Catholic bishops entered the fray. In mid-February 1930, before the government's educational amending bill was published, the six Catholic bishops responsible for Northern Ireland issued a statement claiming that the existing primary educational system in the north pressed with special severity on the Catholics because they could not obtain any aid from public funds towards the erection or equipment of new schools or the expansion of existing schools except on terms which were, on religious grounds, unacceptable. They recognised that the clerics of the various Protestant denominations were not satisfied with the provisions made for provided and transferred schools and that the government had promised them an amending act. The bishops' point was that 'an amending measure of this character unaccompanied by an equitable satisfaction of the Catholic claims would be such an outrage on justice and decency that we hesitate to believe that either the government or the parliament is so dead to all sense of responsibility as that in any circumstances the one would promote and the other enact such a measure'.[64]

Laymen at the traditional St Patrick's day gatherings of the Ancient Order of Hibernians protested against the victimisation of the Catholics on various issues and demanded fair treatment in educational affairs. If the reports of crowd sizes were at all close to being accurate the government had to be aware of the demands: 10,000 Hibernians massed at Omagh and this was only one of several gatherings.[65] Hence, whereas a year previously it had been the Protestant clerics who had been attacking the ministry of education most fiercely, in 1930 it was the Roman Catholics who were fighting hardest.[66]

The king's speech opening the parliamentary session on 11 March 1930 included a promise of an amending bill to secure Bible instruction and to change the constitution of the regional and county borough education committees.[67] A bill to this effect was read for the first time on 1 April.[68] On the same day a deputation of twenty leading Catholics called upon Lord Charlemont. The group was headed by Bishop O'Kane of Derry, and included Archdeacon Tierney, the most important of the Catholic clerical managers, all the Nationalist members of parliament, and Eugene Carraher the president of the Irish national teachers' organisation.[69] The precise nature of the Catholic demands is unknown, but Joseph Devlin's summary provides some indication: 'They asked for precisely the same rights as are being freely conceded to their Protestant fellow-countrymen and fellow-citizens.'[70] By this he probably meant that the Catholics asked for full financial support for their denominational schools on the grounds that the provided and transferred schools, which were fully governmentally supported, were actually Protestant schools.

In any event the deputation gained no satisfaction and the next day the *Irish News* printed an emergency letter to the faithful from Daniel Mageean, bishop of Down and Connor. It was surrounded by a dark black band, usually used for the funeral notices of the most important personages. 'In view of the attack on Catholic interests in education by the bill now before the parliament of the Six Counties, I would ask the clergy of this diocese to say in the mass the prayer Pro qua-cunque Necessitate... and I would request the laity to join with the priest in praying that God may guide and help us in this hour of danger.'[71]

Bishop Mageean realised that although prayer might move mountains, there were more practical ways to move governments. Accordingly he dropped a threat of possible legal action if the amending bill were passed without the Catholics' receiving some concessions. 'There are means within the constitution,' he said, 'to prevent even those in high places from violating its principles. It is laid down in the constitution that no religion may be endowed, and we shall be forced to find in the highest court in the Empire whether the endowment of Protestant schools is in harmony with that constitution.'[72] This threat was an astute move for (as will be discussed later in this chapter) there were serious doubts about the legality of requiring teachers to give 'simple Bible instruction'. It was echoed in the south of Ireland by Sean Lemass, prominent in the Fianna Fail Party, in a speech given at Corrofin, County Clare, less than a week after the bishop's threat. The education bill, Lemass stated, contravened the spirit of article 16 of the Anglo-Irish treaty. Therefore, he asserted that it was the duty of the Irish Free State government to bring the matter to the attention of the government of the United Kingdom.[73]

The debate on the second reading of the amending bill took only two days, 9 and 10 April, but it was an ill-tempered debate.[74] As one political correspondent noted, none of the measures introduced by the government of Northern Ireland since its inception had been the subject of so much preliminary disputation,[75] and neither in the debates in the Commons nor in the arguments outside were the Catholic clerical leaders let down by their lay allies. In the Commons Joseph Devlin was persuasive, amusing, vitriolic by turns; and outside, the *Irish News* poured forth a torrent of propaganda which often became sheer invective.

Although the government's bill passed the second reading with ease a number of events occurred in April and early May which, when added to the threat of legal action by the Catholics, unsettled the government and undercut its confidence. For one thing the primary school teachers of all denominations came out firmly and unmistakably against the amending bill. In March the three unions which represented Northern Ireland's teachers had announced their opposition[76] and after the second reading of the bill the Ulster teachers' union reaffirmed at its annual conference its position and stated that it 'viewed with grave apprehension any attempt to alter the fundamental basis of the education act'.[77]

Further, an unseeming squabble about the amending bill occurred amongst the members of the Belfast corporation, a fray which the government's supporters won, but only after generating a considerable amount of publicity which was embarrassing to the government.[78] Briefly, the Belfast education committee appointed a deputation to inform Lord Charlemont that it did not approve of the clauses in the government's bill which provided for increased clerical representation upon the school management committees and upon regional and borough education committees. The majority of members of the Belfast corporation were enraged by this action and a special meeting was held on 28 April wherein the actions of the Belfast education committee were repudiated by thirty-two votes to twelve. Apparently the meeting was very unpleasant: as a result of the meeting one alderman, Mrs Julia McMordie, a member of the education committee, resigned from the corporation.[79]

Meanwhile Bishop Mageean was replacing his previous threats of legal action (which, presumably, already had made the desired impression) with a suggestion that the four-and-two committee system could be modified to fit with Church principles. If the functions of the four-and-two committee were limited to the purely secular side of education then the Church could enter into such arrangements. The Church managers would, of course, maintain control of all matters relating to religion and morals, including the appointment of the teachers and the selection of textbooks.[80] This was little more than the Protestants were demanding vis-à-vis the provided and transferred schools and the idea began to take hold in some Anglican and some Catholic circles.[81]

Finally, the sum total of all these Roman Catholic pressures —the threat of legal action, the campaign by lay politicians and journalists, the denunciations from the pulpit, and the development of a set of compromise proposals which made the Catholic Church appear reasonable and the government arbitrary—forced Lord Craigavon to grant a major concession. Speaking at an Orange Order luncheon at Warrenpoint on 8 May 1930 he announced that he would have an additional clause added to the education bill then before the Northern Ireland parliament, providing fifty per cent grants for the construction and expansion of privately managed elementary schools.[82] Indisputably, this was a great victory for the Catholics. Naturally, their Catholic spokesman could not exult publicly (Joseph Devlin demanded a seventy-five per cent grant) but the Church authorities worked quietly within the framework of the 1930 act for the better part of the succeeding two decades.

The 1930 education act was a substantial document; for our purposes its provisions may be divided into five segments.[83] The first of these altered the composition of the regional and county borough education committees and of the local school management committees. Specifically, the minister of education was required to appoint up to one quarter of the members of each regional and county borough education committee from among the representatives of those persons or groups in the area who had transferred a school to the committee. In addition, the committee of management established to oversee provided and transferred schools was to draw at least half its members from the transferors of those schools which came under the local management of the committee and from among those persons who were formerly managers of any public elementary school which was superseded by a provided school. Although the act did not mention the clergy directly, the intention of this segment of the 1930 act was to allow the Protestant clergy who had previously been prominent in managing schools to maintain a share in the control of the local elementary schools even though those schools were ostensibly under local civic control.[84]

Secondly, the 1930 act provided that in appointing teachers the local school management committee had the power to narrow the field down to three applicants whose names would then be transmitted to the regional or county borough education committee for a final decision. If, for some reason, the education authority was not satisfied with any of the three candidates, they were to refer the matter to the ministry of education which could pick one of the candidates, refer the matter back to the school management committee for the names of other candidates, or direct that the appointment be readvertised. In the normal case, however, it was assumed that the regional and county borough committee would have no difficulty in accepting one of the three candidates. Although the wording of these provisions was studiously neutral religiously, their meaning becomes clear when juxtaposed with three relevant facts: (1) the local school committees under the terms of the new act effectively were to be dominated by those who had run the former voluntary (read 'denominational') schools; (2) the only schools which would be transferred, or replaced by provided schools, were Protestant schools; and (3) the 1925 education act had removed the prohibition on inquiring into the religious background of teaching candidates. Thus, the result of the appointment clauses of the 1930 act was that Protestant interests were able to ensure that only Protestant teachers were appointed to transferred and provided schools.

Next, the act required that in each provided or transferred elementary school it was the duty of the regional or county education authorities to provide Bible instruction should the parents of not less than ten children demand such instruction. The Bible instruction was to be given under the rules of the 1925 act, which meant that teachers were required to give undenominational Bible instruction, but that the children were not compelled to attend. Hence, the 1930 education act made normative practices which had been only permissive under the 1925 act.

Fourthly, the government's education measure embodied the concession promised the Catholics, namely that the ministry of education was empowered to pay one half of the cost of building and equipping new voluntary schools, and one half of the cost of altering, enlarging, and equipping existing voluntary institutions. Finally, the 1930 act contained a variety of miscellaneous provisions designed to improve compulsory attendance regulations, scholarship schemes, and procedures on dismissal of a teacher.

To place the 1930 act in perspective we must ask a series of questions, not all of which can be definitively answered. In the first place one should ask, was the act equitable as between the two major religious groups? Here the answer has to be a firm no. Under the act two school systems operated, the clientele of one being Protestant, of the other either Protestant or Catholic. In the transferred and provided schools, attended almost exclusively by Protestant children, all capital and daily operating expenses were paid by funds from local and central government sources, whereas the voluntary schools (Protestant and Catholic) received most, but *not* all, of their resources from public sources. Now, there would be nothing inequitable about such an arrangement if the option of operating provided and transferred schools were open equally to both religious faiths; there was no injustice in the case of Protestant voluntary schools which for reasons of preference chose to preserve greater educational independence and to receive less money from civic funds. But this was not the case in relation to the Roman Catholic schools since they did not have the opportunity of becoming transferred institutions: in effect the 1930 act redefined the religious nature of the transferred and provided schools so as to preclude any Catholic school manager who had a strict sense of the law from transferring his school. The provision in the 1930 education act that the request of the parents of ten children compelled the teachers in transferred and provided schools to give simple Bible instruction was tantamount to a requirement that simple Bible instruction had to be given in all transferred and provided schools.

Daniel Mageean, Roman Catholic bishop of Down and Connor, accurately summarised both the Protestant and Roman Catholic theological positions when he declared, 'we

H

cannot transfer our schools. We cannot accept simple Bible teaching. I wish to emphasise this point. Simple Bible teaching is based on the fundamental principle of Protestantism, the interpretation of sacred Scriptures by private judgement.'[85] So embedded in generations of sectarian blindness were the Ulster politicians that it was impossible for the Unionists to recognise that the Catholic viewpoint was completely irreconcilable with the Protestant view and that one had to grant the integrity of the Catholic opinions, even if one disagreed with them on theological grounds. Even Lord Craigavon, who seems at this point to have been trying to accommodate the Catholics as much as politically possible, clearly was incapable of grasping the basis of the Catholic argument. He believed that since the Douay version or other version acceptable to Catholic theologians could be used for Bible reading, the Catholics could have no reasonable objection to Bible instruction.[86] Actually, the reading of any version of the Bible without denominational comment was unacceptable to the Roman Catholics.

Clearly the letter of the law was discriminatory against the Catholics, but let us forget legalities for a moment and ask, were not the Catholic authorities unrealistic in concentrating on what the law said instead of evolving ways of circumventing in practice its unfair provisions? Remember that under the 1930 act at least half of the members of the local school management committees were representatives of the former managers of the transferred schools and that the transferors of any school had the opportunity of writing special conditions into transfer deeds. Nothing prevented the Catholic managers of a voluntary school from specifying in the deed of transfer that an individual school management committee had to be appointed for a given school (thus precluding the dilution of Catholic interests by Protestant representatives) and then appointing staunch Catholics to the management committee where, by virtue of their numbers, they would have control of the management of the school; and the school would then be totally underwritten by local and central government funds. This was precisely what many Protestant school managers were doing and there was nothing preventing the Catholics from doing the same.

But at this point most Catholic spokesmen raised a real, but not insuperable, objection. Quite understandably, the gerrymandering of the early 1920s had destroyed what little faith they might have had in institutions of local government in Northern Ireland.[87] All the county councils, even in predominantly Catholic areas, were under Protestant control with the secondary result that all the regional and borough education committees were Protestant-dominated. But when examined closely the significance of these facts was much greater in appearance than in reality. The regulations of the ministry of education gave the regional and county borough committees no choice but to support financially, according to very strict standards, the local transferred and provided schools in both daily expenses and capital expenditures. Further, the 1930 act gave the local school management committees the right to nominate the three final candidates for vacant teacherships, which meant that the management committee of a school transferred by Catholic authorities could have done exactly what the Protestants did: send up the names of three of their co-religionists. All the teachers in a previously Protestant school remained Protestant and, if the Catholics had wished to operate in a similar fashion, the teachers in a formerly Catholic school would all have been Catholic. Granted, there would inevitably have been squabbles between the Catholic-dominated local school management committees and the Protestant-dominated regional education authorities (disputes arose even when everyone involved on both sides was Protestant); but the fact remains that the Catholic authorities could have gained increased educational grants for Catholic children without endangering the Catholic control of the schools—*if* the clergy had been able to transcend their medieval determination to control the schools singlehandedly and had been willing to enter into partnership with the Catholic laity in controlling the schools through the newly-restructured school management committees.

Yet, it can be argued, even if the Catholic clergy had been willing to trust their laity and even if they had been willing to enter the rough and tumble of Ulster local politics, there was still the danger that the parents of the children in the Catholic-controlled transferred school would ask for simple Bible instruction, and that the teachers perforce would be required to teach Protestantism in the Catholic schools. On a purely legal level there is no denying the validity of this objection. On a practical level, however, it is hard to believe that a Catholic teacher, giving Bible instruction in a transferred school whose management committee was Catholic-dominated, would be giving anything that distantly resembled non-denominational instruction. That, of course, is close to suggesting that the Catholic clerical authorities should have taken the immoral step of publicly assenting to the letter of the rules governing Bible instruction while intending to violate the spirit (and perhaps the letter) of the law. Such a practice, however, had nearly ninety years of precedent, for under the national system of education which prevailed before the partition of Ireland, the school texts were interlarded with allegedly non-denominational moral lessons and with paraphrases of Scripture and yet the Catholic bishops were quite happy. Because these lessons were being interpreted by Catholic teachers (and in spite of the rules of the commissioners of national education), Catholic children were being taught denominational lessons from material which the official regulations stated had to be taught in an undenominational manner.[88]

Whatever the weight of the Catholic authorities' objections to transferring their schools to local management committees there were no objections of merit, either on moral or pragmatic grounds, to entering their schools as four-and-two schools. Under the four-and-two arrangements the Catholic authorities would have had two thirds majority on the committee controlling the local school, would have had complete control over the appointment of teachers, would not have had to allow simple Bible reading, and could have maintained all curricular arrangements as under private management. In return they would have been eligible for building and renovation grants from the local rates in addition to the fifty per cent grant from the ministry of education. The first Roman Catholic school to come under a four-and-two committee did so in 1930 and received seven eighths of the cost of renovation and construction from the Fermanagh regional education committee,[89] but few managers followed this example. Joseph Devlin, the Nationalist leader, unwittingly gave the best argument for entering into four-and-two schemes when he stated that the four-and-two committees were under 'bogus popular control' and that they gave no more popular control than a single managership.[90] Why did the Catholic clergy refuse to enter under the four-and-two schemes? It is impossible to say, but it is undeniable that their unnecessary insistence on maintaining their sole clerical prerogatives in the management of primary schools hurt the Catholic children of Northern Ireland, for it perpetuated the usage of inadequate and outmoded school facilities which under the four-and-two plan could have been improved or replaced, largely through governmental funds.

Finally, let us return to the question of law and ask, was the 1930 education act legal, or did its provision regarding Bible instruction contravene the government of Ireland act, 1920? From our perspective in the 1970s it is hard to see how the requirement that teachers give simple Bible instruction if a small number of parents so desired was anything but an endowing of Protestantism generally, if not an endorsing of any specific Protestant denomination. Therefore it seems to have been *ultra vires* under the 1920 government of Ireland act. At the time of its passage, however, no great issue was made about legality, the Catholic authorities apparently having accepted a tacit agreement with Lord Craigavon that in return for their fifty per cent capital expenditure grants they would drop their threat of appealing to the judicial committee of the privy council for a ruling on the constitutionality of the 1930 education act. The attorney-general for Northern Ireland, Anthony Babington, certified that the 1930 education act did not violate the government of Ireland act and apparently the English legal advisers of the time agreed, although in later controversy no one could produce a copy of their opinion.[91] This approval was dissonant with a 1929 ruling by the Northern Ireland high court of justice in the case of *Londonderry vs McGlade* in which it was decreed that 'the one subject on which no public money is to be expended in state-aided schools is religious instruction ... It is not in the power of our local legislature to provide either paid Roman Catholic or paid Protestant religious instruction in a transferred school.'[92] Nevertheless, the 1930 education act was not challenged. Only in 1945, when the government of Northern Ireland was planning a major education reform, did the issue again arise. Then the attorney-general, John MacDermott, stated categorically that it had been *ultra vires* of the parliament of Northern Ireland to pass the provisions of the 1930 education act requiring teachers in transferred and provided schools to give Bible instruction. He also stated that although the 1925 act was not similarly defective, the transfer deeds approved under it, which required that teachers employed in schools transferred to local education authorities give Bible instruction, were illegal.[93]

6

The Stranmillis Affray, 1930-2

Lords Craigavon and Charlemont must have felt immensely relieved when the 1930 amending act was passed and educational peace prevailed, but they were to have scant respite. The Protestant clerics, having won positions on the various local education committees, also wanted places upon the committee which controlled the management of Stranmillis training college, Belfast, a desire which the Craigavon government for a time resisted and to which it eventually surrendered.

Let us set the stage for the encounter. Historically the training of teachers was a matter relating solely to primary education. The former Irish government had never accepted any responsibility for training teachers for secondary schools, and the Ulster ministry of education adopted this precedent.[1] By the time the Northern Ireland ministry of education assumed control for training primary teachers, the normal mode of entry into the elementary teaching ranks (but not the only method) was through the various teacher training colleges: in 1902 only fifty-five per cent of the Irish elementary school teachers had attended training college, but by 1919-20 the figure was eighty per cent.[2] On the eve of the partitioning of Ireland seven training colleges were in operation. These were the Marlborough Street training college, Dublin (a non-denominational institution with a high proportion of Presbyterian students); the Church of Ireland training college, Kildare Place, Dublin (Anglican); and the following Roman Catholic training colleges: St Patrick's, Dublin; De La Salle, Waterford (both for men students); and Our Lady of Mercy, Blackrock; Mary Immaculate, Limerick; and St Mary's, Belfast (the latter three for women).[3] Notice here that only one institution, St Mary's, Belfast, which specialised in training of Roman Catholic women teachers, fell within the ambit of the Northern Ireland government. Therefore, the new ministry of education had to decide what provisions should be made for the training of Roman Catholic men and Protestant men and women for posts in Northern Ireland's elementary schools.

Simply stated, the Ulster ministry of education had three options. The candidates could be trained in Great Britain, in the Irish Free State, or the Ulster government could found its own training college, or colleges.

Although it at first appeared that there was some possibility of forming an amicable arrangement for the training of northern teachers with the government of the Irish Free State, the door was slammed by the southern government. One of the first actions of the Free State's newly-established ministry of education was to close the non-denominational, but predominantly Presbyterian, Marlborough Street training college.[4] Thus, the only remaining training college in the south which was open to Protestants was the Church of Ireland training college; the Presbyterians were therefore left without adequate provision anywhere in Ireland. Further, when representatives of the Ulster government had approached the southern government with the idea of cooperating in setting the examinations for admission to the various training colleges, they had been more or less ignored. More important, the southern government altered the curriculum of the training colleges in 1922, scheduling the annual examination a month earlier than usual so that the pupils in the colleges could devote the last month of the session to the study of the Irish language and literature.[5] However appropriate the gaelicisation of the training college curriculum was in the south, it was incompatible with the dominant cultural traditions of Northern Ireland.

The only arrangements concluded successfully with the south were made between the Ulster ministry of education and the authorities of the Church of Ireland training college in Dublin. An agreement was struck in April 1922 whereby for two years the Dublin college would train Protestant men and women teachers, until other arrangements could be made. This agreement terminated at the end of the academic year 1923-4.[6]

Understandably, there was within Northern Ireland considerable pressure for the creation of Ulster's own teacher training institution. This pressure stemmed chiefly from the Presbyterian Church and from the primary school teachers (a 'Tibetan policy' a critic called it).[7] On 19 May 1922 Lord Londonderry appointed 'the committee for the training of teachers for Northern Ireland'. This committee, which was under the chairmanship of the man in the Northern Ireland cabinet least amenable to clerical bullying, H. M. Pollock, the minister of finance,[8] set about establishing what was to be known as the Stranmillis training college in Belfast. Moving quickly, Pollock's committee secured the cooperation of the Queen's University and of the Belfast Technical Instruction Committee and by October 1922 was able to admit nearly 200 students to a course of study taught jointly by Queen's professors and by lecturers of the Belfast College of Technology, using the facilities of the two institutions.[9] Eventually in 1929 permanent buildings for Stranmillis college were completed.[10]

For a time it seemed as if the teacher training problem was solved. In 1923 the Ulster teacher training committee had negotiated an agreement with St Mary's training college, Belfast, whereby that college received financial support for training Roman Catholic women in a course of studies subject to the control of the government's teacher training committee.[11] (The denominational control of the college remained unaffected, however.) At first male Catholic teacher candidates enrolled in Stranmillis training college.

Not surprisingly, given the canon law's prohibition of mixed education, the Roman Catholic authorities did not long countenance the training of male Catholic teachers with Protestants in the Stranmillis institution. The Ulster government offered to build a hostel for the Roman Catholic men where they could be supervised in their extra-curricular pursuits by Catholic clergy, if the Catholic students were allowed to continue at Stranmillis. The Catholic authorities refused and claimed that a Catholic men's training college should be founded as well as a Catholic hostel. In turn the ministry refused to meet these demands on the grounds that the number of Catholic men students in training was very small and that in any case there were strong feelings among the northern majority against endowing any specific denomination.[12]

Of necessity, however, the ministry of education had to make some accommodation with the Catholic authorities because the Catholic authorities could frustrate any ministerial plan simply by ordering the school managers not to appoint any teachers trained under a scheme of which they did not approve.

A compromise was reached under which the ministry of education would pay a certain amount per head for male Catholic students trained in the two-year course at St Mary's training college, Strawberry Hill, Middlesex (hereafter contemporary usage is adopted and the institution is referred to as 'Strawberry Hill' to avoid confusion with St Mary's, Belfast, for Catholic women). In April 1925 the secretary of the committee for the training of teachers in Northern Ireland wrote to all the Catholic first-year students who were enrolled in Stranmillis college informing them of the arrangements which had been made and that if they failed to comply with the conditions laid down by the Roman Catholic bishops (ie, that they leave Stranmillis and enrol in Strawberry Hill) it would be very unlikely that they would secure an appointment in a Catholic elementary school anywhere in Northern Ireland.[13] In the following October thirty-one Roman Catholic men, including eleven second-year students, entered the English Catholic training college.[14] Because Roman Catholic men did not attend Stranmillis after 1925,[15] it inevitably became identified as a Protestant institution. Once again the cleavages of Northern Ireland's dual social system had overcome attempts at integration.

Whatever the merits or flaws of a religiously segregated system of teacher training, one fact is clear: that the arrangements were equitable as between Protestants and Catholics. This point has to be made because both groups charged otherwise. The Protestants claimed that the Catholics received larger annual capitation grants than did the Protestants, while the Catholics charged that the arrangements were unfair to them in matters of capital expenditure. Dealing first with the Protestant claims, it should be noted that the capitation grant allotted by the ministry of education for each female student at Stranmillis was identical to that paid to the managers of St Mary's, Belfast, so there was no ground for complaint on that point.[16] As for the men, it was true that the amount paid to the English board of education in respect of those enrolled at Strawberry Hill was somewhat greater than that paid for each man enrolled at Stranmillis. In mid-1927, the rate for men (Catholics) at Strawberry Hill was £76 13s, while the figure for men (Protestants) at Stranmillis was £70. In 1929-30 the figures were respectively, £70 16s and £67 10s; and in 1936-7, £72 7s and £70.[17] Granted, these are differences, but when one recalls that at most forty Catholic men were being trained at any given time, the charges of favouritism become ludicrous, involving a difference of only a few hundred pounds at most each year.

Similarly the Catholic complaints that the Protestants were being favoured because the ministry of education had paid for the construction of the Stranmillis buildings while the Catholic community had to pay for its own buildings were of scant significance. In actual fact, in 1911 the London government had undertaken to pay an annual annuity of £1,000 a year which recouped the Catholic Church for its investment in St Mary's College, Belfast.[18] Further, under the Strawberry Hill arrangements for men the Catholics of Northern Ireland were not required to pay anything for the capital costs of construction of the English college, since the burden of capital expenditures fell upon the shoulders of the English government and the English Catholic Church, not the Northern Ireland government or the Catholic Church in Northern Ireland.[19]

From last chapter's discussion of the successful campaign of the Protestant clergy to gain appointment to the local education committees which controlled the transferred and provided schools, the reader could accurately predict that the same clergymen would attempt to gain some degree of control over Stranmillis training college. In the case of Stranmillis, the clergy were engaged in a stark, undisguised power-grab, which contrasts somewhat with the case of the local schools: whereas in the case of schools transferred from the original clerical owners to local control it was possible to make a plausible argument for continued clerical representation among the governing committees (the churches had, in most cases, built the schools), no similar argument could be made in the case of Stranmillis college, which had been built entirely with state funds and supported for its entire existence from the Northern Ireland exchequer.

  In 1928, when the agitation for a further amendment of the Londonderry act was brewing, some mention had been made of the need for Protestant clerical representation upon the committee for the training of teachers which managed Stranmillis. In particular, the very Reverend Dr Strahan, a former moderator of the Presbyterian assembly, had introduced the question at the Newry presbytery in May 1928 and in the general assembly in June.[20] The deputation representing the

United Education Committee of the Protestant Churches and
of the Orange Lodges had included a demand for 'representation of educational and religious interests' on the Stranmillis
governing board in the list of claims they placed before Lord
Charlemont in early July 1928.[21] As stated in a later (15
February 1929) resolution of the United Committee of the
Protestant Churches: 'without demanding a denominational
training college, we ask as a matter of justice that the conditions under which teachers are trained who are in the future
to be entrusted with the education of Protestant children be
made as acceptable to the Protestant Churches as the conditions under which Roman Catholic teachers being trained
are made acceptable to the Roman Catholic Church.'[22]

Amidst the promises made by Lord Charlemont to the combined deputations of Orangemen and clerical representatives
on 23 April 1929 was a promise that he would create additional places for clergymen on the committee which managed
Stranmillis. It is worth emphasising that Charlemont later
fully admitted making this promise, even though he refused
to keep it.[23] Why did he refuse to keep his word? In the first
instance because there was strong feeling within the cabinet
against so doing. In particular, H. M. Pollock, the minister of
finance and chairman of the committee for the training of
teachers, was doggedly opposed to allowing any clerical representation and in all probability would have resigned from the
committee, amidst great public furore, if the clerics had been
added.[24] Charlemont, faced with this problem, took the extraordinary step of dissolving the committee for the training of
teachers on 16 April 1931. He appointed a full-time principal
of the Stranmillis training college (previously the professor of
education of Queen's had held the post conjointly with his
university position).[25] Significantly, Charlemont did not appoint a new management committee but placed the management under the direct control of the ministry. Thus, he could
argue that his promise to the Protestant clerics was no longer
binding because the pledge had been predicated upon there

being a management committee in existence; he could hardly appoint the Protestant clerics to a committee which did not exist.[26]

But not only was Charlemont avoiding a direct conflict with Pollock when he evaded keeping the undertaking he had given to the Protestants, he was also acting on a newly-found conviction that it was wrong to allow the clergy to claim authority over secular education. The clergy had a right to oversee moral and religious matters, but not secular ones. Hence, in the spring of 1931 the clergy were offered an advisory committee for the supervision of religious training and moral questions at Stranmillis, one which would have no powers over the secular aspect of the college.[27] However, a deputation sent by the United Education Committee of the Protestant Churches (the Reverend Messrs Smyth, Quinn, and William Corkey were again to the fore) made it clear that the clerics would not settle for anything less than the reconstitution of the management committee and the appointment of clergymen upon it, with no restrictions on the sphere of clerical influence.[28] 'The whole system of education is being administered as if there was only one denomination,' charged the Reverend Mr Corkey, 'and that the Roman Catholic. The Presbyterian Church,' he went on, 'always believed in a non-sectarian and unified education all round. But it never believed in giving recognition and state endowments to the Roman Catholic Church when all other denominations were overlooked and given nothing.'[29]

Late in July 1931 Lord Craigavon and Lord Charlemont met with the heads of the United Education Committee of the Protestant Churches. After this meeting a special meeting of the cabinet was held and a letter stating governmental policy was dispatched to William Corkey. The letter contained a compromise offer. The heads of the three Protestant Churches were invited to nominate one representative each to serve on a seven-member departmental committee of management for Stranmillis training college. The parliamentary secretary of the ministry of education, John Hanna Robb, would chair the group. The three clergymen would sit with the other members of the committee only when, in the opinion of the chairman, a religious or moral matter was being considered.[30] Soon thereafter Viscount Charlemont wrote to each of the three Protestant denominations asking for their nominations.[31]

The United Education Committee of the Protestant Churches was far from satisfied with these proposals. On 12 August 1931 the secretaries wrote to Lord Craigavon (note that they no longer were willing to deal with Lord Charlemont) explaining why they continued to be displeased. In the first place, they said, the proposal to add three clerical members to the Stranmillis management committee to advise on religious and moral matters was a far different thing from the promise which the government had made in 1929 to add three clerical members to Pollock's committee without any restrictions on the clerics' involvement in secular matters. Further, the secretaries of the United Protestant Committee took strong exception to the idea that the heads of the Protestant Churches were to nominate members of the committee. Such procedure might be appropriate to the Catholic system but not to the Protestant system of church government.[32]

William Corkey, in a letter to Craigavon of 19 August 1931, amplified the Protestant clerics' objections by asking six questions which are worth summarising because they indicate the clergy's anxieties: (1) since the principal of Stranmillis would be giving Bible instruction, would his appointment be made by the whole committee or just by the secular members? (2) if, for example, the lecturer in history taught in such a way as to undermine morals, would it be within the power of the whole committee to discipline him; and would the clerical members have any say in the appointment of such a lecturer? (3) would applicants for admission to training be required to submit evidence of moral fitness? (4) what redress would there be if the chairman of the management committee, the parliamentary secretary of the ministry of education, failed to convene a full meeting when he should have done so? (5) were matters of religion and morals to be decided solely by the three religious members of the management committee or by all members? (6) would the church representatives have power to decide to increase the time allocated to religious instruction if they so desired?[33] The demands implied by these questions are fascinating. So broadly was the moral sphere defined, and so aggressively were the clerics seeking clerical power over governmentally financed activities, that one has to be reminded that one is reading the claims of Protestant clerics, not of Roman Catholic priests of extreme Ultramontane views.

Lord Craigavon, it appeared, was no longer willing to be hectored. On 21 August he issued a stinging reply to the clerics telling them that Stranmillis training college was the property of the whole people and that no person or association of persons had any right to special representation in the control of that institution. Nevertheless, his government was willing to make some concessions to the Protestant clergy as specified in his earlier proposals. In answer to the Protestant clergy's six questions, Craigavon stated: (1) the principal of the college would be appointed by the minister of education; (2) the minister of education would appoint the lecturers and deal with any problems which arose concerning their conduct; (3) if there was any doubt of the moral fitness of any candidate for admission to the college the matter would be referred to the entire management committee; (4) power would be given to any three members of the management committee, lay or clerical, to convene a meeting; (5) all religious and moral matters would be decided by the whole committee, not by the clerical members; and (6) the amount of religious instruction would be set by the whole committee. The prime minister closed this no-nonsense communication with the directive that 'should your committee require any further explanation of the government's decision I should be glad if you will kindly write to the convener, Mr J. H. Robb'.[34] Craigavon, it seemed, finally had decided that his policy of 'not an inch' was applicable to educational as well as political issues.

At this juncture a split occurred in the ranks of the Protestant campaigners. The Reverend Messrs Smyth, Quinn, and Corkey continued to write abusive letters and make acid speeches about the government's policy.[35] The moderator of the Presbyterian general assembly and the president of the Methodist conference followed the inclinations of the majority of their constituents and refrained from nominating representatives to serve on the Stranmillis management committee.[36] In the Church of Ireland, however, a significant minority refused to approve the actions of the United Education Committee of the Protestant Churches and declined to endorse the policy of non-cooperation with the government. This moderate minority was led by Archbishop D'Arcy who, it will be remembered, had dissented from the extreme tactics of the United Education Committee when it was lobbying for the 1930 amending act. In early July 1931 D'Arcy had written a public letter stating 'there is a great danger, if the demand made by the committee of the Protestant Churches is conceded in the form in which it is presented, that we shall see our new education authority go the way of the old national board'.[37] In another letter published in October, D'Arcy stated that the arrangement proposed by the Northern Ireland government for Stranmillis college was 'an admirable one which should satisfy us all'.[38] As lord primate of all Ireland, therefore, D'Arcy accepted the invitation to nominate a member of the Stranmillis management committee.[39] Although the attitudes of the lord primate were shared by one other prelate, Charles Grierson, the bishop of Down, Connor and Dromore, the moderates were in a minority. They were opposed within the Anglican Church by the Reverends James MacManaway and Joseph Peacocke, respectively bishops of Clogher and of Derry, and by the majority of the Anglican synodsmen. Thus, the diocesan synods of Clogher, Derry and Raphoe, Down, Connor and Dromore, and even of Armagh, passed resolutions endorsing the stance of the United Education Commit-

J

tee of the Protestant Churches.[40]

The meeting of the Armagh diocesan synod was of considerable interest for it provided an opportunity for a statement of the moderates' position and also, because Lord Charlemont was himself a synodsman, the debates provided additional insight into the attitudes of the minister of education. The objections of the moderate clergy to the continued obduracy of the United Education Committee were two-fold. First, as the archbishop of Armagh stated, the demand that the churches have a veto right over secular legislation was a position that was incompatible with the characteristics of the modern state. Secondly, the archdeacon of Armagh added the important pragmatic point that there was no sign that the Orange Order would support the Protestant clerics in their demands. Lord Charlemont in opposing the resolution favouring the United Education Committee's action (that the synod 'request the committee to continue its efforts to secure that conditions under which teachers are trained who are in the future to have the care of Protestant children shall be such as the Protestant Churches can approve of') stated, 'the phraseology of this motion belongs to the thirteenth century'. It was in the thirteenth century, he recalled, that a great Pope issued a famous bull in which he laid down that the Church was supreme over the state, and that the state could not legislate. Nevertheless, the anti-government resolution was adopted by sixty-one votes to fifty-two.[41]

Despite the clerical pressures Lord Craigavon's government seemed determined to stand on its offer of July 1931. But then the clerical agitators shifted tactics. Instead of pressing on alone they now employed the time-tested tactic of using the Orangemen as their foot soldiers. And as in the past they kept doggedly at their attack until the government found itself in a vulnerable position vis-à-vis outside events.

This time events in the Irish Free State strengthened the hands of the Protestant clerical campaigners. On 9 March 1932 Eamon de Valera, the southern Irish politician most

feared in the north, formed a cabinet. He at once began moving to reduce the ties between the Free State and the United
Kingdom. On 20 April a bill was introduced to abolish the
oath of allegiance to the British Crown which had previously
been taken by all members of the Free State parliament, and
more important measures were obviously on tap. The authorities of the Northern Ireland government were unnerved,
because any change in the relations of the United Kingdom
and the Irish Free State was potentially unsettling to the
position of the Ulster Unionist government. Hence, one finds
a leading Unionist newspaper reporting on 23 March that the
government and the churches were again negotiating about
Stranmillis: 'it is understood that the decision to make another
effort to settle the dispute... was dictated by mutual recognition of the seriousness of the situation in Southern Ireland
and the importance of strengthening the government's hands,
in the event of developments affecting Ulster, by closing up
the ranks of the Protestant and Loyalist community.'[42]

An agreement was reached on 23 March, increasing the
number of persons on the Stranmillis management committee
to nine. Each Protestant denomination was given the right to
nominate one representative, the names of the nominees to be
submitted to the minister of education through the medium
of the heads of the three churches. The three clerical representatives were to have the full status and powers enjoyed by
the other members of the committee. The government had
once again surrendered to the Protestant clergymen. The
victors' names appended to the agreement were, on behalf of
the Loyal Orange Lodges, Sir Joseph Davison, and, on the
behalf of the United Education Committee of the Protestant
Churches, the now-familiar Reverends Corkey, Smyth, and
Quinn.[43]

Not only did history repeat itself on the agitators' side of
the transaction, it was also repeated on the governmental side.
Just as the prime minister had conducted the surrender of
1925 when Lord Londonderry was absent, so he directed this

one without Charlemont's presence. During the month of March approaches were made to the United Education Committee of the Protestant Churches by John M. Andrews, the minister of labour.[44] The surrender to the churches was negotiated by Andrews and by Craigavon. Charlemont was kept informed by telegraph (precisely where he was and why is unclear) just as, in 1925, Lord Londonderry had been informed by telegraph of the government's surrender. And Lord Charlemont telegraphed his approval,[45] just as Lord Londonderry had done in 1925, but he can only have felt betrayed. Charlemont wrote to William Corkey: 'I feel that it would be hardly fair on my part not to give you my congratulations on your famous victory at the Battle of Stranmillis. Personally, of course, I think that had I commanded on the field in person the results might have been different, but equally they might not.'[46]

And just as in 1925 and in 1930, the primary school teachers of Ulster felt they had been deserted by the government and left more than ever dependent upon the vagaries of the Protestant clergy. The annual congress of the Ulster teachers' union protested 'the abject surrender of the government in acceding to the reactionary demands of the joint committee of the Protestant Churches. . .'.[47] The Belfast branch of the Irish national teachers' organisation condemned the government's admitting the principle of sectarian control of an institution built and maintained entirely out of public funds.[48]

Their protests were in vain. The new Stranmillis management committee as duly constituted in mid-July 1933 included the following three clerical representatives: the Anglican W. S. Kerr (who had served the United Education Committee earlier by writing an anti-government pamphlet), the Methodist W. H. Smith, and the Presbyterian William Corkey.[49] Thus, the chief clerical agitators had won not only a victory for their cause, but considerable powers for themselves.[50]

The Stranmillis affray was no more than a footnote to the greater school controversy of 1929-30, but consider the results:

the Protestant clergy had managed to assert their right to sit, solely by virtue of their position as clergymen, on a committee which managed an institution that was created by the state and maintained entirely by public funds. Ironically, to the modern observer it seems almost as if in the 1930s the Protestant clergy of Ulster were close to achieving the ancient Roman Catholic ideal of clerical control over all forms of schooling.

7

Depression and Revitalisation, 1931-44

Northern Ireland has always been highly vulnerable to economic fluctuations and the depression years were especially painful. The employment situation was worse in Ulster than in England and Scotland and nearly as bad as in Wales. Whereas in Great Britain as a whole the peak year for unemployment, 1933, found 23.0 per cent of the insured male workers unemployed, in Northern Ireland the corresponding figure was 31.4 per cent. And, unlike the situation in Great Britain, unemployment in Northern Ireland did not drop sharply after 1933: in 1939 24.8 per cent of the insured males in Northern Ireland were still out of work whereas in Great Britain the figure had dropped to 10.7 per cent.[1] The government of Northern Ireland naturally followed the lead of London and pared governmental expenditures whenever possible. Education was affected, but in viewing the effect of the depression upon Northern Ireland's education system it will become clear that the school system was not severely damaged. The real effect of the depression was not so much actually to deprive the educational system of resources but to lower morale and to stifle initiatives for the improvement of the system.

The question of the primary teachers' salaries illustrates the point that the financial stringency of the depression years did more damage to morale than to structure. In the early days of the parliamentary session of 1931-2 Lord Craigavon threw out what he termed 'a friendly warning' to the elementary school teachers that their wages would be cut.[2] Soon it was announced that the cut would be approximately 7½ per cent, a figure which was equal to the cut experienced by members of the Royal Ulster Constabulary and, as Craigavon emphasised, half that undergone by cabinet members, parliamentary secretaries, and members of the House of Commons and the Senate of Northern Ireland.[3] The cumulative effect of a previous cut in 1926 and that of 1931 was to reduce elementary teachers' salaries by roughly fourteen per cent. On the other hand, the salary of the average civil servant in Northern Ireland had been cut slightly more than one third since 1920.[4] In any case, when one realises that the retail price index for the United Kingdom for 1931 was less than sixty per cent of what it had been in 1920, it becomes clear that despite the cuts in money wages the primary school teachers had a much higher real wage in the 1930s than they had had in the early 1920s.[5]

Nevertheless, the teachers could hardly have been expected to be pleased with the pay-cut, and the ill-feeling such a cut naturally engendered was exacerbated by the government's insensitivity in effecting the cuts. The reductions were simply promulgated by statutory notice without the government's consulting the teachers. Lord Craigavon's explanation for the peremptory nature of the decision was that the cuts had to be made quickly in order to save money during the present financial year.[6] Further, the officials of the ministry of education were tactless in their discussion of the salary cuts. The following statement is from the ministry's report for the year 1931-2:

It is interesting to note that in view of the reduction effected in teachers' salaries—first in 1926, and then last year—the cost of our education system, notwithstanding the very considerable improvements and the great extension of educational facilities effected in the last ten years, does not now bulk any larger in the parliamentary votes than it did eight or nine years ago.[7]

Interesting? Not, certainly, the word the teachers used to describe the salary reductions.

In 1935, after the English government restored the salary cuts which had been made in its school system, the Ulster elementary school teachers began pressing for a return to their previous income levels.[8] The Irish national teachers' organisation was especially active in agitating for salary changes.[9] In the spring of 1936 the government responded to the teachers' campaign, which had considerable parliamentary support, by offering to restore as of 1 July approximately one half the cut made in 1931 and to introduce a lump sum gratuity for all retiring teachers.[10] The salary increment figure was later fixed at $4\frac{1}{3}$ per cent.[11] The teachers were far from satisfied. Their chief spokesman in parliament, John Beattie (Pottinger, Belfast), made a vigorous, albeit predictably unsuccessful, attempt to have the government censured for keeping the primary teachers' salaries approximately ten per cent below the 1920 scales.[12] The two major teachers' unions, the Ulster teachers' union and the Irish national teachers' organisation, joined forces in a vigorous campaign[13] and finally as of 1 July 1937 the government restored in full the salary cuts made in 1931.[14]

The morale of the elementary school teachers was further affected by the difficulties young teachers had in obtaining posts. On the surface the problem was not serious, for on 31 March 1931 only about fifty of the approximately 1,500 elementary school teachers in Ulster were unemployed. But thirty of these were recent graduates of St Mary's training college.[15] In 1936 it was reported that of the total of 175 men trained at Stranmillis in the preceding five years, twenty-eight were unemployed and of these eighteen had not been able to find even any temporary work. Of the 349 women trained in the same period, twenty-six were unemployed.[16] A survey of all the students who graduated from any of the three recognised training colleges between 1930 and 1936 revealed that sixty-nine were unemployed on 31 March 1936 and that thirty of these ex-students had never at any time had any employment[17]—this in relation to an output of about 160 students from the training colleges in a typical year.

Women teachers as a group suffered most from the employment situation. In the early 1930s regional and county borough education committees began introducing prohibitions against the employment of married women teachers. These restrictions stemmed solely from economic considerations, for married women had taught in the Ulster schools previously and there was no evidence that they were less successful as educators than men or unmarried women. Nevertheless, when in the autumn of 1931 the Belfast education committee resolved to prohibit in the future the appointment of married female teachers, the course of events was set. The Belfast education authority was the largest single employer of teachers: it engaged about 900 total personnel of whom, in 1931, about eighty were married women. These women kept their posts, but the new rule prohibited not only the new appointment of married women teachers, but also required that in the event of a woman teacher's marrying, she had to tender her resignation.[18] The banning of married women increasingly became general and by the late thirties most local education authorities enforced such a regulation.[19]

As the job market tightened one practice which appears to have become especially prevalent (although by no means limited to the depression years) was the teachers' canvassing for jobs. The procedure approved by the ministry of education in filling a post in a provided or a transferred elementary school was for the appointing board (usually the local school committee) to advertise for positions, review credentials, interview candidates, and rank them in order of merit. In actual practice a candidate usually did not have much hope of appointment unless he individually canvassed each member of the appointing body and brought whatever influence his family or acquaintances had to bear upon the group. Moreover, since most appointments were initiated by school management committees who selected a short list of three candidates and then made final by the regional education committee, canvassing was often practised at both local and regional levels. By the late 1920s the situation had become disgraceful in many areas. At the Armagh diocesan synod of 1929 the Reverend Mr Mayes made a considerable impression by suggesting that henceforth 'the appointment of teachers should be left to the ministry, and not to any committee, as during the five years that have passed since the [1925 amending] act became law, local appointments are usually given to those who can pull the most wires'.[20] The problem had been accentuated, not alleviated, by the 1930 amending act which gave increased power in the appointive process to the local school committees and this change, when coupled with the tight employment market during the depression years, made canvassing for work an unpleasant necessity for many members of the teaching profession. In 1933 the ministry of education was forced to investigate the appointments made to the model school at Enniskillen, the largest elementary school in County Fermanagh.[21] Investigation revealed that the regional education committee for the county had chosen the number two candidate for the post (as ranked by the local management committee) over the number one candidate because influence was brought to bear on individual members of the regional committee. The ministry thereupon was forced to nullify the proceedings and appointed the number one candidate.[22] When late in the decade the protest of leading members of the Church of Ireland against the prevalence of canvassing for teacherships in provided and transferred schools was called to the attention of the government, the parliamentary secretary of the ministry of education answered weakly that while the ministry strongly deprecated canvassing there was no evidence to show that the appointment procedures did not, in general, work satisfactorily.[23]

It would be a mistake to ascribe the tight employment situation solely to budgetary pressures. The Northern Ireland school system during the 1930s was also influenced by a decline in the birth rate which had originated in the late 1920s.[24] Thus, whereas the enrolment in public elementary schools was above 208,000 in 1933, it had declined to under 193,000 in 1939 (see Appendix, Table III). Declining enrolment affected the teachers by reducing the attendance of some small schools below the number required for governmental recognition and by lowering the attendance in some larger schools to the point at which the number of assistant teachers had to be reduced. Hence, between 31 March 1935 and 31 December 1937 eighty-nine elementary school teachers lost their positions as a result of falling school enrolments. All but eighteen of these had found other teaching jobs by 31 March 1938, but the fact of their re-employment probably had less impact upon their fellow-teachers than the fact that between 31 December 1935 and 31 December 1937, 396 teachers in small elementary schools were issued with notices threatening them with loss of position in the near future unless the enrolment at their individual schools increased.[25] Late in the decade the ministry of education attempted to cushion the effects of reduced enrolment by awarding teachers threatened with loss of position a twelve-month delay in actual withdrawal of salary during which time they could seek other posts should the attendance in their schools not recover.[26] In 1938 the grace period was extended to a year and a half.[27] Humane as these regulations were, they did not obscure the fact that during the 1930s the primary educational system was experiencing a period of contraction.

The best indication that the Ulster community was aware

of the contraction in the primary educational system during the depression years is the fact that during the 1930s there was a falling off in the number of men candidates for entrance to the elementary training college. In the case of Stranmillis there were also complaints that the quality of male applicants was falling markedly.[28]

After all the energy which had been expended by the Protestant clergy in forcing the passage of the 1930 education amending act, it was strange to note that a considerable proportion of the managers of the Protestant voluntary schools still refused to transfer them to local civic administration. Transfer was especially slow in the city of Londonderry and in Counties Fermanagh, Londonderry, and Tyrone.[29] As of 31 December 1937 there were 1,166 non-Catholic schools in operation and of these 142 were provided schools and 511 were transferred schools. If we exclude from the total number of non-Catholic schools the provided schools, it becomes clear that only half of the non-Catholic elementary schools (511 of 1022) had been transferred to the local authorities.[30]

The only segment of the elementary education system which expanded during the depression years was the complement of provided schools, that is schools built jointly by the ministry of education and the local education authorities and managed by the local authorities. Whereas in 1931 there were only thirty-three provided schools in operation, the number in 1939 was 188. When, in 1943, the last provided school building begun before the outbreak of war was completed, the number was raised to 195 schools, accommodating over 48,000 children.[31] The conclusion which any alert educational planner could have drawn from contrasting the near-failure of the transfer programme and the considerable success of the provided school programme was that in the future the government should ignore the demands of the Protestant clerical authorities for modifications in the conditions of transfer (since many of them refused to transfer their schools despite accommodations made for them) and concentrate instead upon aiding the local education authorities in building new facilities.

No Catholic schools were transferred to local civic control[32] although, as of 31 December 1937, nine of the 561 schools under Roman Catholic managership were under four-and-two committees. Under the terms of the 1930 education amending act the Catholic school managers had received, by 31 March 1938, £184,731 for the building of new voluntary schools and for the remodelling of old ones.[33] This was somewhat more than half of the construction costs the school managers incurred, but it still left the Catholic population to bear a large burden for school construction. Not surprisingly during the 1930s the Nationalist members of parliament pressed the point that the educational system was unfair to Catholics and that the Catholic schools had a right to a full school construction grant. (The quality of the education debates in the Commons reached a remarkably low state in the depression years; witness the staunch declaration of Cahir Healy, Nationalist MP for South Fermanagh, in reply to a suggestion by another member of parliament that the Catholics should transfer their schools:

> The hon. member for Antrim suggests the question of transferring the schools. He might as well ask a Catholic to eat meat on Friday as transfer his school.[34]

Nothing in educational debates within the house, however, matched the infamous rant delivered outside by Cardinal MacRory: 'The Protestant Church in Ireland,' he declared, '—and the same is true of the Protestant Church anywhere else—is not only not the rightful representative of the early Irish Church, but it is not even a part of the Church of Christ.' [35])

Even during the worst years of the depression there were indications of latent energy and vitality in Ulster's educational system. For example, a major departmental committee studied the curriculum of the primary school in 1931 and suggested changes which became effective in 1932 and which remained in force until the middle 1950s.[36] That the committee's changes seem trifling to the modern observer—the group recommended only a slight revision in the programme as previously defined in 1927, and, indeed, still seemed to be operating within the framework of William Starkie's 'revised programme' of 1900—is of less importance than the fact that improvement seemed to be occurring; a counter-theme was emerging in educational affairs in opposition to the general tone of disappointment and discouragement.

Similarly, when in 1936 the system of inspection was altered, the change was interpreted by contemporaries as a significant educational improvement. Before the reform a general inspection of the work of each member of the staff of a primary school occurred triennially, in alternate years, or annually according to the circumstances of the school. The inspector assigned a mark to the teacher in each subject and also gave a general estimate of the teacher's efficiency, known as the merit rating. The highest ratings entitled the teachers to additional emoluments and the lowest involved financial penalties.[37] This system had been a grievance of the teachers since the earliest days of the Ulster ministry and in 1936 a conference was finally arranged between the officers of the ministry of education and the representatives of the teachers' unions. As a result a new approach to inspection was introduced in 1937 which, while preserving the overall merit marks and the financial corollaries of these marks, attempted to evaluate each teacher's educational efficiency in the widest sense rather than mechanically averaging the teacher's performance in each specific subject. The effect of these changes on the teachers' outlook was not immediate, although an atmosphere somewhat more conducive to pedagogic freedom was created.[38] Educationalists, however, when dealing with matters of curriculum, almost invariably interpret change as improvement and in the depression years even the appearance of educational improvement was a hopeful event.

Also, two technical changes in the qualifications required of primary school teachers were hopeful omens: the ministry's staffing code of 1936 prohibited appointments of additional untrained junior assistant mistresses, and the ministry required that after 1 January 1937 all members of religious orders who took up teaching had to possess the same training qualifications as lay teachers. These rules marked the final step in the elimination of the untrained teacher in Northern Ireland.[39]

An admixture of success and disappointment characterised the ministry's continued attempts to amalgamate small primary schools. From 1931 through 1939 the number of children on the roll of an average elementary school rose from 109 to 114 (see Appendix, Table III). But even this modest improvement was hard-won for it will be remembered that declining birth rates were annually reducing the total number of children enrolled in the Northern Ireland elementary education network. To make matters smoother in cases in which provided or transferred schools were amalgamated, or in which provided schools superseded other institutions, an act of 1935 allowed the education committees to appoint a teacher or teachers from the superseded institution to the new school directly, without advertising the post or opening the position to general competition. This made amalgamations of schools easier and served to protect further the teachers' position.[40]

During the 1930s the amalgamation of schools was hindered not only by the localism of the rural Ulsterman but also by a new obstructiveness on the part of the Roman Catholics. When pressed, the Protestant school managers were willing to accept the government's regulation requiring the amalgamation of neighbouring boys' and girls' schools when either had an average attendance under fifty. But the Catholic authorities tenaciously defended sexual segregation.[41] Doubtless some of the Catholic opposition to coeducation stemmed from the extreme sexual asceticism which had reigned in Catholic farming communities since the Great Famine of the nineteenth century, but more directly responsible were the pronouncements of Pius XI (1922-39) on education. 'The amalgamation of boys' and girls' schools has been condemned by his Holiness Pope Pius XI,' one Catholic spokesman informed the Senate, and added, 'and by the medical profession generally.'[42] Thomas J. Campbell, who had succeeded Joseph Devlin as the Nationalist leader, told the House of Commons:

> You are, I say, rashly and recklessly insisting on the amalgamation of the schools, with the result that the education of these Catholic boys and girls is to be conducted under a system to which Catholics have the strongest objection. I appeal to you to consider Catholic feeling on educational, moral and religious grounds, and yet cry a halt in regard to this order. Hitler would not treat the Jews of Germany in the same way as you are treating these schools.
>
> You may ask what is our objection. I may put it in a sentence. These Catholic parents do object to the promiscuous training of their children, boys and girls, in schools particularly at that decisive and delicate period of their lives as evil and pernicious; and if you proceed with the enforcement of this order the Catholic parents will have to consult their consciences.[43]

The officials of the ministry of education heeded the threat implied in the Catholic attitude and did not press them to amalgamate their schools with the same zealousness they employed when dealing with Protestants. On 31 December 1937 there were about eighty instances, representing a total of 160 schools, of adjoining boys' and girls' public elementary schools. Four of these schools were under the management of local education authorities, ten under Protestant management, and 146 under Roman Catholic management.[44]

Near the end of the thirties the Northern Ireland government decided to take a major step forward educationally. In 1936 the English government had passed a bill raising the school leaving age to fifteen, effective in September 1939 (in actual fact the war prevented the English act's taking effect, but that was in the future). Pressure, most notably from the Presbyterian general assembly, was immediately applied to the Ulster government for a similar statute,[45] and because the Unionist government was wedded to preserving at least the illusion of parity with Great Britain in social legislation, it was susceptible to these pressures. Viscount Craigavon included a promise to raise the school leaving age to fifteen in his manifesto for the general election of 1938,[46] and a bill purporting to carry out this promise was passed during the 1938 session.[47] Actually, as the minister of education admitted, the measure to raise the school-leaving age was 'not exactly that in practice'. What was intended, he explained, was 'that all those for whom there is provision in schools and who are not required by the necessities of their parents or who have no opportunities of beneficial employment, shall continue to receive education suited to their needs up to the age of fifteen'.[48] The act provided that a young person had to stay in full-time education in an elementary, secondary, or technical school until age fifteen with the following exceptions: (1) if he were attending technical and/or agricultural classes for fifteen hours weekly; (2) were fourteen years old, attending school for six hours a week and 'beneficially employed' (there were complicated procedures for certifying beneficial employment, but in essence if a boy or girl had a job he or she had only to attend night school); or (3) were needed in either domestic or agricultural employment by his or her parents. In practical terms the act extended compulsory attendance to age fifteen for unemployed, town-dwelling adolescents. Even in Belfast it was estimated that the exceptions for young persons fourteen to fifteen would be fifty per cent of the age group.[49] This act was scheduled to become effective for the academic year 1939-40, but the advent of World War II prevented the application of the Northern Ireland statute.

If, as we shall see in a moment, the beginning of World War II raised the curtain on a new era in Ulster educational affairs, the curtain was rung down on the old by the exit,

K

shortly before the war began, of several of the stalwart characters. Lord Charlemont fell ill in 1937 and resigned. With his resignation the patina of noble elegance imparted to the education ministry since its founding, successively by Lords Londonderry and Charlemont, faded. Charlemont's successor, John Hanna Robb, was a competent parliamentarian who had served faithfully since the mid-1920s as the parliamentary secretary of the ministry and as chief spokesman for education in the House of Commons. Robb was appointed to the Senate and assumed Charlemont's previous role as leader of the Senate. His place in the lower house as parliamentary secretary was taken by Mrs Dehra Parker, an energetic, well-born, often tactless individual, whose zeal was destined to bring about an intra-governmental conflict during the war years. Most important, that peerless civil servant, A. N. Bonaparte Wyse, permanent secretary to the ministry, underwent a serious operation late in the autumn of 1938 and the next year found it necessary to retire. He was replaced by Reginald S. Brownell, a former assistant secretary of high ability, but lacking Wyse's magnetic qualities.[50]

World War II's impact upon the educational system of Northern Ireland was paradoxical: it was directly destructive, but simultaneously it refocused the attention of the electorate and the government upon the schools, re-energised the administrators and teachers, and eventually led to a restructuring of the entire educational system.

Although Northern Ireland experienced painful air raids in 1941, the direct damage to the region from military attack was relatively slight.[51] Indirect damage, such as that occurring through the over-utilisation of agricultural land and the diversion of resources from consumption goods to military uses, was probably greater than the direct damage. But even here the harm done to Northern Ireland is not so clear, for the war brought an industrial resurgence to Ulster, especially in shipbuilding, and the region's previously very high unemployment rate dropped. The greatest effects of the war upon Northern Ireland were chiefly social and psychological.

Four facets of the social and psychological impact of the war upon Northern Ireland are noteworthy. The first of these is the way in which the Unionist government tried desperately to be included fully in the wartime activities and experiences occurring elsewhere in the United Kingdom. Lord Craigavon was accurately representing the feelings of the majority of his Protestant people when he pleaded with the British to extend military conscription to Northern Ireland. Secondly, the Unionists had to become accustomed to the highly disappointing fact that the British government was not willing to accept Ulster as a full partner in the war. Fear of the combined powers of the de Valera government in the south and the Roman Catholic populace in the north had convinced the London authorities that conscription could not be applied to Northern Ireland. (The fury of the Unionists at being denied conscription was as nothing compared to their reaction had they known that in 1940 Winston Churchill attempted to barter Ulster for Eire's participation in the war against Germany.)[52] Throughout the war major strategic decisions about the use of Northern Irish ports and land facilities were made without consultation with the Stormont government.

The third effect of the war was to alienate even farther from one another the Protestants and the Roman Catholics. This is not to deny that the war, by lessening unemployment, temporarily reduced intra-communal violence, but in the long run the Catholic refusal as a group to join the war effort deeply embittered the Protestants. The pronouncement against conscription of the Catholic bishops of Northern Ireland was seared into the Protestant memory: 'Our people have already been subjected to the gravest injustice in being cut off from one of the oldest nations in Europe and in being deprived of their fundamental rights as citizens in their own land. In such circumstances to compel them to fight for their oppressor would be likely to raise them to indignation and resistance.'[53] It was very hard for the Protestants to forget that the Catholic bishops considered the Unionists, not the Nazis, as the oppressors. In matters of educational reform the question was whether or not the Unionists would be able to forget their resentment and would frame reforms in which the Catholics could share. Fourthly, the war affected the outlook of the Ulster populace by accustoming the citizenry to massive governmental intervention in their daily lives. The power of government became more obvious and the use of these powers more acceptable to the population. As in Great Britain, the citizens of Northern Ireland came to expect that once the war was won the powers of government should be used to shape a more comfortable, secure, and just society.

As far as the direct effect of the war upon the schools was concerned, the first impact was the postponement of improvements in the elementary school network. Except in a few urgent cases school construction was suspended in early 1940 for the duration of the war.[54] Further, the school leaving act of 1938 was supposed to become operative on 1 September 1939, but it had to be postponed, at first for a year, and subsequently indefinitely.[55]

The most dramatic bit of action associated with the elementary school system was the evacuation of school children attempted in 1940 and 1941. The official historian of wartime activity in Northern Ireland has indicated in a dignified understatement that 'evacuation makes one of the most disappointing stories in the war history of Ulster...'[56] The plans for the evacuation of young children, which were supervised by the ministry of home affairs until June 1940 and thereafter by the ministry of public security, were certainly elaborate. As early as the spring of 1939 the ministry of home affairs was issuing tentative plans for the evacuation of children.[57] In practical terms evacuation meant the removal of children from Belfast to the surrounding rural districts. The original plan laid down the principle that the elementary school population should be the base population to be removed, although children under five who had siblings in an elementary school were to have a right to be added to the evacuation lists as well as the mother or any other female relative who wished to accompany them.[58] During the summer of 1939 tests were held establishing, it was believed, that evacuation could be carried out successfully,[59] and officials from the ministry of home affairs exhorted local government officials in rural areas to find accommodation for the thousands of Belfast school children who would be evacuated.[60] Although the evacuation was to be voluntary—parents were not to be compelled to part with their children—the ministry of home affairs reported that 50,000 persons said they and their children wished to evacuate Belfast in case of emergency.[61]

But when war came the Ulster government did not activate its elaborate mechanism for clearing Belfast. On 1 September 1939 school children began to be evacuated from London and other large English cities, and it was naturally expected that the Northern Ireland government would quickly follow suit. Instead, a business-as-usual attitude prevailed and the government announced that evacuation would begin only if and when the cabinet thought it necessary.[62] The ministry of home affairs boasted that it could evacuate 70,000 children if necessary, 37,000 of them within forty-eight hours of the start signal[63] but the government contented itself with passing a law making it the duty of education authorities in 'reception' areas to provide schooling for evacuated children and to provide for the reassignment of teachers; all this was contingent upon an evacuation occurring.[64] But no evacuation was ordered and although this decision was correct in the short run (there were no raids in the autumn and winter of 1939-40) the refusal of the government to put the existing plan immediately into force when war broke out quite possibly encouraged parents to believe that the chance of air raids was small and that evacuation was an unnecessary inconvenience.[65] Parental scepticism became the greatest impediment to the success of future efforts.

Early in 1940 the ministry of home affairs decided, for reasons which are obscure, to scrap the existing evacuation plan and to introduce a new one. Previously each school was to be transferred together, but under the new scheme parents were given the right to 'pre-select' billets for their children, meaning that they could specify that the children be sent to relatives or friends in the countryside. All of Northern Ireland outside Belfast and Derry was designated as reception areas. Obviously the provisions allowing parents to designate where their children were to be sent (anywhere in Northern Ireland where there were friends or relatives) meant that the preservation of the integrity of individual schools was impossible.[66] Parents were required to re-register their children under the new scheme and whereas 70,000 children eventually had been registered for evacuation under the original plan, only 20,000 were registered under the revised scheme.[67] Explanations for the comparative failure of the new plan ranged from allegations of parental lethargy to inadequate governmental publicity to bungling officials having conducted evacuation rehearsals in such bad weather that the children nearly drowned so that when the parents were asked to consent to evacuation the majority refused to have anything to do with it![68]

Events progressed from farce unto failure when, on short notice, the ministry of public security (which had taken over direction of the evacuation in June 1940) ordered an evacuation of Belfast school children on 7 and 8 July 1940. Elaborate orders were issued involving 2,000 workers, thirty-five special trains, 200 motor cars, and an estimated 18,000 children.[69] Actually only 5,638 evacuees and 947 conductors of children turned up.[70] Having learned very little from its July effort, the ministry of public security scheduled yet another mass evacuation of Belfast children for 29 August 1940: 1,490 children plus 169 adults reported.[71]

Immediately after the onset of German raids on Belfast in

April 1941 the attitude of the population changed drastically and thousands of parents demanded immediate evacuation of their children. Whereas the ministry of public security had previously been over-prepared, it was now under-prepared. In addition to those signed on for the government's scheme, thousands of house-holders and their children streamed into rural areas under their own initiative, making control almost impossible.[72] Altogether upwards of 30,000 children (all were from Belfast excepting a few from Londonderry) flooded into the rural areas.[73]

The educational problems resulting from this influx were immense. Granted, few areas were as hard hit as the village of Dromara, County Down, whose five hundred inhabitants under the guidance of the local schoolmaster had to find accommodation for two thousand refugees.[74] In most places evacuated children were able to find places in existing schools although this naturally raised the probability of overcrowding. In some districts double shifts were necessary and in others the limited school accommodation had to be supplemented by hired halls and equipment obtained on loan from Belfast.[75] Unfortunately for the children involved, there was a great deal of difficulty in getting sufficient desks removed from Belfast to the country and not every child had a desk. But, as Mrs Parker glibly explained, 'there is no harm whatever in a class standing for certain lessons as was the custom years ago; indeed, I think a child will often obtain more rest and freedom from fidgets if it stands for a time after a long period of sitting'.[76] More than half the Belfast teachers, about five hundred in number, were temporarily transferred to the reception areas. The Belfast schools reopened shortly after the main raids, and despite public warnings of the danger, gradually the students trickled back. The number of displaced children dropped to 7,351 by the end of 1942, to 3,032 at the close of 1943, to 1,557 by the end of 1944, and to 278 in 1945.[77]

The effect of unfamiliar home situations, interrupted schooling, overcrowded and inadequately equipped schools upon the children can only have been educationally dysfunctional. This is not to deny the fact that for some children the move into the countryside and away from their parents was positively beneficial[78] and not to deny that the influx of city children into rural areas was socially educational for rural parents and children alike; but to overemphasise the direct educational benefits of evacuation would be unjustified romanticism. The decline in average daily attendance which had begun in 1933 accelerated under wartime conditions: between 31 December 1939 and 31 December 1942 attendance dropped almost ten per cent. Even more indicative of the dislocated situation was the fact that the average number of children in daily attendance, expressed as a percentage of children on the rolls, dropped from 86.4 per cent in 1939 to a low of 79.6 per cent in 1941, and had recovered only to 83.8 per cent by the end of the war (see Appendix, Table IV). Obviously not only were those children who attended school being educated under strained conditions, but some thousands of children who would have been in school during peacetime were absenting themselves from the schools.

The war also damaged the primary schools by affecting the teachers. During the summer of 1938 the ministry of education ruled that teachers were permitted to join the territorial army or the officer training corps and were to be granted a leave of absence from their school duties to take part in annual training, without penalty and without being required to provide a substitute.[79] Significantly, the absence of conscription in Northern Ireland resulted in very few teachers actually undertaking military service: only 102 men teachers and twenty-seven women joined the forces out of a cohort of 1,456 men and 3,467 women primary school teachers.[80] The real impact of the war upon the teaching profession came through attrition. Immediately after the war broke out the ministry of education decided to discontinue training men teachers. No new king's scholarships for first-year men were awarded in

1939 and for a time the ministry even contemplated preventing those men who had completed their first year of training from completing the second year of the course, although on this point it later relented.[81] The premises of Stranmillis training college were taken over by various government agencies and the personnel evacuated to Portrush, sixty miles from Belfast, early in 1940. From 1940 through 1942 only a handful of men teachers were training (a few had been admitted in 1940 to help replace those on war service), and the number of women candidates both at Stranmillis and St Mary's, Belfast, was greatly reduced.[82]

A teacher shortage soon developed and the government came increasingly under pressure to reinstitute training for men and to expand opportunities for women. Both the Presbyterian Church and the Church of Ireland complained of the difficulty of finding qualified personnel for their respective schools.[83] Hence in 1943 nineteen men were called to training, twenty-four in the next year and in 1945 a contingent of 119. Of the latter group sixty-three men went to Stranmillis, six to St Mary's, Middlesex, and fifty by special arrangement to St Mary's, Belfast, the Catholic women's training college. These efforts were too late, however. 'The virtual suspension of the training of men teachers from 1939 to 1942 had led by 1945 to a grave shortage of trained teachers in the schools.'[84]

Turning to the effects of the war upon the central administration one finds that most damage was indirect: the sending of several of the principal officers to other departments for war service meant that the ministry of education was understaffed, especially in view of the new work it took on, such as managing the girls' training corps.[85] After Tyrone House, the headquarters of the ministry of education, was damaged in the air raids of 1941, headquarters were moved to Castle Erin, Portrush. The senior and junior officials as well as all important documents were transferred and the only officials remaining in the old headquarters were the private secretary to the minister of education, two inspectors, and from July 1943 the principal officer and staff in charge of youth welfare activities.[86] Both the staffing problems and the removal of the department from the seat of government obviously impeded the efficient operation of the ministry, although precisely how much is impossible to determine. (One of the results of the understaffing was that the ministry was unable to render its annual reports, a fact which indicates that its efficiency was seriously reduced and, simultaneously, frustrates the historian who is left without any official report of the war years.)[87]

Despite all the problems the war caused for Ulster's primary education system, it yielded one massive advantage: it jogged educators, civil servants, and parliamentarians out of their set approaches to educational matters and forced them to re-examine both the assumptions and the methods of the educational process:

> No marked changes with regard to teaching methods or the range of subjects in the schools has occurred during the past few years, but an inclination to examine and question the old and formalised curriculum and methods of instruction has been growing in recent years; new ideas and modern methods have been gaining ground and a spirit of enterprise and experiment is abroad.[88]

The genesis of a spirit of educational enterprise was understandable if not entirely predictable. For example, it is easy to see how the experience of serving as guardians of the entire welfare of scores of evacuated children would force a school teacher to redefine his assumption about an educator's responsibilities to his charges. Similarly when, as in the case of Belfast, the chief billeting officer for an entire city was a school teacher and when all the planning for the evacuation area was left to the teachers,[89] or when the schools of Belfast were organised to accommodate an estimated 12,000 to 15,000 homeless persons,[90] the citizens, their elected officials, and civil servants naturally came to view the educators as something more than child-minders. The new definitions of educational responsibility and the new spirit of initiative were not entities which can be demonstrated statistically, but they were none-theless real. It is impossible to understand the post-war changes in the school system unless one is cognisant of the energy liberated by the war experience.

The conclusion that the war energised, and thus benefited, the educational system more than it debilitated it is reinforced when one turns to the technical schools. Although at first the technical school enrolment dropped because of wartime con-ditions, it soon recovered and actually increased. The growth was especially large in evening classes related to the now pros-pering engineering industry. So healthy was the technical education scene that a new programme of trade scholarships was instituted in 1942. Because of the nature of the instruction given in the technical schools it was relatively simple for the schools to adapt their activities to wartime work, such as radio mechanics and aircraft technology. In addition to the influx of civilian students, the technical schools of Northern Ireland conducted courses for servicemen and women in mechanics, drafting, fire control, radio mechanics, and production control. Unlike the primary schools the technical schools experienced no shortage of teachers. The result of the technical schools blossoming during the war was that when plans were being made for post-war reconstruction the technical school system was allocated more resources and given more attention than it had ever received.

The path of the secondary schools was not as smooth as that of the technical schools, but they too prospered. Granted, there was a shortage of men teachers and many secondary school buildings were overcrowded and underequipped. But the overcrowding and the scarcity of equipment were more a result of the healthy state of the schools than of wartime in-jury: whereas in the academic year 1939-40 there were 14,557 children enrolled in the secondary schools and their associate preparatory departments, the number for 1944-5 was 18,854.[91] The secondary school teachers, unlike their primary school counterparts, did not have any duties imposed upon them by the evacuation plans and the proportion of secondary school children evacuated from Belfast was very low. The cardinal point which the wartime experience taught the secondary school authorities was that in the post-war world more pupils than ever would be seeking admission.[92]

Even if Northern Ireland had existed in a vacuum, un-influenced by events occurring elsewhere in the British Isles, the experience of World War II doubtless would have yielded major reforms in the educational system. Northern Ireland, however, was tied to England directly by the social parity policy and by a predisposition of the Unionist government to take English actions as models to be emulated. The British wartime experience was too complex to summarise here[93] but it suffices to note that direct impact of World War II on English education was much greater than upon Ulster and that the political response to this dislocation was to propose major post-war reforms. Significantly, even before the war started there existed a body of policy statements on educational reform which were simultaneously conservative enough to be accept-able to the educational establishment and liberal enough on matters of democracy and equality to satisfy most innovators. Specifically, the ground work for English wartime educational reforms had been laid by the appearance in 1926 of *The Education of the Adolescent*. This was a major report by the English board of education's consultative committee, chaired by W. H. Hadow. The report, which marked a watershed in English educational history, stated emphatically that all normal children should receive some kind of post-primary education. To implement this suggestion the report posited two major types of post-primary schools: selective academic grammar schools and schools giving an education with a practical bias (the latter became known as 'modern schools'). The Hadow report propounded the necessity for a sharp break at the age of '11-plus' between primary and post-primary schooling. The Hadow report met with a large measure of public approval and by the onset of the war approximately two thirds of England's school children were in schools re-organised along Hadow lines. Then, just on the eve of the war another major report was issued by the board of education's consultative committee, now under the chairmanship of Will Spens. Whereas the Hadow report had suggested that post-primary education take place in grammar schools and modern schools, the Spens report recommended that, in addition, children should have the option of entering the technical schools at the same age and according to the same examination by which they were admitted to the grammar or to the modern schools. Thus, 'trilateralism' became a widely accepted educational prescription.

When we juxtapose the instinctive turning to educational improvement under wartime stress and the pre-existence of a progressive body of official wisdom on desirable reform, another point follows naturally: that under the pressure of wartime events the pre-war educational reform ideas were crystallised into legal form. The great educational reform act of 1944, the Butler act, provided that all children were to receive post-primary education. The full-time attendance age was to be raised to fifteen and, at some date in the future, part-time attendance was to be required to age eighteen. The trilateral system of grammar, modern, and technical schools was not written into the Butler act because these were matters of administrative fiat rather than of statute law, but the statements of the government's intentions made it clear that trilateralism was an implied feature of the new education act.

It is obvious why these English developments were destined to have a major impact upon educational practices in Northern Ireland. The Ulster government and the majority of the population were predisposed to look to England for a lead in most matters of social legislation. And the English education reforms were articulated before the Northern Ireland government turned its full attention to educational reconstruction.

'The general assembly is convinced that any less a measure of reform in Northern Ireland than that now secured for England would be disastrous to the well-being of the people of Northern Ireland': so went a resolution of the Presbyterian Church's general assembly passed in June 1944.[94] Less than a year earlier the Ulster teachers' union had responded to the English government's plans for educational reconstruction by advocating that the Ulster government establish a committee to consider educational reconstruction in Northern Ireland so as 'to keep step by step with proposed reforms outlined in the English white paper'.[95] And in October 1943 a private member's motion had been introduced into the Stormont House of Commons and passed (a rare occurrence) resolving that the house, having taken note of the proposals for educational reconstruction embodied in the English white paper on education of July 1943, was of the opinion that the government of Northern Ireland should declare its intention to introduce a scheme for commensurate advances in Ulster at the earliest possible moment.[96] In looking to England the Northern Ireland authorities acquired not only ideas but vigour as well. England had itself undergone massive educational dislocations which, even more than in Northern Ireland, had liberated enormous amounts of energy. A synodic effect occurred: like a small wave subsumed by a larger one of identical periodicity, the enthusiasm for educational change in Northern Ireland was heightened greatly by English events.

At this point it should be re-emphasised that not all pressures for educational change in Northern Ireland were derived from the English proposals. With a view to post-war reforms, the Presbyterian general assembly had resolved in June 1942 that in the future 'the fullest opportunities of education, suitable to their gifts, should be made available to all children, irrespective of the means of their parents or guardians'.[97] Later in the same month the parliamentary secretary of the ministry of education, Dehra Parker, concluded her presentation of the year's education estimates by making the government's first important statement about education reform. She said, in very general terms, that the equality of opportunity in relation to ability and intelligence was to be the goal and that development was necessary especially in the areas of technical education, non-academic post-primary schooling, and in nursery schooling for young children.[98]

The combination of indigenous pressures with those emanating from England led the government to announce in the king's speech, opening the parliamentary session of 1944-5, that a white paper dealing with educational reconstruction was being prepared.[99] The planning process behind the white paper was an intra-governmental affair. No expert committee was struck. Instead the civil servants and the minister of education framed the document. The paper, *Educational Reconstruction in Northern Ireland,* was finished in December 1944 and its completion marks the point at which it became certain that Lord Londonderry's system of education, which had existed for somewhat more than two decades, would be replaced by new structures.[100]

The major structural recommendations of the white paper were predictable.[101] The school leaving age was to be raised to fifteen without exceptions. A break between primary and post-primary education was to occur at the age of 11-plus (confusingly, 'secondary' education which previously had been a term reserved for academic post-primary schooling was applied to all forms of post-primary schooling). After the age of 11-plus the children were to be divided into two streams: free 'junior secondary schools' (the equivalent of the English secondary modern schools), and fee-charging 'senior secondary schools' (the equivalent of the English grammar schools).

Significantly, the Northern Ireland authorities, in contrast to their English counterparts, did not recommend full trilateralism. Free 'junior technical schools' were to operate as a distinctive form of schooling, but they were not to admit pupils until the age of 13-plus which meant that most of them would have to transfer from junior secondary schools. Also in contrast to the English situation, very few of the Ulster grammar schools were under the control of local education authorities. There was, therefore, no chance of abolishing fees or even demanding that all entrants be admitted by standardised procedures. The white paper proposed that each school receiving government aid be permitted to reserve up to twenty per cent of its annual intake for pupils to be selected by any means the headmaster desired, the remaining eighty per cent to be chosen by means of the 11-plus examination. Although fees were not abolished, children whose parents had limited means were to be granted scholarships by the local education committees.

The white paper's most potentially divisive proposals had to do with religion. One of the recommendations involved an increase of from fifty per cent to sixty-five per cent of the total capital costs of the building grants made by the ministry of education to voluntary primary schools and the new group of junior secondary schools under the management of four-and-two committees. The white paper suggested also that the local education authorities should assume responsibility for the full cost of heating, cleaning, lighting, and general maintenance of these schools. A second group of proposals recommended that English precedents be followed and that every primary and secondary school in Northern Ireland, voluntary or civic-controlled, begin the day with a collective act of worship and that religious instruction be given in every school. In the voluntary schools the worship and the religious instruction normally would be denominational, but in the schools under the management of local education authorities the collective worship and the religious instruction which were obligatory were not to be distinctive of any particular denomination. The clergyman's right to visit the local education authority schools to give denominational instruction was not to be affected. An invisible clause behind all the white paper's proposals was that almost all existing education statutes should be repealed, including those of 1925 and 1930 upon which the Protestant clerics placed so much emphasis. Any contemporary educationist reading the government's religious proposals could have been expected to shudder, for the one inescapable fact of Northern Ireland's educational development has been that the raising of the subject of religious education has always initiated bitter religious controversy.

8

Not Peace, but the Sword, 1945-50

Unlike his predecessors, Lieutenant-Colonel Samuel H. Hall-Thompson, minister of education from spring 1944 to late 1949, sat in the Commons, not the Senate, and was therefore subjected to the rough-and-tumble style of the lower house. Because the parliamentary secretaryship to the minister of education was left vacant after Mrs Parker's exit in March 1944, the entire burden of presenting the government's plan for educational reconstruction fell to Hall-Thompson. Civil servants who worked for Hall-Thompson during this period remember him as a quiet gentlemanly man, an idealist in educational matters, who was not politically astute.[1]

In defending the government's policy on education reconstruction Hall-Thompson had to meet a certain amount of criticism stemming from purely educational considerations. Some observers objected to the age of 11-plus as the time in a child's life to transfer him from primary to secondary school;[2] other critics believed that the separation of children into two distinct streams of post-primary schooling would involve social class discrimination and would be unfair and undemocratic;[3] and the association of principals of technical institutions pressed for full trilateralism, as in England, instead of the

162

Northern Ireland plan of reserving admission to technical schools to age 13-plus.[4] All these were rational criticisms which could be responded to in a logical and reasonable manner. But, as a member of parliament noted during the marathon four-day debate on the white paper on educational reconstruction, 'it is perfectly obvious that ninety-five per cent of the debate on the education proposals in this house, outside it, and in the press, has ranged round the religious instruction question, and . . . it has overshadowed all the other proposals which the government has made with regard to the improvement of education facilities'.[5]

When Professor Robert Corkey had been discharged from the post of minister of education in February 1944 for alleged inattention to his duties, he had countercharged that he was being removed because he clashed with permanent officials of the ministry on questions of religious policy. But even without the Corkey episode the tensions about religious education were high. As early as the spring of 1940 several Protestant clergy and laymen of the Belfast education committee had called attention to what they claimed was a decline in the Christian teaching in the schools and to the resultant rise in juvenile crime.[6] A little later Professor Corkey (still at that time a private member), demanded that the Ulster government follow the English and Scottish example and introduce specialists in religious instruction into the schools.[7] In March 1942 a deputation representing the Church of Ireland, the Presbyterian Church, and the Methodist conference, waited on J. H. Robb and Mrs Parker and asked that the ministry of education recognise the time spent in the schools on non-sectarian religious instruction (meaning Bible instruction) as being part of the normal teaching hours of the schoolteachers. Further, they asked that religious knowledge be included as an optional subject on the secondary school certificate examinations. Although at the time of the meeting the minister of education refused their requests,[8] Robb later on, in early May, issued regulations modifying the previous requirement that secondary teachers give at least eighteen hours of secular instruction a week to require that they teach at least eighteen hours per week of which sixteen had to be secular instruction.[9]

The churches wanted more, however. Considerable publicity was given to the statement on secondary education in a report of the general assembly of the Presbyterian Church that in secondary schools the spiritual nature of true education was being ignored and that the situation was undignified and educationally indefensible.[10] During the autumn of 1942 a private member gave notice of a motion that 'the ministry of education should take immediate steps to ensure that boys and girls in all secondary schools in Northern Ireland receive religious instruction'.[11] He was persuaded to postpone the motion only after the prime minister agreed to receive a deputation from the Protestant Churches to discuss the entire matter.[12] Whether or not the meeting ever took place is unclear from available records[13] but it is certain that the Protestant anxieties were not allayed. When Dr Renshaw's motion of October 1943 prodding the government to declare its intentions on educational reconstruction was passed, a phrase was added in debate declaring that such plans should include 'provision for the fullest possible facilities for religious instruction'.[14]

Late in March 1944 the northern education committee of the Church of Ireland asked the government to instigate discussions before the white paper on educational reconstruction was published between the ministry of education and various interested parties, including of course the representatives of the various churches.[15] Between April and September 1944 there were numerous conferences between the ministry and the United Education Committee of the Protestant Churches. The Protestant Churches desired a collective act of worship at the beginning of the school day in all schools; and provision for religious instructions for all children in whatever type of school they attended.[16] The discussion broke down because, although the government was willing to require a daily collective act of worship and daily religious instruction, it required that the churches should agree to the repeal of the rules for Bible instruction framed under the 1930 education act.[17]

The white paper appeared on 11 December 1944. The Protestant's United Education Committee declared in response that although it approved of the white paper in principle, it regretted that it had not been possible for the ministry of education to reach an agreement with the churches prior to publication. Any abrogation of the 1930 religious settlement, the Protestant committee declared, would be totally unacceptable.[18] Protestant objection came to focus upon three topics: (1) the repeal of previous statutes which had regulated the conditions of religious instruction in public elementary schools and in particular in schools transferred from clerical managers; (2) the proposed conscience clause for the teachers; and (3) the increased grants proposed for four-and-two schools.

The government's intention of repealing almost all existing educational statutes as a prelude to forming a new system was brought clearly to the attention of the public not in a convincing piece of explanatory rhetoric but in the declaration of the attorney-general for Northern Ireland, John C. MacDermott, that the religious provisions of the 1930 act were *ultra vires* and that the transfer deeds written under the 1925 and 1930 acts were illegal if they included provisions compelling teachers paid with public funds to give Bible instruction.[19] This opinion greatly rankled many members of the Northern Ireland parliament and members of the clergy. On the weekend of 20-21 June 1945, the United Education Committee of the Protestant Churches published a statement declaring, among other things, that it could not 'agree to the repeal of the provisions for Bible instruction for pupils in public elementary schools which were embodied in the 1930 act by the late Lord Craigavon and which granted statutory safeguards to the Protestant parents of Northern Ireland whose children attended transferred and provided schools...'.[20]

The Protestant clerics and MPs were also uneasy about the government proposal to protect the liberty of conscience of individual teachers in schools under the management of local civic authorities by allowing them to be excused from giving religious teaching or leading collective worship if they were conscientiously opposed to so doing. The fears of many Protestants were succinctly stated by one member of the House of Commons who said, 'I am afraid that if that conscience clause is inserted in the education bill, too many teachers will take advantage of it and make religious instruction a very difficult subject to be taught in the schools'.[21] The government's rejoinder was that if this happened extra staff could be engaged to conduct religious instruction and worship. The worries about the conscience clause were related to the anxieties about the repeal of the education acts of 1925 and 1930. Under those acts the deeds of transfer of most of the elementary schools originally managed by Protestant religious groups stated that Bible instruction was to be given by members of the school staff as part of their employment agreements. The possibility that teachers would no longer be compelled to give Bible instruction raised the old fear that if the Roman Catholics secured a majority on a regional or county borough education committee they could appoint Catholic teachers to transferred and provided schools even though the schools were attended by Protestant children and even though the provided schools had been built with Protestant funds; and that the Roman Catholic authorities would then forbid the Catholic teachers to give Bible instruction.[22] The Protestant fears were reinforced by clear hints in the government's white paper on educational reconstruction that the primary school management committees would lose some of their powers in the appointment of teachers.[23]

In a statement of 20-21 January 1945 the United Education Committee of the Protestant Churches blandly noted, without explanation, that it opposed the government's plan to increase the construction grant from the previous fifty per cent to sixty-five per cent of total costs for schools managed by four-and-two committees, and to raise the heating, cleaning, and maintenance grant from the previous fifty per cent to one hundred per cent.[24] No explanation was necessary: the government was trying to entice the Roman Catholic school managers to place their schools under four-and-two committees and the increment was intended as a boon to the Catholic schools.

And what about the Catholics? Were they pleased with the government's plan? Absolutely not. The features of the white paper affecting the Catholics as a denominational group were double-edged. Academic secondary schools under voluntary management were to receive sixty-five per cent capital construction grants from the exchequer, and primary and junior secondary schools which agreed to establish a four-and-two management committee were to receive capital construction grants of sixty-five per cent plus full cost of heating, cleaning, and lighting, and all other maintenance expenses. Against these potential benefits was an offsetting increment in responsibilities. The raising of the school leaving age to fifteen, combined with the reorganisation of the old elementary school network into a primary school-junior secondary school pattern, implied considerable expenses for the Roman Catholic authorities.

The Catholic civic leader who most clearly articulated Catholic misgivings was Thomas Campbell, a Belfast MP. According to Campbell, 'one aim of the white paper is further to ostracise the Catholic voluntary schools and to tear up the managerial system by the roots'.[25] What was to be gained by the Catholics surrendering their private managerships for four-and-two committees? Only an increase of fifteen per cent of the total capital costs and fifty per cent of the maintenance expenses—hardly a sufficient sum to exchange for educational freedom. Campbell wanted complete government financing of all these expenses for the voluntary schools and because they were not granted he denounced the white paper as a direct denial of educational equality and a denial of educational freedom. As for compulsory non-denominational religious instruction in local authority schools this was simple Bible instruction and was unacceptable ('religious education with the vitamins left out'). An agreed syllabus was equally unacceptable ('the only agreed syllabus for Catholics is the catechism of their Church').[26]

Cardinal MacRory, in his lenten pastoral for 1945, said that the first thing which struck him when reading the government's white paper was the vast additional expenditure which would be required to carry out the suggested changes. He objected to the reconstruction scheme on the general grounds that it was not then, at war's end, the appropriate time to spend so much public money and on the specific ground that it proposed to continue 'the utterly unjust treatment of a large portion of the population on account of their religious convictions'.[27] The bishop of Down and Connor, Daniel Mageean, charged in his lenten pastoral that the object of the white paper was to 'establish a colossal system of state-controlled education'. The ordinary citizen, however, would not countenance this plan, Mageean said, for 'from bitter experience he knew what had happened in other countries when the state took control of youth . . .'.[28] The anti-state theme was elaborated at a higher level of abstraction in the lenten message of Bishop Eugene O'Callaghan of Clogher who argued that in educational matters it was the duty of the state to safeguard the natural rights of parents and of the church and to facilitate parents and church in exercising those rights.[29] Bishop Farren of Derry claimed that the government's reason for having civic and parental representatives on a school management committee was a hollow one because the Catholic clerical school manager was not just an individual but the holder of a religious office, and as such was automatically taken by the Catholic people as their representative.[30] And Bishop O'Doherty of Dromore promised that the Church would not surrender its present control even if greater sacrifices than made at present were required.[31]

Acting collectively the Catholic bishops of Northern Ireland issued a closely reasoned statement concerning the white paper on education, because 'its proposals are so inimical to Catholic interests that we feel it necessary to issue a joint statement, re-affirming the Catholic position'.[32] The statement began on a theoretical level, stating that the family and the Church have a divine mission to educate children, but that the state does not: the power of the state in the field of education was held to be derivative from the authority the state has from God to promote the common temporal welfare, something quite different from the direct heaven-sent mission of the family and the Church in regard to children. The state in exercising its authority in matters of education should, the bishops declared, be governed by two principles: it should respect the prior rights of the children, the family, and the Church, and it should act in accordance with the demands of distributive justice which had been articulated by Pius XI. Whenever the state tried to force neutral or mixed state schools upon a section of the community or tried to extinguish free denominational schools by refusing to give denominational schools adequate financial assistance, the state violated the two-fold duty postulated by the bishops.

Turning specifically to the white paper, the bishops were very sceptical of the government's proposal to make it a duty of the civic education authorities to provide nursery classes for children aged two to five years in the areas where the ministry of education felt such provision was required. (In essence, this was a proposal to care for the children of women who worked in the Belfast and Londonderry textile factories.) The bishops' opinion was that a public nursery was a poor substitute for a good Catholic home. 'If the mother is unable to look after her baby,' they said, 'she should get the necessary assistance or instruction; if economic conditions make the home unsuitable, they should be remedied by the provision of a living family wage. It is only in rare cases, and by way of exception, that clinics and nurseries may be tolerated.'[33] Based on the prescription that 'it is necessary that all the teaching and the whole organisation of the school, and its teachers, syllabus and textbooks in every branch be regulated by the Christian spirit, under the direction and material supervision of the Church',[34] the bishops made it clear that Catholic children could not attend schools under civic control without violence to the children's consciences. Next, the placing of Catholic schools under four-and-two committees was declared unacceptable. 'We reject them,' the bishops said, 'because we fear that these committees are but an instalment to the complete transfer of our schools...'.[35] As for the realignment of existing elementary schools into primary schools and junior secondary schools, with the break at 11-plus, the bishops objected because unlike the existing schools they would not be organised on a parish basis.

The bishops' counter-proposals were simple: the government should give the Catholic schools the same financial support (meaning complete subventions for all expenses) it gave the provided and transferred schools. In other words, the government should formally institute a denominational system based on the separate-but-equal principle.

How terribly difficult the educational planners' position was is obvious when one contrasts the view of the Protestant educational campaigners with that of the Roman Catholic bishops. The former demanded that the state schools be Protestant in staffing and in curriculum, but would not admit the principle of denominationalism. The latter would be satisfied with nothing less than full acceptance of the principle of denominationalism. Between these two views there was no middle ground. A compromise that would satisfy both groups was an impossibility.

'Unless the minister is prepared to meet the bodies outside this house and reach an agreement this bill cannot go through this house,' a crusty backbencher informed Hall-Thompson during the debates on the government white paper. 'Let us see who are the people outside,' he continued. 'They are the three great Protestant Churches... Surely the minister of education, before driving a bill through this house, should be at peace with the churches.'[36] This was excellent advice from a political standpoint because the leaders of the United Education Committee of the Protestant Churches were already lobbying: on 23 January a delegation from the churches' committee, led by the archbishop of Armagh, John A. F. Gregg, had met with various Unionist MPs.[37] Hall-Thompson, realising the potential danger, twice invited the clerical gentlemen to enter into direct negotiation, but by early March still had not received an acceptance.[38] He extended yet another invitation in mid-March and this finally led to direct negotiations.[39]

Now, as in previous contests between the government and the Protestant clerics, the clerics multiplied their leverage by striking hard as a general election approached. Circulars were sent to candidates standing in the mid-June general election for the Stormont parliament asking their pledge to vote against the government's plan to repeal the religious instruction clauses of the 1930 education act.[40] When, on 1 June 1945, Sir Basil Brooke, the prime minister of Northern Ireland, John E. Warnock, minister of home affairs, Hall-Thompson, and various education officials met a deputation of the Protestant Churches and the Orange Order (the attorney-general, it should be noted, was not present), an agreement was reached on the basis of which the Protestant clerics cancelled their election circulars.

The agreement formulated at the 1 June meeting was subject to various interpretations and later became the focus of a bitter government-clerical split in 1945-56. The central clause was that the rights enjoyed by parents and by school management committees under the 1925 and 1930 acts would remain unaltered *subject to a conscience clause* formulated to protect the teachers from compulsion in matters of religion.[41] The clause 'agreed' to by both sides was as follows:

Where a teacher who has been appointed to give Bible instruction finds himself unable on grounds of religious belief to continue to give Bible instruction conscientiously and makes application in writing to the appointing body that he be excused from doing so, the appointing body if satisfied that the application is *bona fide* shall not refuse the application nor shall a teacher so excused be prejudiced in any way thereby provided always that that part of the teacher's duty shall be discharged by a qualified member of the teaching staff of the same school, or if this is not practicable, by another qualified teacher. Where a teacher had not been appointed to give Bible instruction he shall not be required to give such instruction.[42]

This later behaviour of the Church representatives makes it clear that they were under the impression that, subject to minor verbal changes, this clause would be included in the government's forthcoming education bill and that this clause was not subject to referral to the attorney-general or to alterations needed to make it conform with the government of Ireland act of 1920.

What the government negotiators understood about the 'agreed' conscience clause is far less clear. Presenting a record of the meeting slightly more than six months later, eleven members of the Protestant delegation attested that Hall-Thompson had said, 'Of course all we have done is subject to the government of Ireland act, 1920, section 5.' But in their judgement 'this remark by Colonel Hall-Thompson was not considered of any consequence'. This because they understood that Warnock, the home affairs minister, represented the attorney-general, and because the prime minister had declared, after polling Warnock and Hall-Thompson, 'that then is a government decision'. But the Protestant negotiators admitted that after saying 'that then is a government decision' (note that the words were not the unequivocal 'that then is *the* government's decision'), the prime minister said to Warnock, 'you will of course let the attorney-general see what you have agreed to', a phrase which to the historian implies that the clause was to be submitted to the attorney-general for his approval or disapproval.[43]

That the government and the churches were operating on different wavelengths did not become clear until the late autumn of 1945, although there had been a hint of this fact in late July when Hall-Thompson responded to a question by saying that an agreement was reached 'on the principle of a conscience clause for teachers in provided and transferred schools'.[44] He did not say that a specific conscience clause had been defined. In any case, by late December 1945 it had become clear to the Protestant educationists that Hall-Thompson was intent upon modifying the conscience clause as 'agreed' between the parties, and a public letter signed by eleven of the members of the original delegation was addressed to the archbishop of Armagh informing him of the government's alleged breach of faith.[45] The Protestant campaign remained quiet for a time, but resolutions of the general synod of the Church of Ireland in May 1946 and of the general assembly of the Presbyterian Church in June condemned the government's alleged duplicity.[46]

The anti-government phalanx, it was clear, was saving its major salvos until the education bill was before the legislature. When the bill was published on 28 September 1946 it contained a conscience clause which was considerably different from the one which the Protestant Churches' committee claimed had been originally promised:

> If a teacher in a county school [meaning provided or transferred school under the old terminology] who has been required by the local education authority to conduct or attend collective worship in the school or to give undenominational religious instruction in the school, requests the school management committee that he be wholly or partly excused from conducting or attending such worship, or from giving such instruction, or both from conducting and attending such worship and from giving such instruction and, at the same time, furnishes to the committee, for submission to the local education authority, a statutory declaration that his request to be excused is made solely on grounds of religious belief, then,

until the request is withdrawn, the teacher shall be excused accordingly.[47]

(Subsequent subsections prohibited authorities from penalising the teacher for his invoking the conscience clause.) Whereas the clause which the churches believed had been agreed to allowed the school management committee to decide if a teacher's conscientious objection claim was *bona fide*, the government's clause left them no discretion in the matter.

Equally disturbing to the Protestant education interests was the minister of education's statement that the new bill would not re-enact the provisions of the 1930 education act which allowed management committees of transferred schools to require that a candidate for a vacant teaching post express his willingness to give Bible instruction. This decision was taken 'because we insist on complying with the written law of the government of Ireland act and the unwritten law of decency...'.[48] During the second reading debate Herbert Quin, a member for the Queen's University, neatly summarised the churches' anxiety on this matter in noting:

When property was transferred from the churches to enable the government through the ministry of education and the local authorities, to have what one might call the state school, the property was transferred on certain conditions. There is nothing in the bill which will ensure that those conditions will be carried out as a statutory obligation.[49]

The storm which had been brewing broke at a meeting held by the United Education Committee of the Protestant Churches on 8 November in a packed Wellington Hall, Belfast. Opponents of the government's education bill covered a wide range, from those who opposed the bill because it would make some rural children walk three or four miles to new post-primary schools to those who opposed concessions to Roman Catholics as well as those concerned about the government's alleged reneging on its promise not to modify the 1930 educational settlement. The meeting protested against those provisions which would deprive the management committees of their 'complete freedom to decide when Protestant teachers are required to teach Protestant children and to give Bible instruction...'. An appeal was made for a £20,000 campaign fund to help to bring the government to its senses.[50] This meeting was followed by Protestant meetings of a similar nature in Londonderry, Portadown, Bangor, Newtownards, as well as a handful of additional meetings in churches in Belfast.[51]

When Lieutenant Colonel Hall-Thompson tried to explain the government's position to the Ulster women's Unionist council at Unionist headquarters, Belfast, on 9 November 1946, he was met with cries of 'resign', and 'throw him out!' He managed to speak for a time and explained that the original conscience clause as tentatively agreed to at the 1 June 1945 meeting had been altered for two reasons: the legal authorities had declared that the original version was legally unacceptable because it put the teacher through a religious test; further, the leaders of the teachers' unions had declared that the teachers would not accept the clause as originally drafted. So rowdy was the reception given Hall-Thompson that Lady Clark, who presided, asked to be excused and left the chair. After the minister had departed from the headquarters those present concluded festivities by singing 'Derry's Walls!' and the national anthem.[52]

During the committee stage in parliament, Herbert Quin attempted to have the bill amended to give the former managers of transferred schools the right to reclaim the schools if, in their own opinion, the conditions of transfer were not being fully carried out. The amendment received no support from members of the house and was negatived.[53] Quin also attempted to have introduced an ingenious clause stating 'nor shall a teacher be required to give denominational religious instruction unless at the time of the teacher's appointment it has been specifically set out in the teacher's agreement with the local education authority as one of the subjects which the teacher has been appointed to teach'. On the surface this proposal appeared to be designed to protect the teacher, but actually it did the opposite, for it legitimated, by implication, an education committee's compelling a teacher to give religious instruction so long as it was part of the original contract. If passed, this amendment would have made the conscience clause almost totally inoperative; Hall-Thompson, therefore, had it negatived.[54]

Early in December debate in the Commons became very unpleasant. John Nixon, a right-wing Unionist member for Woodvale, Belfast, accused the government of having broken its word to the Protestant Churches. He claimed that the government had tricked the clergy and the Orangemen for the sake of winning an election and had then betrayed them.[55] Sir Basil Brooke, the prime minister, replied that the agreement with the Churches had been specifically predicated upon the approval of the attorney-general being obtained.[56] Brooke expanded this interpretation in a later debate and was backed up by Mr Warnock and Hall-Thompson, which was to be expected; but of some note was the fact that William F. McKoy, KC, who had served as the Protestant delegation's unofficial legal counsel, corroborated the prime minister's story. However, another member of the Churches' delegation, John M. Andrews, former prime minister of Northern Ireland, stated that he had thought the decisions made on 1 June 1945 were final.[57] The conflicting perceptions of these two men, McCoy and Andrews, who had been on the same side of the negotiating table, indicates that in all probability the long skein of recrimination, ill will, and conflict which followed from the meeting of 1 June 1945 was the result not of bad faith on the part of either the government or of the Churches, but of a basic misunderstanding of the terms of the original agreement.

Now, to draw the curtain on this narrative of unnecessary controversy one point should be underscored: the government's education act, whose rough passage was completed when it received the royal assent on 27 March 1947, contained the same conscience clause included in the original bill.[58] For the first time since 1925 the government of Northern Ireland had not altered its course in the face of an agitation by the more volatile Protestant elements.[59]

'The trouble about us here in Ulster,' said Lord Glentoran during the debate on the second reading of the education bill, 'is that we get excited about education and drink.'[60] One aspect of the education excitement of 1946-7 which bears special notice was the arrangement for the Roman Catholic schools. Between the issuance of the white paper on educational reconstruction and the publication of the education bill, the government had decided, in response to Roman Catholic complaints, to raise the grant for capital expenditure for all voluntary schools from the previous fifty per cent to sixty-five per cent, without requiring that they be placed under four-and-two committees. Grants for the maintenance, heating, and lighting of voluntary primary schools and of the non-academic secondary schools, which were to be formed from the old all-age primary schools, were also to be raised from fifty per cent to sixty-five per cent.[61]

These concessions to the Catholics were introduced at an unfortunate time in Ulster's history, for community relations in Northern Ireland were deteriorating. Winston Churchill had both articulated and reinforced the bitterness of many Unionists when, in a radio broadcast of 13 May 1945, he denounced the government of Southern Ireland for its neutrality during the war. He said among other things: 'We left the de Valera government to frolic with the Germans and later with the Japanese representatives to their heart's content.'[62] In the Ulster context anything which exacerbated relations with the south *mutatis mutandis* increased domestic tension between Protestants and Roman Catholics. In the months that followed ugly sparks were generated by the

M

interjection of the partition issue into the Stormont parliament's debates. Therefore, at the time the education bill appeared Ulster Protestants were even more highly sensitised than usual to alleged Catholic aggressiveness.

Further, aside from the increased capital construction and school maintenance grants, certain features of the government's education bill elicited strong anti-Catholic responses from the Protestant Churches' education committee. In arguing against the repeal of the 1925 and 1930 acts the Protestant clerics, it will be recalled, had been concerned about the situation in certain border areas where, conceivably, the Catholic population might gain control over the local education committee and appoint Catholic teachers to previously Protestant schools. In addition, some of the opposition to the introduction of the government's conscience clause on the part of the Protestant critics stemmed from the fear that the clause opened the possibility of Catholics being appointed to teach Protestant children despite the best efforts of a Protestant school committee. For example, the Reverend Professor Corkey, former minister of education, argued persuasively that if a teacher was being appointed to a one-teacher school in a remote Protestant district and if the only applicant happened to be a person, such as a Roman Catholic, who refused to give non-denominational religious instruction, then the school committee would have no power to block his appointment. Their hands would be tied.[63] Much less persuasive was the argument of Senator William Wilton who declared that under the conscience clause, 'the education authority will have to appoint a teacher without regard to his religious views. He may be a Jew—although I am not saying anything against Jews—he may be a Roman Catholic, or even a member of the IRA.'[64] (Hall-Thompson's dismissal of this argument was crushing: 'If Senator Wilton knows an IRA gunman who is a qualified teacher, and if he knows a school management committee of Protestant clergymen who would put a gunman on their short list of three, then I cannot stop them; but I have yet to meet such a committee.')[65]

Thus, the clauses which augmented the grants to voluntary schools, an increment universally recognised as a concession to the Catholics, elicited a hyper-response.[66] When the clarion call was sounded for the great Wellington Hall education meeting of 11 November 1946, it was mingled with tones of anti-Catholicism, including a charge that the government was attempting to endow Roman Catholicism.[67] At the Wellington Hall meeting Herbert Quin, MP, charged that raising the grant to voluntary schools meant an endowment of £2,000,000 to the Roman Catholic Church, and a resolution was passed opposing the increase.[68] The opponents of the sixty-five per cent grant did not moderate their tactics within the halls of Stormont. 'I feel there has been a betrayal of Protestantism,' Quin declared in the Commons, and added a bit later that he would absent himself from the second reading as the only means within his power to protest against the endowment of the Roman Catholic Church and the discrimination by the government against the Protestant transferors of schools.[69] Even more dogged in his opposition was Harry Midgley, Commonwealth Labour member for Willowfield, Belfast, who tirelessly bearded Hall-Thompson (whom he was to replace as minister of education early in 1950). Midgley managed the difficult task of being continually on record as a proponent of social class equality in education and as an implacable opponent of increased grants to Catholic voluntary schools. Midgley's chief point was that grants to these schools should not be increased without a quid pro quo, by which he meant increased secular control over their management.[70]

Merely because many Protestants were opposed to increasing the grant to voluntary schools one should not assume that the Catholics were happy. The reply of Michael McGurk, Nationalist member for mid-Tyrone, to a statement by Harry Midgley that the original fifty per cent grant given under the 1930 education act was a mistake, capsulised the Catholic position: 'We admit that it was a mistake; it should have been 100 per cent.'[71] Such quotations could be multiplied by the score. The point is that the government, in increasing its grants to Roman Catholic schools, suffered the venom of the extreme Protestants while reaping precious little gratitude from the Roman Catholics.

Too much discussion of the sectarian bickering that surrounded the 1947 education act can obscure its complicated architecture. Turning, then, to the act itself, one must begin by explaining that between the presentation of the white paper on educational reconstruction and the publication of the education bill the government redefined its vocabulary.[72] Schools were categorised along two axes according to how they were controlled and also according to the level of education they provided. On the first axis, schools of all levels and under the control of local education authorities were designated 'county schools' and those not controlled by local education authorities were called 'voluntary schools'. On the other axis schools were divided into primary schools and secondary schools. There were three types of secondary schools: intermediate schools (called junior secondary schools in the white paper) which were free of charge and which provided a non-academic secondary education; grammar schools (called senior secondary schools in the white paper) which were the existing selective academic schools in which fees continued to be charged; and technical intermediate schools (the junior technical schools of the white paper) which charged no fees but which usually did not take pupils until the age of 13-plus, in contrast to the other intermediate and grammar schools whose intake was at 11-plus.[73]

In essence the 1947 act framed a dual system comprising local civic institutions alongside which was articulated a parallel set of voluntary institutions. The heart of the civic stream of the system was the local education authority formed under each county and county borough council. The regional education committees in the Counties Antrim, Londonderry, and Tyrone were abolished (in Armagh, Down, and Fermanagh previously there had been one regional education committee for the entire county). Thus, the number of education authorities, previously eighteen, was shrunk to eight, one for each county and one each for Londonderry and for Belfast. Most of the members of these committees were appointed by the local county council or county borough council. As in the case of the former regional education committees, members were appointed from among county and borough councillors, from nominees selected by the urban and rural district councils within the county, and from among other persons interested in education. In addition, the minister of education was to appoint up to one quarter of the total committee members from among the representatives of the transferors of those schools within the area under the jurisdiction of the county or county borough education committee which had been transferred to the control of the authority.[74]

At the elementary school level, management of county primary schools (previously called provided or transferred public elementary schools) continued much as before. School management committees were constituted exactly as they had been under the 1930 act with the exception that the teachers' representative on the committee was now required to be the principal of the school. Running parallel to this section of the civic educational system were the privately managed voluntary primary schools and those under the four-and-two committees; these schools continued to be managed just as they had previously.[75]

The extension of the age of compulsory education to fifteen, with no exceptions, combined with the requirement that children leave primary school at age 11-plus and enter some form of secondary education, allowed the formation of a new form of school, the intermediate school. In practical terms the creation of this new form of institution meant that the local education authorities, in the case of county primary schools, and the individual school managers, in the case of voluntary primary schools, had to decide whether they wished their schools to continue as elementary schools serving children up to age 11-plus, or to become intermediate schools specialising in non-academic education from age 11-plus to fifteen. As for the management of the county intermediate schools, the school management committees were to be composed in a form effectively identical to that of the primary school committees. Hence, in the case of any county primary school which was converted into an intermediate school, the rights of the groups which had originally built the school and subsequently transferred it to the local education committees were to be protected by their representatives being appointed to at least one half the seats on the new committee. Unlike the voluntary primary schools, the voluntary intermediate schools were required to be under the management of a committee, rather than of a single school manager. This was a small move away from clerical control of the voluntary schools, but more symbolic than functional.[76]

Local education authorities were given the power to oversee county grammar schools through the medium of school management committees appointed by the authority; the specific composition of each management committee was to be negotiated between the local authority and the ministry of education.[77] Because in 1947 only nine of the seventy-five recognised grammar schools were managed by local authorities, provisions for voluntary grammar schools were more important.[78] Voluntary grammar schools stayed under the existing managers and were eligible to receive sixty-five per cent capital expenditure grants if they gave up eighty per cent of their places to local authority pupils. (These provisions, which seemed benign at the time, became the focus of bitter controversy in 1949 and 1950, a situation which will be discussed later.)

The framers of the 1947 act fitted the technical schools into their basic scheme without being tyrannised by demands for administrative neatness. There was, to begin with, the gap between the primary schools and the technical schools. Children left the primary schools at age 11-plus and did not enter the technical schools until 13-plus, which meant that they had to spend at least two years in an intermediate school before going on to vocational training. Nevertheless, administrative order was preserved by placing the technical schools under the jurisdiction of the local education authorities who managed them through the medium of local school committees. Thus (with the exception of the towns of Bangor, Larne, and Newry, which temporarily continued to act as technical education authorities), the technical education system was at last brought within the same management system as the primary school system.[79] This was a goal which Lord Londonderry wished to have attained in 1923, but from which he was blocked by political forces.

Underlying the financial details of the 1947 education act was a set of financial relationships so complex as almost to preclude description. This is not to say that the relations between the various local education authorities and the schools, and between the schools and the ministry of education, were not clear-cut; they were. But the relations between the Northern Ireland exchequer, the ministry of education, and the local education authorities, when superimposed upon Ulster's byzantine system of local finance, were nearly impenetrable. Under the Londonderry act the ministry of education paid all primary teachers' salaries and made substantial grants towards the salaries of teachers in post-primary schools. The regional education committees were liable for general expenses (for which they received a two thirds rebate from the central government up to a ceiling equal to the produce of 8d in £1 on local rates) and for an educational levy by the central government under the finance act of 1932 equal to 1s in £1 towards the costs of educational services in general.

Under the 1947 act the basic division of financial responsibilities between the ministry of education and the local authorities stayed the same, but the sixth schedule to the act introduced the principle of transferring local rate revenues from the richer to the poorer education authorities. In practice Belfast was heavily taxed to pay for educational developments in rural areas. This policy, when combined with the heavy derating of rural areas, meant that Belfast educators and aldermen could argue quite plausibly that Belfast was over-taxed in educational matters. The grievances of Belfast's representatives under this financial system should be noted for future reference, for their dissatisfaction was to be one of the causes of the acrimonious ousting of Lieutenant Colonel Hall-Thompson from the ministership of education late in 1949.[80]

The complexity of bringing into operation the 1947 education act should not be underestimated. While it was a relatively simple matter to have most ancillary features of the act in effect by the end of 1948,[81] a great deal of effort and planning was necessary to effect the raising of the school leaving age to fifteen and to establish a full, new network of intermediate schools. The raising of the leaving age and the creation of a new form of schooling were intertwined problems; and the difficulty of achieving simultaneously these two ends was several times greater than the difficulty of achieving either end by itself. The ministry of education estimated that 100 county and ninety voluntary intermediate schools would be needed.[82] Yet, by the end of the academic year 1950-51, only twelve intermediate schools were in operation (see Appendix, Table VIII). None of these were specially constructed for the purposes but were converted primary and technical schools, and, in one case, a former private residence. The first specially constructed intermediate school was not opened until September 1952.[83] The ministry of education had a difficult task in overcoming the educational conservatism of the Northern Ireland populace, especially in rural areas. This rural conservatism more than any other factor explains why Counties Armagh and Tyrone were without a single intermediate school for seven years after the act was passed and County Fermanagh for eight.[84]

As a corollary of this slow progress in reorganising the schools, it was necessary continually to postpone raising the school leaving age, since the bulk of the incremental student population was to be allocated to intermediate schools. The 1947 act set a deadline of 1 April 1951 for raising the age, but in 1951 the date was deferred by parliament until 1 April 1953. And in 1953 it was further deferred to 1 April 1957 when it finally became operative.[85]

In contrast to the intermediate schools, the former technical schools found their niche in the new arrangements without difficulty, chiefly because very little restructuring was required. The former junior technical schools were named 'technical intermediate schools' (but were usually referred to simply as technical schools) and those former technical schools which had been chiefly engaged in giving commercial or domestic science courses were placed on notice that eventually they would be converted into intermediate schools.[86] The number of technical schools was not great, there being twenty-nine such schools in operation in 1950-51 (see Appendix, Table VIII).

Even without a raising of the school leaving age the greatest problem confronting the grammar schools was the rapid increase in enrolments (see Appendix, Tables VII and VIII). This was partially due to a secular trend towards increased parental demand for grammar school places for their children, partially to the new scholarship system, and partially to the lowering of the normal age of entry for grammar schools from 12-plus to 11-plus. Shortages of staff and buildings were the result of the increased enrolments.[87]

Nevertheless, considering the complexity of reconstructing the Northern Ireland educational system, reasonable progress was being made, and Lieutenant Colonel Hall-Thompson had reason to be pleased. He scarcely could have foreseen that in May 1949 his proposing a bill to deal with minor financial matters[88] would set in motion a train of events which in a few months' time would shake the Northern Ireland government and result in his own ouster from office. The portion of the ill-fated 'education (miscellaneous provisions) bill' which was destined to cause trouble was a clause drafted in response to the claims of some voluntary school managers that the government, which paid the full salaries of the primary and intermediate school teachers, should also pay the employer's portion of the teacher's national insurance contributions, rather than leave the employer's contribution to be paid by the school manager. Hall-Thompson proposed to have the employer's insurance contributions for all primary, intermediate, and county grammar school teachers paid in full from public funds in the proportion of sixty-five per cent from the exchequer and thirty-five per cent from the rates. Simultaneously, he had framed a similar arrangement for the employer's contributions under the teachers' superannuation scheme. He also added a section providing that a portion of the cost of training teachers, which previously had been borne entirely by the central government, be met from the rates.[89]

In moving the second reading Hall-Thompson stated: 'The education bill which I present for second reading to this house is not controversial in the sense which we in Northern Ireland usually understand when considering education bills, and I do not anticipate that it will excite the same interest as the last measure I had the honour of presenting.'[90] His illusions soon were shattered, however, for when the money resolution for his bill was introduced, Hall-Thompson suffered a humiliation rare for a Unionist minister; the money resolution was not passed and instead was indefinitely postponed.[91]

Why did the opposition to this apparently innocuous measure arise? First, because Hall-Thompson proposed that the costs of paying the employer's portion of the insurance stamps be placed upon the sixth schedule of the 1947 act. In practical terms this meant that the ratepayers of Belfast would bear a high proportion of the expense. Secondly, the proposal to pay the entire insurance and superannuation contribution of the teachers in voluntary primary and intermediate schools resurrected all the parliamentary hostility to augmenting grants to voluntary schools which had fumed forth during the debates on the 1947 education act. Hall-Thompson, it will be recalled, had raised the capital costs' grant to voluntary schools from fifty per cent of total costs to sixty-five per cent. Many Unionist backbenchers were furious and had resolved not to give another farthing to the voluntary schools. Thirdly, the opposition to Hall-Thompson's bill was related to the recrudescence of religious tensions in Northern Ireland. Specifically, the government of southern Ireland had declared itself a republic in 1948 and had severed its last ties with the British Commonwealth, while simultaneously maintaining its claim to be the rightful government of all Ireland. Relations between the two governments were tense for several succeeding years; the physics of the Northern Ireland social situation translated north–south tensions into Protestant–Catholic tensions. Given the fact that all of the Catholic primary and intermediate schools were voluntary schools, the opposition to increasing the aid to the voluntary schools stemmed in part from these political tensions.[92]

In contrast to every preceding educational controversy which had occurred since the formation of the Northern Ireland government this agitation was led by laymen instead of clerics. Indeed, the board of education of the Presbyterian Church endorsed Hall-Thompson's bill.[93] Within the parliament the most vigorous opponent was Harry Midgley, MP for Woodvale, Belfast, who in 1947 had been one of the most articulate opponents of the augmented capital construction grants for voluntary schools. Outside the legislature, Mr Norman Porter led a small band of extreme militants, the national union of Protestants.[94] The government decided to reintroduce the money resolution in December 1949 and Sir Basil Brooke attempted to compose the differences between the cabinet and its backbench critics at a Unionist Party meeting on the thirteenth, but to no avail. The cabinet, it was reported the next day, had decided to force the issue.[95]

Then matters took an unpredictable turn. The half-yearly annual meeting of the Grand Orange Lodge of Ireland took place on the morning[96] of 14 December at the Sandy Row Orange Hall, and the education issue was discussed. The prime minister attended and some transaction occurred whereby it was decided that the education bill would be amended and that Hall-Thompson would resign.[97] The next day Brooke announced the resignation of the minister of education and then, with great dignity, Hall-Thompson carried on with the passage of his amended bill. The provision for placing a portion of the costs of training teachers on the rates was deleted and Hall-Thompson himself introduced a manuscript amendment (obviously part of a pre-arranged compromise) limiting to 31 March 1951 the period during which the teachers' insurance would be paid in full from public funds.[98] In other words, Hall-Thompson's successor would have to work out a permanent arrangement. The eventual compromise struck by Hall-Thompson's successor in 1951 was that the exchequer paid sixty-five per cent of the employer's insurance contribution for teachers in voluntary primary and intermediate schools and that the school managers paid the remainder.[99]

Hall-Thompson's successor? It was Harry Midgley, socialist, trade unionist, anti-clericalist, Orangeman, longtime member of the Belfast education committee, minister of public security in Sir Basil Brooke's government from 1943 until the end of the war, stalwart of the Commonwealth Labour Party, defender of the working man, vigorous anti-Catholic, bedeviller of Lieutenant Colonel Hall-Thompson, who, on 12 January 1950, was confirmed a minister of education in a Unionist government.[100]

Midgley settled the insurance contribution conflict fairly easily by splitting the insurance contribution between state and local agencies on a sixty-five/thirty-five per cent basis, but he had a more difficult time dealing with the financing of the voluntary grammar schools, an issue which he had himself helped raise while still a private member. The white paper on educational reconstruction and the governmental statement introducing the new educational system, it will be recalled, had emphasised that each child in Northern Ireland would receive secondary education in the form of institution most suited to his ability. This rhetoric raised parental expectations to a high level, and when it was discovered that the number of grammar school places in Belfast was less than the number of qualified children, resentment against the grammar school arrangements mounted.[101]

Some of the resentment against the grammar school system was focused directly at the inadequacy of space, some upon the 11-plus examination which in the overcrowded situation became not a test of educational aptitude but a competitive examination,[102] but most was channelled into a campaign against the means test for grammar school scholarships. When the Presbyterian general assembly protested in early June 1949 that the government had failed to give the people of Northern Ireland equal educational treatment with Great Britain and called for the prompt abolition of the means test for grammar school scholarships,[103] prescient politicians realised that a live political issue was at hand. One of those politicians was Harry Midgley who on 21 June raised the question for debate in the House of Commons.[104] No decision was reached at that time, but one of Hall-Thompson's last actions as education minister was to announce on 20 December 1949 that some weeks earlier the government had decided in principle to abolish the means test, although the details had yet to be agreed upon.[105]

So the details were left to the new minister, Harry Midgley. The abolition of the means test for grammar school scholarships meant that the local education authorities became responsible for the fees of at least eighty per cent of all pupils attending the voluntary grammar schools. This did not increase the total revenue of the grammar schools (previously the parents had paid the portion of the fees now assumed by the civic authorities), but the government scrutinised these revenues more carefully since they now came mostly from public sources. And once Midgley and his associates fell to scrutinising the fees they asked the crucial question: are school fees to be set so as to cover only the cost of tuition or could they legitimately include charges for capital outlays such as new buildings and renovations?[106] Midgley's answer was that the managers could not include capital costs in school fees. His reasoning was that under the 1947 education act the ministry granted a sixty-five per cent building grant to voluntary grammar schools, but if the schools were allowed to include an additional levy towards capital costs in the school fees which now were to be paid chiefly by public scholarship funds, then the voluntary schools could conceivably arrive at a position where all capital expenses were paid by public funds, a situation clearly not intended by parliament when it passed the 1947 act.[107]

Persuasive as this reasoning was, it came as a complete shock to the headmasters and governors of Northern Ireland's grammar schools who were jealous of their schools' independence and reluctant to go cap-in-hand to the government every time a classroom was renovated or a new extension added to their buildings. The grammar school authorities were well organised, because in 1944, in bringing pressure to bear on the government over the plans for educational reconstruction, they had formed the Association of Governing Bodies of Secondary Schools in Northern Ireland (renamed the Association of Governing Bodies of Grammar Schools in Northern Ireland after the 1947 education act altered educational terminology). This group was heavily influenced by persons associated with the Royal Belfast Academical Institution, a school justly proud of its high standards and highly resistant to the meddling of civil servants.[108]

After nearly a full year of bitter negotiations a compromise was struck whereby each grammar school in Northern Ireland was given the choice of entering one of two categories of state aid and regulation. 'Group A' schools were to reserve at least eighty per cent of their spaces for children sponsored by the local education authorities. The scholarships provided from public funds for these children were to equal the cost of tuition only and the school was prohibited from using revenue from these scholarships for capital costs. The schools were, however, permitted to charge the parents fees of up to £3 a year per pupil as a capital levy. Schools which chose to enter Group A were to receive sixty-five per cent of all capital costs from the Northern Ireland exchequer. 'Group B' schools, in contrast, were to receive no money for capital construction costs but were to have complete freedom to charge whatever fees they wished and to use the revenues in any way they desired. Group B schools were not required to reserve a specific number of spaces for children sponsored by the local education authorities, but the local authorities were empowered to provide scholarships for children attending these schools, the amount of the scholarship to be less than the total fees charged by the school and to be determined in the case of each institution by the ministry of education.[109] By the end of the academic year 1950-51, thirty-one of Northern Ireland's voluntary grammar schools had opted for Group A, thirty-three for Group B.[110] The choice of Group B status by more than half of Northern Ireland's voluntary grammar schools represented a major setback for the principles enunciated under the 1947 education act, and in particular for the ideal of providing a network of grammar schools accessible to all pupils of ability regardless of their parents' financial means. Ironically, Harry Midgley's undeniable failure in this matter in his role as minister of education was the result of a train of events which had been shaped and energised by Harry Midgley, the private member and freelance education critic.

Midgley died in office in 1957 with good intentions and competent administration to his credit, but few striking achievements. His experience as minister typified the tone of the entire range of post-war education activities: it was a period in which high ideals and high expectations produced great educational change, but in which the momentum of reform was too often dissipated as useless friction and profitless controversy.

9

What Other Hope?

At this point I am no longer writing about history in isolation from present events. Instead, I would like to tie some historical observations to policy suggestions concerning Northern Ireland's future educational development. The policy suggestions are not prescriptions and are put forward most tentatively; it is easy for an outsider to criticise the Ulster situation, but when he realises the complexity of the region's problems, he also recognises that to propound any simple solution would be arrogance. Whether or not these suggestions make sense to the reader, I hope he will allow the historical chapters which precede this one to stand or fall on their own merits, since their content was dictated by historical data and not by policy considerations. As for the structural developments in Northern Ireland's educational system between 1950 and the present, they can legitimately be summarised as the working out in practice of the principles of the 1947 act. By the mid-1960s the system which had been visualised in the era of educational reconstruction was substantially a reality.[1]

The most important theme running through Northern Ireland's educational history has been the seemingly irresistible demand for segregated schooling. The theme has stemmed

N

from two sources, clerical and social. Despite their detestation of each other, the educational principles of Protestant and Catholic clergymen have been remarkably similar on pivotal issues. For example, if one compares the words and actions which the Protestant clerical leaders directed against the vaguely ecumenical provisions of the Londonderry act of 1923 with the educational premises articulated in Catholic canon law one finds that the religious leaders of both groups believed that Ulster's children should be taught by teachers of their own denomination, that children should attend school with their co-religionists, and that religious instruction should be woven into the school curriculum.

The second pressure towards educational segregation has come from Northern Ireland's dual social structure. Laymen among the Protestant and Catholic populations have consistently established institutions and followed social patterns which have minimised the intermingling of the two major religious blocs. Thus, pro-segregation activities, which almost invariably have been led by clerics, have been backed readily enough by Ulster laymen of both faiths.

After the passage of the 1947 act Protestant primary school managers, despite their carping about the statute's provisions, transferred almost all of their schools to civic managership. This action, combined with the Catholics' continued refusal to transfer any schools, brought to its logical conclusion the trend towards self-encapsulated systems demarcated on religious lines. The pattern is clearly revealed in the following figures for children on the rolls of primary schools as of January 1964:[2]

	R.C.	Other denominations
County schools	837	96,673
Four-and-Two	905	3,424
Voluntary, under single managership	87,439	987

Crucially, the pressures on Northern Ireland's educational development have created not only a system of religious segre-

gation, but one which is separate *and* unequal. Chapters 3–8
of this book demonstrated that the Protestant clergy were
successful in twisting the state primary schools into Protestant
institutions, fully dependent upon public funds, while the
Catholic schools received less than full public support. This
is not to 'blame' the Protestant clerics (whether or not the
reader finds their action praiseworthy or opprobrious will
depend on his own outlook), but it is to make the historical
statement that in a power struggle the Protestant clerics had
greater leverage than did their opponents.

Actually, the Protestant clerics triumphed not only over
their religious rivals, but over the state as well, a fact which
leads one to observe that, ironically, the partition of Ireland
did not change the basic state–Church conflict in education,
but only the groups involved in the fray. In the years before
partition the contest for control of the schools was between
the Roman Catholic authorities and the state officials, with
the religious authorities being prepotent; in Ulster after partition it was between the Protestant clerical authorities and
the state officials, with the clergy being generally victorious.
Granted, there have been important differences between
Protestant pressures in Ulster and Catholic pressures in pre-
partition Ireland. In particular, the Protestants have been
satisfied with a more diffuse, although no less pervasive, style
of control over the educational institutions. (Doubtless this
relates to the contrasting degrees of centralisation in the
Catholic and Protestant polities.) But such differences should
not blind us to the fact that the substantive issues in Church–
state relations and the relative powers of the two combatants
have changed surprisingly little, for the Protestant clergy in
the north have followed the same strategy of maximising their
own powers that always has been followed by the Roman
Catholic clergy in the south.

An almost Newtonian countercurrent of events implied
that as the Protestant clerics bent the state system more and
more into the shape of a Protestant school system, the govern-

ment, either under the impress of the demands of equity or in an attempt to quiet a tempestuous minority, regularly improved the financial conditions under which the voluntary schools operated. Thus, in 1930 Lord Craigavon balanced his concession to the Protestant clerics by introducing a fifty per cent building grant for voluntary primary schools, a category into which all Catholic elementary schools fell. This grant was increased to sixty-five per cent in Hall-Thompson's 1947 education act. The latest extension of this trend came with an amending act of 1968 which raised the capital construction grant from sixy-five per cent to eighty per cent for primary and intermediate schools under four-and-two committees.[3] This plan for 'maintained schools' (the new name for four-and-two schools) overcame the reluctance of many managers of clerically managed schools: by the end of 1969, 200 of the 615 voluntary primary schools had become maintained schools[4] and since then there have been regular additions to this list from the ranks of the previously privately managed Catholic schools.

Here let us use this countercurrent to extrapolate one suggestion for future educational arrangements in Northern Ireland which at least would have the virtue of equity as between religious denominations: this is simply that grants for maintained schools of all levels should be raised to 100 per cent of capital construction costs, which would mean that the maintained schools, like the state schools, would have all their expenses paid from public resources. Whether this suggestion is politically feasible is a difficult question to answer, but it is worth noting that a large sample survey conducted in 1968, before the recent troubles began, revealed that sixty-four per cent of the Protestants surveyed favoured the government giving as much public money to Catholic schools as to Protestant.[5]

An opponent of equal grants for Catholic schools could, I think, make three clear arguments against such an undertaking. The first of these, that these proposed arrangements would benefit the Roman Catholic Church and therefore should be opposed by all true Protestants, is not a position with which one can deal rationally, rooted as it is in prejudice. The second is more to the point, that the maintained schools (that is, the schools under the four-and-two committees) would not be sufficiently responsive to local civic authorities, since on almost all matters their governors deal directly with the ministry of education. There is some merit in this argument, but it should be pointed out that under the 1947 act the management committees of individual (Protestant) schools transferred to the local education authorities were constituted so as to minimise the intervention of the civic authorities in the management of the transferred school. A third objection to the full grant for maintained schools is that the managing boards of those schools do not necessarily have enough lay representation. This is a fair point. Nothing prevents the local parish priest from naming his curate and the clerics from the neighbouring parishes as his representatives on the four-and-two management committee. If a school is to be supported entirely by public funds—resources which stem almost entirely from taxes on the laity—it seems only reasonable to require that laymen have a majority of seats on the management committee of the maintained school. Whether or not the Catholic clerical authorities would accept such a proviso is uncertain.[6]

Even though the separate-but-equal system has attractions, specifically from the standpoint of equity, the effect of segregated schooling upon Northern Ireland's social configuration at least deserves study. Here, unfortunately, there is a minimum of data. Granted, there is a mass of evidence from foreign countries suggesting that the segregated education of the young increases social prejudices[7] but arguing from analogy is dangerous, particularly because most of the studies in other nations have dealt with segregation of racial (ie, black–white) or linguistic groups; in Northern Ireland the segregation occurs along religious lines in a population which shares the same skin colour and language.

One can, as I have done, examine the textbooks used in Catholic and Protestant schools and one will come to the conclusions originally formulated by Barritt and Carter in their study of community relations in Northern Ireland:[8] that the Protestant schools teach history from an English viewpoint, that Catholic schools teach it from an Irish viewpoint; that the presence of the Irish language in Catholic secondary schools and its almost complete absence from Protestant schools imparts an entirely different tone to much of the curriculum of the Catholic schools—not a surprising result since all of the texts are prepared in the Irish Republic.[9] Quite wisely, in view of the irreconcilable pressures under which it operates, the ministry of education has allowed the schools considerable latitude in the choice of textbooks, a policy which increases the tendency towards substantive differences in the curricula of the Protestant and Catholic schools. But noting these differences in the curricula of the two halves of the segregated school system is not the same as concluding that the segregated schooling arrangements heighten prejudices or communal differences. Schools are much less influential than parents and peers in shaping the attitudes of children, and conceivably the same mixture of dogmatism and prejudice which characterises inter-group relations within Northern Ireland would result even if the schools had identical curricula.

The only study of which I am aware which sheds any light on the effect of Ulster's schools upon inter-group relations is the imaginative study done in the city of Derry by the students of Bishop Grosseteste, College of Education, Lincoln, under the direction of Alan Robinson. One thousand children were asked some very simple but highly revealing questions. What country is Derry situated in? Seventy-three per cent of the Catholic primary school pupils said 'Ireland', while sixty per cent of the Protestant primary school pupils said 'Northern Ireland'. What is the capital of the country in which Derry is situated? Fifty-six per cent of the Catholic secondary school pupils said 'Dublin', and seventy-five per cent of the Protestant pupils said 'Belfast'. Other questions were asked about historical knowledge, leading citizens, etc. Significantly, on some important items sectarian divisions of opinion were more marked during the secondary school years than during the primary years.[10] Robinson's conclusion is that 'clearly schools in Northern Ireland do not cause the conflict between Catholics and Protestants, but in reinforcing the dichotomy they may affect adversely the relations between both groups'.[11] It seems apparent, therefore, that the schools as a whole do nothing to reduce ill feeling and misunderstanding between Protestants and Catholics.

A most striking individual indication of the pressure of a segregated system on the mind of a child is found in the autobiography of Bernadette Devlin. (Whether one approves or disapproves of her politics is irrelevant; the potential impact upon the outlook of a child by her immersion in a segregated school system is the point at issue.) Miss Devlin attended St Patrick's Academy, Dungannon, which was a 'militantly republican school', under the hegemony of a Mother Benignus to whom, according to Miss Devlin, 'everything English was bad'. This dominant figure was a zealot for Irish culture and although she did not hate Protestants (unlike the English whom she did hate), she believed they could not be tolerated because they were not Irish. Under this nun's regime the school athletic teams were prohibited from inter-scholastic sport competitions with Protestant schools because the children would have had to stand for the national anthem. History in this school seems to have been taught as a narrative of English crimes against Ireland. The textbooks used for this subject were a series published in the south of Ireland and specifically forbidden by the ministry of education. Even before she left the academy Miss Devlin came to perceive the reverend mother as a bigot, but the impact of such a teacher upon the minds of less resilient children can easily be imagined.[12] One suspects that instances of the inculcation of prejudice, both consciously and unconsciously, in Northern Ireland's schools could be multiplied by the thousands, in Catholic and Protestant institutions alike. However, until further research is done this must remain a conjecture.

Given the present state of our knowledge, a judicious conservative conclusion would be that it is *certain* that the schools of Northern Ireland are almost completely segregated, that it is *highly probable* that the segregated schools do nothing to neutralise hostile and prejudicial attitudes between religious groups, and that it is *probable* (but by no means proved) that the segregated school system exacerbates inter-group frictions.

But be careful: it is deceptively and dangerously easy to slide from the conclusion that the segregated schools system does no good and probably does considerable harm to group relations, to murmuring 'integration' as if it were a magic word. That mixing of children in integrated schools can produce an improvement in the attitudes each side holds towards the other is undeniable; what is often forgotten is that integration can also increase social tensions and worsen group relations.

Recall for a moment the fact that Northern Ireland's dual social system is also a dual system of religio-politico-ethnic beliefs. Each side has a set of ideas about its own position and about the nature of the other side, which, if lacking in logical consistency, have a psychological unity. In each of these nearly closed belief systems threats from the outside usually produce dogmatism on the inside. If a randomly chosen set of children (and by association their parents) are mixed by fiat and without adequate counselling and extra-classroom support, the result is apt to be painful. Members of each group will perceive the other solely in terms of threat, and each group will become more dogmatic in their intolerant beliefs to the opposite side.[13]

If an integrated school is to have any chance of success I would suggest that it must have four characteristics. The first of these is that it must be voluntary in the sense that only children of parents who actively desire their attendance are admitted. Any degree of compulsion would probably raise the threat response and cancel completely any benefit that might come from mixing children of the two faiths.[14] Secondly, to be successful an integrated institution should be constituted of children of parents who have some shared beliefs in common, despite diverging religious views; to a considerable extent the desire to send a child to an integrated school implies certain shared beliefs about communal harmony being more important than religious purity.[15] Similarity in parental occupations or at least social class is also important if the two sets of parents are not to view each other as alien species. This implies, unfortunately, that for the foreseeable future the successfully integrated schools probably will be class-bound institutions. Thirdly, even if the children of an integrated school and their parents are constituted so that each side is minimally threatening to the other, it will still be necessary to introduce a variety of supportive techniques, such as frequent parent-teacher conferences, a wide range of activities to bond the children (ranging from cooperative academic projects to a programme of competitive sports against other institutions), and probably a school sociologist, social worker, or psychologist will be required. Finally, given the realities of Northern Ireland's educational structure, an integrated school to be successful must in its managerial arrangements stay clear of both the local government authorities and of the authorities of all religious denominations. Very few Catholic parents would have anything to do with the local government agencies, most of which in the past have been vigorously anti-Catholic, and few Protestant parents would send their children to a school over which the Catholic clergy held a commanding position (and that is the only position the clergy will accept). Thus, it would be necessary for an integrated primary or intermediate school to opt for 'maintained status' and to be controlled by the parents and by the ministry of education, with other vested interests excluded.[16]

One could wish less for Northern Ireland than to desire in the future that for the sake of justice all children, Roman Catholic and Protestant alike, receive the same educational benefits from the government and that for the sake of Christian charity some hopeful careful experiments in integration are attempted.

Statistical Appendix

Compilation of complete series of statistics for Northern Ireland's educational system is difficult for several reasons. First, the education system was established during a chaotic period in Ireland's history by men who were competent, but overworked. Understandably, some statistical series began one year, others began another. Not until 1926 did the ministry's statistical procedures become stable and thorough. Secondly, the history of the Northern Irish educational system in the years 1920-50 was really the history of three successive systems: that inherited from the British, that operative under the Londonderry act from 1923-47, and that created by the 1947 act. The data generated during each of these three stages differed considerably from the others, because data appropriate to one set of educational structures was often inadequate for describing another. Thirdly, World War II left the ministry woefully understaffed and no full-scale accounting was done during the years 1939-44. Fourthly, the civil servants of the ministry were sometimes guilty of obscurantism in defining statistical categories and were occasionally inconsistent in procedures between one year's statistics and the next's.

With these points in mind, the following tables are presented. In order to make the individual series as complete as possible in several places I have had to complete minor accounting operations which the ministry performed some years, but not others; this is the only way to maintain comparability of data. Also, the reader will note that I have defined the categories in certain cases not in the official vocabulary of the ministry of education but in layman's terms. For example, in Table III the aggregate of provided and of transferred elementary schools is labelled 'state schools' although until 1947 there was no official name for them, when aggregated. I have then kept that term even after 1947 when the term 'county school' became the inclusive term for provided and transferred schools. This procedure seems to me to be preferable to the anachronistic alternative of using the official term 'county school' to apply to the years 1922-47. In any case, the labels of categories in the tables which follow are self-explanatory and where the reader finds that they differ somewhat from the official vocabulary I hope he will be indulgent, since my purpose is to extend the run of data available.

One series which is unfortunately missing from the tables is that on technical education up to 1947. From the data available I found it impossible to develop a series on full-time technical schools and their enrolment which would have been comparable to the series on elementary and on post-primary schools.

The sources of the tables are the annual reports of the ministry of education. The sources of each individual table are specified in the Notes (see p 271) with a year, which refers to the ministry's report, and a page number. Thus, '1937-8 (p 104)' refers to the *Report of the Ministry of Education for the year 1937-8*, p 104.

TABLE I

EDUCATIONAL EXPENDITURE BORNE ON THE PARLIAMENTARY VOTES, 1922-50[1]

(Fiscal Year, 1 April to 31 March)

Year	Ministry of education salaries and administrative expenses	Elementary education	Academic secondary education	Technical education	University education	Grants in aid to local authorities	Grand total
1922–3	Breakdown not available	Breakdown not available					£1,903,630
1923–4	Breakdown not available	Breakdown not available					2,180,705
1924–5	Breakdown not available	Breakdown not available					2,158,660
1925–6	£69,138	£1,556,982	£116,026	£65,142	£36,000	£ 69,040	1,912,328
1926–7	67,733	1,452,033	108,970	64,406	36,000	110,960	1,840,102
1927–8	69,487	1,461,769	115,653	67,256	36,000	137,417	1,887,582
1928–9	66,513	1,466,884	128,866	68,738	38,000	137,374	1,906,375
1929–30	68,695	1,469,893	142,548	69,140	40,000	162,708	1,952,984
1930–31	70,162	1,467,892	156,521	71,421	40,000	164,301	1,970,297
1931–2	66,587	1,369,058	160,033	71,075	40,000	177,155	1,884,208
1932–3	63,269	1,376,743	155,679	67,954	40,000	173,816	1,877,461
1933–4	63,621	1,360,269	163,016	69,274	40,000	173,160	1,869,340
1934–5	62,920	1,367,155	169,403	71,121	40,000	174,431	1,885,030
1935–6	63,750	1,366,028	173,549	71,794	40,000	179,042	1,894,163

continued on next page

TABLE 1 *continued*

Year	Ministry of Education salaries and administrative expenses	Elementary education	Academic secondary education	Technical education	University education	Grants in aid to local authorities	Grand total
1936–7	65,586	1,402,694	179,115	73,186	40,000	180,378	1,940,959
1937–8	66,787	1,461,759	194,839	73,748	40,000	237,453	2,074,586
1938–9	68,226	1,481,519	203,894	80,984	57,500	242,129	2,134,252
1939–40	64,843	1,481,964	210,354	83,546	62,500	247,486	2,150,693
1940–41	63,137	1,490,005	214,798	80,268	62,500	250,340	2,161,048
1941–2	64,338	1,520,678	226,800	81,388	62,500	244,188	2,199,892
1942–3	70,934	1,575,343	263,900	97,545	62,500	255,397	2,325,519
1943–4	76,657	1,608,194	291,657	102,329	62,500	274,980	2,416,317
1944–5	83,702	1,690,897	311,488	114,319	62,500	302,065	2,564,971
1945–6	94,412	2,288,757	385,332	132,711	62,500	347,806	3,311,518
1946–7	100,522	2,172,120	381,980	192,908	62,500	334,639	3,244,669
1947–8	113,770	2,328,719	465,325	222,065	67,500	378,712	3,776,091
1948–9	126,522	Breakdown not available; total spent on education services:					£4,869,514
1949–50	138,197	Breakdown not available; total spent on education services:					£5,206,287
1950–51	150,105	Breakdown not available; total spent on education services:					£5,495,563

TABLE II

RECEIPTS OF LOCAL EDUCATION AUTHORITIES FROM LOCAL SOURCES
(RATES AND SCHOOL FEES) 1925–48[2]
Fiscal Year, 1 April to 31 March

1922–3 through 1924–5	Not available
1925–6	£ 63,896
1926–7	77,950
1927–8	110,410
1928–9	117,403
1929–30	95,951
1930–31	105,963
1931–2	122,728
1932–3	131,770
1933–4	137,627
1934–5	137,724
1935–6	140,984
1936–7	161,258
1937–8	145,050
1938–9 through 1943–4	Not available
1944–5	282,135
1945–6	321,444
1946–7	395,684
1947–8	458,294
1948–9ff	Not available

TABLE III

NUMBER OF ELEMENTARY SCHOOLS OF VARIOUS TYPES AND THEIR RESPECTIVE ENROLMENTS, 1922–50[8]

(as of 31 December each year)

Year	No of provided schools	Average no on rolls, calendar year	No of transferred schools	Average no on rolls, calendar year	Total no state schools	Total average no children on rolls, calendar year	No vol schools under statutory committees	Average no of children on rolls, calendar year	No of vol schools not under statutory committees	Average no of children on rolls, calendar year	Grand total: No of schools	Grand total: average no of children on roll, calendar year
1922	Pre-Londonderry system, categories not relevant										2,066	200,368
1923	Pre-Londonderry system, categories not relevant										2,054	200,910
1924	Breakdown not tabulated by the ministry										2,041	200,447
1925	Breakdown not tabulated by the ministry										2,006	201,969
1926	6	2,584	75	13,132	81	15,716	88	11,048	1,801	175,734	1,970	202,498
1927	10	4,056	194	32,248	204	36,304	108	13,493	1,636	151,891	1,948	201,688
1928	13	4,786	323	46,606	336	51,392	109	12,653	1,488	136,874	1,933	200,919
1929	21	6,844	403	53,816	424	60,660	93	10,665	1,403	129,375	1,920	200,700
1930	33	10,964	440	71,529	473	82,493	99	11,176	1,321	107,402	1,893	201,071
1931	63	17,440	448	60,235	511	77,675	78	9,734	1,279	116,068	1,868	203,477
1932	79	23,023	474	62,522	551	85,545	81	10,425	1,203	126,980	1,837	205,630
1933	93	25,455	498	70,397	591	95,852	76	9,255	1,147	103,214	1,814	208,321

Year												
1934	115	…	…	…	…	…	…	…	1,…	…	1,…	…
1935	117	29,708	509	64,250	626	93,958	65	8,902	1,084	100,465	1,775	203,325
1936	129	31,562	512	62,165	641	93,727	63	8,569	1,049	97,446	1,753	199,742
1937	142	33,889	511	61,078	653	94,967	55	7,509	1,019	94,363	1,727	196,839
1938	166	38,261	489	57,348	655	95,609	54	6,873	991	91,510	1,700	193,992
1939	188	N/A	479	N/A	667	N/A	Breakdown not available total no vol schools:			1,024	1,691	192,793
1940	193	N/A	478	N/A	671	N/A	Ditto:			1,015	1,686	189,669
1941	193	N/A	483	N/A	676	N/A	Ditto:			1,005	1,681	192,049
1942	194	N/A	483	N/A	677	N/A	Ditto:			996	1,673	185,595
1943	195	N/A	485	N/A	680	N/A	Ditto:			987	1,667	185,919
1944	195	N/A	490	N/A	685	N/A	Ditto:			980	1,665	186,426
1945	196	39,930	493	54,744	689	94,674	48	5,659	924	85,613	1,661	185,940
1946	201	41,128	495	55,023	696	96,150	52	5,925	912	85,528	1,660	187,604
1947	200	40,918	497	54,716	697	95,634	51	5,866	905	85,092	1,653	186,592
1948	N/A	N/A	N/A	N/A	690	92,988	72	6,932	873	84,338	1,635	184,258
1949	N/A	N/A	N/A	N/A	699	94,529	92	7,480	841	84,413	1,632	186,422
1950	N/A	N/A	N/A	N/A	713	N/A	105	N/A	813	N/A	1,631	N/A

P

TABLE IV

ELEMENTARY SCHOOL ATTENDANCE 1922–50[2]
(for year ending 31 December)

Year	Average number on rolls	Average daily attendance	Percentage
1922	200,368	152,517	76.1%
1923	200,910	155,748	77.5
1924	200,447	158,057	78.4
1925	201,969	164,541	81.5
1926	202,498	169,610	83.3
1927	201,688	168,990	83.8
1928	200,919	169,027	84.1
1929	200,700	167,502	83.4
1930	201,071	171,732	85.4
1931	203,477	173,835	85.4
1932	205,630	176,863	86.0
1933	208,321	177,208	85.1

Year			
1935	203,325	172,112	84.7
1936	199,692	170,549	85.4
1937	196,754	167,101	84.9
1938	193,902	166,025	85.6
1939	192,793	166,657	86.4
1940	189,669	159,954	84.1
1941	192,049	152,925	79.6
1942	185,595	150,395	81.0
1943	185,919	152,035	81.7
1944	186,426	155,669	83.0
1945	185,940	155,910	83.8
1946	187,604	157,102	83.7
1947	186,592	155,444	85.2
1948	184,258	158,040	85.8
1949	186,422	160,182	85.9
1950	189,221	162,074	85.7

TABLE V

SIZE OF ELEMENTARY SCHOOLS, SELECTED YEARS[5]

(as of 31 December each year)

Average Daily Attendances

	less than 10	10–19	20–29	30–34	35–39	40–49	50–69	70–94	95–119	120–139	140–159	160–184	185–229	230–239	240–274	275–319	320–364	365 and over	Total
1923	5	88	205	159	209	332	423	181	130	66	52	42	53	13	26	30	15	25	2,054
1925	4	62	157	121	178	348	451	200	129	55	72	40	63	14	31	31	19	31	2,006
1930	2	64	126	144	146	328	403	201	118	43	55	48	60	11	34	26	30	54	1,893
1935	0	79	124	159	141	288	355	180	87	55	41	39	53	13	29	29	25	77	1,774
1938	2	67	160	128	160	274	329	164	89	40	38	29	41	10	33	27	25	84	1,700
1945	8	129	161	127	158	257	300	126	81	40	29	34	47	14	18	24	23	85	1,661
1950	3	77	131	91	107	208	306	218	96	58	44	35	42	14	21	38	26	116	1,631

RELIGIOUS PROFESSIONS OF CHILDREN IN ELEMENTARY SCHOOLS, 1922–50[6]

(as of 31 December each year)

Year	Roman Catholic	Presbyterian	Anglican	Methodist	Other	Total
1922	68,959	66,665	51,743	6,648	4,370	198,385
1923	67,925	65,605	51,553	6,621	4,311	196,015
1924	69,166	65,595	52,313	6,872	4,647	198,593
1925	70,232	65,954	52,334	6,844	4,923	200,287
1926	Not available					
1927	72,143	64,285	51,484	6,792	4,856	199,560
1928	71,998	64,405	51,618	6,634	4,856	199,511
1929	72,068	63,825	51,944	6,743	4,980	199,560
1930	72,872	63,921	52,686	7,056	5,148	201,683
1931	73,291	64,978	53,470	7,272	5,389	204,400
1932	74,443	64,879	54,638	7,439	5,337	206,736
1933	75,150	64,011	54,887	7,286	5,500	206,834
1934	74,517	62,628	54,126	7,263	5,409	203,943
1935	73,838	61,050	53,103	7,145	5,471	200,607
1936	72,964	59,320	52,509	7,093	5,467	197,353
1937	72,259	57,949	51,726	7,008	5,495	194,347
1938	71,789	56,807	50,929	7,002	5,335	191,862
1939–44	Not available					
1945	73,242	52,573	47,878	6,914	4,863	185,470
1946	74,369	52,891	48,015	7,052	4,934	187,261
1947	73,814	52,280	47,125	7,199	5,000	185,418
1948	75,083	51,211	45,104	7,031	5,016	183,445
1949	76,335	51,810	45,138	7,245	5,184	185,712
1950	77,653	52,447	45,164	7,389	5,338	187,991

TABLE VII

EDUCATION IN ACADEMIC POST-PRIMARY SCHOOLS AND
IN PREPARTORY DEPARTMENTS RELATED THERETO, 1921–48[7]

School year	Number of schools	Total enrolment
1921–2	54	4,784
1922–3	76	6,206
1923–4	72	8,677
1924–5	72	9,357
1925–6	69	8,460
1926–7	70	9,012
1927–8	71	9,913
1928–9	72	10,611
1929–30	74	11,618
1930–31	73	12,094
1931–2	73	12,267
1932–3	72	12,339
1933–4	73	12,710
1934–5	74	12,974
1935–6	73	13,165
1936–7	73	13,440
1937–8	76	13,683
1938–9	76	14,083
1930–40	75	14,557
1940–41	75	14,493
1941–2	75	14,772
1942–3	75	16,023
1943–4	76	17,535
1944–5	76	18,854
1945–6	76	19,861
1946–7	76	21,021
1947–8	77	21,973

TABLE VIII

POST-PRIMARY EDUCATION, 1948–51[8]

	Intermediate Schools				Technical Intermediate Schools			Grammar Schools										All Secondary Schools	
	Number of Schools		Number of Pupils		Number of Schools	Number of Pupils		Number of Schools		Number of Pupils								Total Number of Schools	Total Number of Pupils
										Preparatory Department		Secondary Department				Preparatory and Secondary Departments			
												Lower Division		Upper Division					
	County	Voluntary	Boys	Girls		Boys	Girls	County	Voluntary	Boys	Girls	Boys	Girls	Boys	Girls	Boys	Girls		
1948–9	8	2	2,568	2,225	28	2,244	2,238	10	67	2,009	3,023	7,096	7,334	2,607	2,349	11,712	12,706	115	33,693
1949–50	9	2	3,060	2,844	28	2,504	2,025	15	64	2,124	3,132	8,052	8,202	2,817	2,408	12,993	13,742	118	37,168
1950–51	10	2	3,360	3,336	29	2,596	1,982	15	64	2,123	3,089	8,885	8,966	2,893	2,430	13,901	14,485	120	39,660

Notes

CHAPTER 1, pp 9-18

1 *Seventy-First Report of the Commissioners of National Education in Ireland, for the Year 1904*, pp 13-14 [Cd. 2567], H.C. 1905, xxviii

2 On the conflict see especially *Minutes of the Proceedings of the Commissioners of National Education Relating to Rule 127 (b) and Cognate Rules*, H.C. 1905 (184), lx; *Seventy-First Report of the Commissioners of National Education in Ireland, for the Year 1904*, pp 9-13; 'Statements and Resolutions of the Irish Hierarchy at Maynooth Meeting June 21', *Irish Ecclesiastical Record*, 4 series, vol XXVII, no 7 (July 1910), p 92

3 *Seventy-Seventh Report of the Commissioners of National Education in Ireland, School Year 1910-11*, p 16 [Cd. 5903], H.C. 1911, xxi; *Eighty-Sixth Report of the Commissioners of National Education in Ireland, School Year 1919-20*, p 16 [Cmd. 1476], H.C. 1921, xi

4 On the basic flaws in the act see Donald H. Akenson, *The Irish Education Experiment: The National System of Education in the Nineteenth Century* (London: Routledge & Kegan Paul, and Toronto: University of Toronto Press, 1970), pp 344-9, 361

5 I am sorry that limitations of space have precluded my discussing in detail what is really a very complex matter. For the reader who wishes to go into the subject, a useful beginning can be made with the following: *Report of Mr F. H. Dale, His Majesty's Inspector of Schools, Board of Education, on Primary Education in Ireland* [Cd. 1981], H.C. 1904, xx; *Report of the Vice-Regal Committee of Inquiry into Primary Education (Ireland) 1918* [Cmd. 60], H.C. 1919, cxi; *Report of the Vice-Regal Committee on the Conditions of*

Service and Remuneration of Teachers in Intermediate Schools and the Distribution of Grants from Public Funds for Intermediate Education in Ireland [Cmd. 66], H.C. 1919, xxi

The four bills referred to are: *A Bill to Provide for the Establishment and Functions of an Administrative Council in Ireland and for other purposes connected therewith*, H.C. 1907 (182), ii; *A Bill to Make Further Provision with Respect to Education in Ireland and for other purposes connected therewith*, H.C. 1919 (214), i; *A Bill to Make Better Provision for Primary Education in the City of Belfast*, H.C. 1919 (24), ii; *A Bill to Make Further Provision with Respect to Education of Ireland, and for other purposes connected therewith*, H.C. 1920 (35), i.

A good deal of relevant material is found throughout David W. Miller's 'The Politics of Faith and Fatherland: The Catholic Church and Nationalism in Ireland, 1898-1918' (unpublished PhD Thesis, University of Chicago, 1968). Also see Dr Miller's, 'Educational Reform and the Realities of Irish Politics in the Early Twentieth Century' (unpublished paper presented to the American Historical Association, 30 December 1969). See also: 'Catholic Clerical Managers Association, Meeting of Central Council', *Irish Educational Review*, vol II, no 10 (July 1909), pp 629-32; 'Control of Primary Education in Ireland', *Irish Educational Review*, vol I, no 12 (September 1908), pp 729-36; 'Pastoral Address of the Irish Bishops on the Managership of Catholic Schools', *Irish Ecclesiastical Record*, 4 series, vol IV, no 367 (July 1898), pp 75-8; 'Pronouncement of the Irish Hierarchy at a General Meeting held at Maynooth on Tuesday, January 27th', *Irish Ecclesiastical Record*, 5 series, vol XV, no 2 (February 1920), pp 150-52; 'Statement of the Standing Committee of the Irish Bishops on the Proposed Education Bill for Ireland', *Irish Ecclesiastical Record*, 5 series, vol XIV, no 12 (December 1919), pp 504-7

6 *Report of Messrs F. H. Dale and T. A. Stephens, His Majesty's Inspectors of Schools, Board of Education, on Intermediate Education in Ireland*, p 85 [Cd. 2546], H.C 1905, xxviii

7 Unfortunately, no thorough study of the intermediate system has been published. The best study is an unpublished thesis by T. J. McElligott, 'Intermediate Education and the

Work of the Commissioners, 1870-1922' (unpublished MLitt thesis, Trinity College, Dublin, 1969)

8 Ibid, pp 125-6, 145; *Report of Messrs F. H. Dale and T. A. Stephens, His Majesty's Inspectors of Schools, Board of Education, on Intermediate Education in Ireland*, pp 11, 41-4, 85

9 See: McElligott, p 127; *Report of the Intermediate Education Board for Ireland under the Intermediate Education (Ireland) Act 1914, as to the Application of the Teachers' Salaries Grant*, p 3 [Cd. 8724], H.C. 1917-18, xi; *Report of Messrs F. H. Dale and T. A. Stephens, His Majesty's Inspectors of Schools, Board of Education, on Intermediate Education in Ireland*, pp 43-4, 85; *Report of the Vice-Regal Committee on the Conditions of Service and Remuneration of Teachers in Intermediate Schools, and on the Distribution of Grants from Public Funds for Intermediate Education in Ireland*, p 17

10 *Report of the Intermediate Education Board for Ireland for the Year 1920*, p. x [Cmd. 1398], H.C. 1921, xi

11 For the outlines of the new department see 62 and 63 Victoria C. 50; *First Annual General Report of the Department of Agriculture and Technical Instruction for Ireland, 1900-1901* [Cd. 838], H.C. 1902, xx; *Second Annual General Report of the Department of Agriculture and Technical Instruction for Ireland*, 1901-2 [Cd. 1314], H.C. 1902, xx

12 See note 5, above

CHAPTER 2, pp 19-38

1 A valuable article on the subject is John E. Sayers's 'The Political Parties and the Social Background', in Thomas Wilson (ed), *Ulster under Home Rule: A Study of the Political and Economic Problems of Northern Ireland* (London: Oxford University Press, 1955), pp 55-78

2 James Craig, 'Ulster is British', *Spectator*, no 4,991 (23 February 1924), p 277

3 The stultifying effect of a political situation in which a permanent majority tilted with a permanent minority about matters of constitutional loyalty can be seen by glancing through any volume of the debates of the Northern Ireland House of Commons. An especially picturesque sample of

the bitter, cyclical, unproductive debates is found in the
reports of the Commons debate, vol XVI (1933-4), cols 1072-
1128. This was a debate in which Basil Brooke endeavoured
to establish that the Catholics were ninety-nine per cent
disloyal, and Cahir Healy for the Nationalists suggested that
Hitler had not persecuted the Jews so subtly or so long as
the Unionists had persecuted the Catholics in the six counties.

One should also note that the prepotency of constitutional questions over matters of ideology and the domina-
tion of religious loyalties over social class ties has meant
that the Labour Party movement in Northern Ireland has
been weak. Only in the largest urban areas has the party
evinced any drawing power. In the period with which this
study is chiefly concerned, 1921-50, the Labour Party held
only one, two, or three seats in the Northern Ireland House
of Commons. The Labour Party was hurt by the abolition of
proportional representation in 1929. Further, the party was
debilitated by its collective inability to decide whether it was
for or against the union. Only in 1949 did it finally decide
that no alteration in the constitutional position of Northern
Ireland should be made without the assent of the majority
of the population. As far as educational matters were concerned, individual members of the Labour Party in the
Northern Ireland Commons acted as independent spokesmen and as political prophets, but the party as a unit was
a cipher
4 Nicholas Mansergh, *The Government of Northern Ireland:
A Study in Devolution* (London: George Allen & Unwin
Ltd, 1936), pp 248-53
5 On the problems of the Nationalist Party in the years prior
to World War II see David Kennedy, 'Catholics in Northern
Ireland, 1926-39', in Francis MacManus (ed), *The Years of
the Great Test, 1926-39* (Cork: Mercier Press, 1967), pp
139-45
6 10 and 11 Geo. 5, C. 67
7 The articles of agreement for an Anglo-Irish treaty, signed
in December 1921, were negotiated over the heads of the
northern leaders and it was necessary for the north to formally opt out of the Irish Free State within a month after the
Free State's establishment. This step was taken by the northern government on 7 December 1922

8 The following books on the governmental structure are valuable: Harry Calvert, *Constitutional Law in Northern Ireland: A Study in Regional Government* (London: Stevens & Sons Ltd, and Belfast: Northern Ireland Legal Quarterly Inc, 1968); Nicholas Mansergh, *The Government of Northern Ireland: A Study in Devolution* (London: George Allen & Unwin Ltd, 1936); and Arthur S. Queckett, *The Constitution of Northern Ireland* (Belfast: HMSO, 1928), 2 vols

9 For a thorough analytic study of the Northern Ireland Senate see Patrick F. McGill, 'The Senate in Northern Ireland, 1921-62' (unpublished PhD thesis, Queen's University, Belfast, 1965)

10 Denis P. Barritt and Charles F. Carter, *The Northern Ireland Problem: A Study in Group Relations* (London: Oxford University Press, 1962), p 21

11 Compiled from the Government of Eire, *Statistical Abstract of Ireland 1966* (Dublin: The Stationery Office, 1966), pp 350, 358, and from Government of Northern Ireland, *Ulster Year Book 1966-8* (Belfast: HMSO, 1967), p 10

12 John M. Mogey, 'The Community in Northern Ireland', *Man*, vol XLVIII (1948), p 86

13 Rosemary L. Harris, 'Social Relations and Attitudes in a N. Irish Rural Area—Ballygawley' (unpublished MA thesis, University of London, 1954), p 216

14 On Belfast see Jones, *A Social Geography of Belfast* (London: Oxford University Press, 1960), *passim*

   For maps of religious segregation patterns in Belfast as of the mid-1920s see E. Estyn Evans, 'Belfast: The Site and the City', *Ulster Journal of Archaeology*, 3 series, vol VII (1944), pp 25-9.

   Derry's residential pattern is treated in Alan Robinson's 'A Social Geography of the City of Londonderry' (unpublished MA thesis, Queen's University, Belfast, 1967), pp 115-21.

   A recent study of Lurgan is Thomas Kirk's 'The Religious Distributions of Lurgan with Special Reference to Segregational Ecology' (unpublished MA thesis, Queen's University, Belfast, 1967)

15 Barritt and Carter, pp 33-4, 143-51. The authors' evidence was gathered in the late 1950s and early 1960s. Because I am not aware of a similar study conducted during the years 1920-50, I am performing the ahistorical operation of pro-

jecting their results backwards in time. Actually, my reading in contemporary newspapers and magazines convinces me that the differences in social styles between the two faiths were even greater in the 1920-50 period than in the years studied by Barritt and Carter

16 Jones, *A Social Geography of Belfast*, pp 176 ff
17 Robinson, pp 115-17
18 Harris, quoted in Barritt and Carter, p 55
19 Barritt and Carter, p 96
20 Mogey, p 87
21 Owen Dudley Edwards, *The Sins of Our Fathers: Roots of Conflict in Northern Ireland* (Dublin: Gill & MacMillan, 1970), p 190
22 Barritt and Carter, p 96; *Oxford Dictionary of the Christian Church*, pp 947-8
23 Compiled from Joseph E. Canavan, 'The Future of Protestantism in Ireland', *Studies*, vol XXXIV, no 134 (June 1945), p 234
24 M. P. Cleary, 'The Church of Ireland and Birth Control', *Irish Ecclesiastical Record*, 5 series, vol XXXVIII, no 12 (December 1931), pp 622-9
25 Canavan, p 235
26 Kirk, pp 9 ff
27 Quoted in M. W. Heslinga, *The Irish Border as a Cultural Divide: A Contribution to the Study of Regionalism in the British Isles* (Assen: Van Gorcum & Co, 1962), p 74
28 Harris, pp 224-6
29 Ever since the establishment of the government of Northern Ireland, elections for the thirteen Ulster members of the United Kingdom parliament (reduced to twelve members when the university seats were abolished in the United Kingdom in 1949) were conducted under the same franchise rules that prevailed in England. To some extent the rules favoured Protestants by virtue of their privileged economic position. Until 1928 a woman could vote only if thirty years of age or over and then only if she and her husband possessed or occupied property of an annual value of £5; and until the Labour Party's post-war reforms persons owning business premises and those who were graduates of the Queen's University had plural votes. But this was not a conscious attempt to discriminate against Catholics. Further, the constituency boundaries were set by United Kingdom statutes and re-

viewed by the United Kingdom electoral boundary commission, a body with no vested interest in the Ulster scene. Nevertheless, a person hypersensitive on matters of discrimination might point to a typical election, 1931 for example, in which eleven of the thirteen seats were won by Protestants and conclude that gross discrimination was occurring against the Roman Catholics who comprised roughly one third of the population. Actually these election results were a product of the United Kingdom's system of single-seat constituencies rather than of any electoral manoeuvring by the Ulster Protestants. As long as single-seat constituencies were the rule, and as long as the Catholic population was dispersed within the larger population, Catholics were inevitably under-represented at Westminster. In point of fact, the United Kingdom elections were treated as a matter of indifference by most Ulstermen. In 1931 an electorate of approximately 785,000 bothered to cast only about 135,000 votes. In only four of the constituencies were elections actually contested (Mansergh, p 142). The United Kingdom electoral system was not a significant Catholic grievance.

Nor was the provincial electoral system a legitimate grievance, although, like the United Kingdom electoral system, on the surface it appeared to be so. Under the government of Ireland act of 1920, the fifty-two seats in the Ulster parliament were to be filled by proportional representation, an electoral scheme thought to be especially protective of minority rights. This method was abolished as of the 1929 election by the Unionist government in an attempt to prevent the multiplication of parties. Abolition was opposed by the Catholics on the grounds that their rights now would be violated more easily by the Protestants (Mansergh, pp 128-37). Actually the system of single-seat constituencies elected on a simple majority basis produced results almost identical to those of the proportional representation system. Listed below are the numbers of anti-partition candidates (meaning Catholic candidates) elected in the first four Northern Ireland general elections (Barritt & Carter, p 41):

1921	12
1925	12
1929	11
1933	11

The franchise for the Northern Ireland elections was the

same as that of the United Kingdom parliament until after World War II when Northern Ireland maintained business votes and university franchise for provincial elections, even though they were abolished for United Kingdom elections. Thus the franchise was biased somewhat in favour of property and education, and thereby towards Protestant interests. Still, the effect was minor. There were about 912,000 electors on the register in 1964, including less than 14,000 university second votes and under 13,000 business second votes (Timothy P. Coogan, *Ireland since the Rising* [London: Pall Mall Press, 1966], p 321). In reality, it is hard to argue that a significant degree of anti-Catholic manipulation occurred in either the United Kingdom or provincial electoral systems

30 Mansergh, pp 127, 138-40, argues that even in areas where a large Protestant majority made gerrymandering unnecessary the minority lost representation through the abolition of proportional representation. However, it appears that it was gerrymandering rather than the change to the simple-majority system which most damaged minority interests.

The association of change in the electoral system with the practice of gerrymandering in the local government alteration of 1922 explains why the Catholic politicians so strongly opposed the abolition in 1929 of proportional representation for provincial elections

31 Mansergh, p 139

32 T. J. Campbell, *Fifty Years of Ulster, 1890-1940* (Belfast: The Irish News Ltd, 1941), p 326

33 Admittedly, there was a theoretical, if inadequate, explanation for some of the Unionist gerrymandering. This was that ward boundaries for local government areas had to be based on the principle of equalising rateable values, not equalising the electorate. Therefore, because the Catholics had less rateable property their wards were larger. See Government of Northern Ireland, *Disturbances in Northern Ireland* [Cmd. 532] (Belfast: HMSO, 1969), pp 59-60

34 Mansergh, p 280

35 For statistics on housing in six local government areas, compiled during the 1950s, see Barritt and Carter, pp 113-14. Two points should be emphasised. First, not all areas discriminated. Belfast and Newry employed an equitable 'points' system. Secondly, Catholic-controlled councils, for example Strabane and Downpatrick, discriminated just as

heavily against Protestants as the Protestant-controlled councils discriminated against Catholics

36 At this point it should be made clear that the social services managed by Stormont or United Kingdom authorities did not discriminate against Catholics. Indeed, such services as old age pensions and unemployment allowances were of greater benefit to the Catholic community than to the Protestant because of the Catholics' relatively depressed economic conditions

37 Patrick J. Gannon, 'In the Catacombs of Belfast', *Studies*, vol XI, no 42 (June 1922), pp 294-5

38 *Disturbances in Northern Ireland*, pp 60-61. Interestingly, in the case of the Omagh urban district council, a body controlled through gerrymandering by Protestants, no pattern of discrimination was found. Thus, the connection of gerrymandering with gross employment discrimination is not inevitable

39 Barritt and Carter, p 96

40 Ibid, p 96

41 Campbell, p 97

42 To complete the picture it is necessary to note that there has been no pattern of discrimination in those branches of the United Kingdom civil service, such as the inland revenue department, the post-telegraphs, etc, which operate in Northern Ireland. This is the conclusion drawn by Barritt and Carter from evidence gathered in the late 1950s (p 97). I have found no evidence to suggest that it is not a valid statement of the situation from the 1920s onward

43 At this point let it be strongly suggested that the reader *not* be drawn into contemplating the validity or fallacy of the following argument: that although there have been shocking individual instances of discrimination, the overall allocation of jobs and economic status between religious groups in Northern Ireland has not been unjust; that even if there had been no religious discrimination in employment in Northern Ireland—that is even if the employment market had been perfectly efficient and just from an economic point of view—the division of jobs and social status between the two major religious groups would have been the same as it actually was; a just economic mechanism would have allocated the best qualified persons to the most lucrative and esteemed jobs and the least qualified to the least desirable

jobs, or to no jobs whatsoever if the economy were below the full employment level; in the twentieth century the chief determinant of an individual's economic qualifications is his education and the Protestants have been better educated.

Evaluating such an argument is a fool's task because one would have to discover why the Catholics have been less well schooled, and to answer that question one would have to determine the interaction of four factors, none of which can be defined, much less analysed in relation to the other three. First, one would have to decide to what extent the Roman Catholic schools' having received less state aid than the Protestant schools was the result of legitimate fears of the state by the Catholic clergy, to what degree a function of valid religious dogmas, and to what extent the product of selfishness in preserving their prerogatives on the part of the Catholic clergy. Much of this book is relevant to this question, but how one evaluates the data presented depends a good deal on one's own theological and moral preconceptions. Secondly, one would have to determine to what extent the disadvantaged educational position of the Catholics was the result of social class discrimination in the system, rather than religious discrimination. Next, recalling the differences in family patterns between religions, one would have to deal with the extremely difficult matter of the effect of family size upon the educatability of children. Children of large families are in general at an educational disadvantage. Some of this is purely economic, because parents have less money to spend on schooling, but much is cultural and biological as well. Children of large families are often handicapped in the acquisition of verbal skills simply because they receive less attention in this crucial area than do children of smaller families. Further, medical studies have shown that the vitality of both the mother and the child declines markedly after several births and that the younger siblings of large families tend to be physically and intellectually weaker than early born children. Finally, one would have to deal with the nearly impossible cultural question of whether the Catholics in Northern Ireland as a group have placed as much emphasis upon education and are as willing to sacrifice for their children's schooling as are Protestant parents. Thus, instead of being led into an intellectual labyrinth dictated by the abstract question of economic discrimination and

Q

economic justice, it is best to note simply the social fact of individual discrimination and the undeniable personal injustices which thereby occurred.

For recent studies see Jere E. Brophy, 'Mothers as Teachers of their own Pre-School Children: The Influence of Socioeconomic Status and Task Structure on Teaching Specificity', *Child Development*, vol XLI, no 1 (March 1970), pp 79-94; Charles H. Miley, 'Birth Order Research 1963-7: Bibliography and Index', *Journal of Individual Psychology*, vol XXV, no 1 (1970), pp 64-70; Gordon W. Miller, 'Factors in School Achievement and Social Class', *Journal of Educational Psychology*, vol LXI, no 4, part 1 (August 1970), pp 260-69; Robert C. Nichols, 'Heredity, Environment and School Achievement', *Measurement and Evaluation in Guidance*, vol I, no 2 (1968), pp 122-9; Mark Oberlander, Noel Jenkin, Kevin Houlihan, and John Jackson, 'Family Size and Birth Order as Determinants of Scholastic Aptitude and Achievement in a Sample of Eighth Graders', *Journal of Consulting and Clinical Psychology*, vol XXXIV, no 1 (January 1970), pp 19-21; William H. Sewell, Archibald O. Haller, and Alejandro Portes, 'The Educational and Early Occupational Attainment Process', *American Sociological Review*, vol XXXIV, no 1 (January 1969), pp 82-92; Philip S. Very and Richard W. Prull, 'Birth Order, Personality Development, and the Choice of Law as a Profession', *Journal of Genetic Psychology*, vol CXVI, no 2 (June 1970), pp 219-21

44 For a summary of the code see Calvert, pp 380-89

45 I am aware that Protestants living under the Southern Irish government often have remarked publicly upon how well they are treated in the south. These statements, however, have had little impact on the views of the northern Protestants

CHAPTER 3, pp 39-71

1 The legal formalities in the formation of the government of Northern Ireland were as follows. The day appointed for the establishment of the parliaments of Northern Ireland and of Southern Ireland was 3 May 1921. The southern parliament was never to come fully into existence because

the Irish Nationalists looked to the autochthonous Dail Eireann, but on 4 May 1921 writs were issued by Viscount Fitzalan, the lord lieutenant, for the calling of the parliament of Northern Ireland. Elections were held late in May and forty of the fifty-two Commons seats went to Unionists. The Commons assembled on 7 June in the Belfast city hall which for years was to be the site of its meetings. After electing Major Hugh O'Neill speaker, the members took the oath of allegiance and proceeded to choose the twenty-four elective members of the Senate. Thereupon they adjourned to await the formal opening of parliament by King George V. The Senate first met on 20 June and after electing the Marquess of Dufferin and Ava speaker, they adjourned until the 22nd when both houses of the parliament were opened by the king. The legal formalities were completed on 9 December 1922 with the appointment of the Duke of Abercorn as the first governor of Northern Ireland. See Arthur S. Queckett, *The Constitution of Northern Ireland* (Belfast: HMSO, 1928), vol I, pp 18-21, 34-5

2 Carson's acceptance of the judicial post was not announced until the day of the Ulster elections. *(Belfast News-Letter,* 25 May 1921.) In reality, Craig had been chosen his successor in February 1921

3 *Belfast Gazette,* 7 June 1921; Queckett, vol I, p 20

4 For biographical data on Northern Ireland politicians, see, in addition to *Who's Who* and the *DNB*, the serial publication *Ulster Who's Who Handbook*. Alistair Cooke of the Institute of Irish Studies, the Queen's University of Belfast, is preparing a biographical dictionary of Northern Ireland's politicians, 1920 to the present day

5 A statement of Londonderry's beliefs about the union is found in his article, 'The Irish Problem, 1922', *Nineteenth Century and After*, vol XCII, no 550 (December 1922), pp 895-8

6 The description is from the diary of Lady Spencer, wife of the secretary to the Northern Ireland cabinet, entry for 24 June 1921. I am indebted to Alistair Cooke for the quotation

7 I am indebted to James Scott, esq, OBE, Whitehead, County Antrim, for a great deal of information about the operation of the ministry of education in Northern Ireland. Mr Scott, a retired senior official of the ministry, was in its service almost from its foundation. One of his first posts was assist-

ant private secretary to Lord Londonderry
8 (Copy), Lord Londonderry to Arthur A. Baumann, 13 October 1927. Durham County Record Office, D/Lo/C/236 (6). In all probability 'this country' meant the United Kingdom
9 *Belfast Gazette*, 7 June 1921
10 Senate I: 47-8, 21 September 1921. See also the report of Lord Londonderry's earlier speech delivered in Portadown. *Belfast News-Letter*, 3 September 1921
11 Ministry of Education, *Report of the Ministry of Education for the Year 1922-3* [Cmd. 16] (Belfast: HMSO, 1923), p 68
12 Ibid, p 2
13 It will be recalled that the Unionist politicians had been frustrated in their attempts to establish a united ministry of education in 1920. Thus, they were committed to creating a single ministry in Ulster as soon as the government of Ireland act, 1920, came into effect.

In March 1921 a conference representative chiefly of Protestant primary and intermediate school teachers held in Belfast had called specifically for the establishment of 'a proper department of education for Northern Ireland', instead of 'temporary departments for primary, secondary, and technical education' (*Times Educational Supplement*, 31 March 1921).

The only impediment to the unification process was that for a time the law adviser to the chief secretary for Ireland held that it would be necessary for the northern government to establish its own commissioners of primary and intermediate education, and commissioners for endowed schools, before the educational services could be transferred legally to the Ulster government. Arrangements were made, however, to circumvent this objection. See Commons I: 104-5, 21 September 1921; 510-11, 9 December 1921
14 *Times Educational Supplement*, 6 August 1921
15 For details of Wyse's career see Chapter 5, pp 96-7
16 'Transfer of Educational Services. Circular to Managers of Schools, Local Committees, Teachers', reproduced in *Report of the Ministry of Education for the Year 1922-3*, pp 67-8
17 *Belfast News-Letter*, 21 February 1922
18 St John Ervine, *Craigavon: Ulsterman* (London: George Allen & Unwin Ltd, 1949), pp 462-3
19 Commons II: 555-6, 18 May 1922; *Irish News*, 3 May 1923; *Report of the Ministry of Education for the Year 1922-3*, p 3

20 *Irish News*, 27 February 1922

21 *Times Educational Supplement*, 9 December 1922

22 Commons III: 663-5, 2 May 1923; *Report of the Ministry of Education for the Year 1922-3*, p 3

23 Thomas J. McElligott, 'Intermediate Education and the Work of the Commissioners, 1870-1922' (unpublished MLitt thesis, Trinity College, Dublin, 1969), p 177

24 Commons II: 527, 17 May 1922. See also the *Times Educational Supplement*, 25 February 1922

25 *Report of the Ministry of Education for the Year 1922-3*, p 16. Cf to pp 30-33

26 McElligott, p 177

27 *Report of the Ministry of Education for the Year 1922-3*, p 16

28 Ibid, p 17; *Times Educational Supplement*, 16 December 1922. For the conditions and programmes to which the Catholic managers agreed in accepting the authority of the ministry of education, see, Ministry of Education, *Rules and Schedule containing the Programme of Intermediate Examinations for 1923* (H.C. 18) (Belfast: HMSO, 1922)

29 *Report of the Ministry of Education for the Year 1922-3*, p 35

30 One measure was introduced twice, essentially unchanged. Compare *A Bill to Make Further Provision with Respect to Education in Ireland and for other purposes connected therewith*, H.C. 1919 (214), i and *A Bill to Make Further Provision with Respect to Education in Ireland, and for other purposes connected therewith*, H.C. 1920 (35), i. The Belfast bill was entitled, *A Bill to Make Better Provision for Primary Education in the City of Belfast*, H.C. 1919 (24), ii

31 *Times Educational Supplement*, 20 January 1921

32 Senate III: 297, 14 June 1923

33 J. J. Campbell in his pamphlet *Catholic Schools: A Survey of a Northern Ireland Problem* (Belfast: Fallons Educational Supply Co, c 1964), correctly attacks the Lynn committee's assertion that there was a 'general desire' for rate aid and for local control of education. However, while rejecting the implication that the demand for rate aid and local control was nearly universal, one should not miss the fact that most citizens of Ulster (crudely, the Protestant majority) as represented by their MPs, desired local civic involvement in education and wished to aid the schools through the local rates.

Campbell's pamphlet, which is based on articles published in the *Irish Ecclesiastical Record* in 1951 and 1952; is the most cogent and analytic presentation of the Catholic viewpoint on Ulster's educational development

34 *Journal of Education and School World,* May 1921, p 286; July 1921, p 456; *Times Educational Supplement,* 31 March 1921, 7 April 1921, 28 May 1921, 18 June 1921, and 2 July 1921

35 *Belfast News-Letter,* 14 October 1922

36 M. W. Dewar, John Brown, and S. E. Long, *Orangeism: A New Historical Appreciation* (Belfast: Grand Orange Lodge of Ireland, 1967), p 181

37 Commons III: 663, 2 May 1923

38 Jones's educational views and policies as head of Inst are discussed in detail in John Jamieson's, *The History of the Royal Belfast Academical Institution, 1810-1960* (Belfast: for the Royal Belfast Academical Institution by William Mullan & Son, Ltd, 1959), pp 136-60

39 Ibid, p 156

40 *Belfast News-Letter,* 6 October 1921; *Times Educational Supplement,* 22 October 1921, 17 December 1921

41 Ministry of Education, *Interim Report of the Departmental Committee on the Educational Services in Northern Ireland* [Cmd. 6] (Belfast: HMSO, 1922), p 9

42 *Journal of Education and School World,* November 1921, p 714

43 *Times Educational Supplement,* 29 October 1921. See also, 5 November 1921

44 See Owen Dudley Edwards, *The Sins of Our Fathers: Roots of Conflict in Northern Ireland* (Dublin: Gill & MacMillan, 1970), p 96

45 *Interim Report of the Departmental Committee on the Educational Services in Northern Ireland,* p 9

46 I am grateful to Mr Sean McMenamin of the Public Record Office of Northern Ireland for calling my attention to the as yet uncatalogued 'Minutebook of the Departmental Committee on the Educational Services in Northern Ireland', in the keeping of the Public Record Office of Northern Ireland (hereafter PRONI)

47 The Presbyterian's case was presented by the representatives of the general assembly's board of education. As was to be the case with all the important witnesses before the Lynn

committee, the Presbyterians assumed that the secondary school structure would not be altered fundamentally. Therefore, they concentrated on the primary school. The Presbyterians approved of striking a rate to aid the primary schools and believed in local control through county education committees and school management committees. The county education committees, the representatives of the Presbyterian Church declared, should be elected by the county councils on the principle of proportional representation. The Presbyterian spokesmen, the Reverend William Corkey and the Reverend Thomas Haslett, were rather vague about the composition of local school management committees. As a norm they suggested that owners or managers of the school should have majority representation, an especially important point because they argued that the local school committees, not the county committees, should control the appointment of teachers. The Presbyterian representatives suggested that schools built with rate aid should be under stricter local civic control than schools built upon church grounds by religious bodies. Awkwardly and almost unwittingly, the Presbyterian spokesmen were affirming the doctrine upon which the Londonderry act was to be based, that the degree of local civic control should be in proportion to the amount of governmental financial support extended to the individual school. As for the matter of religious instruction, the Presbyterians desired that no major changes be made in the existing rules, save that the right of entry by religious teachers should be made absolute in all schools, including the non-vested schools wherein the right previously did not exist. The Presbyterian board of education was in favour of an 'agreed scheme of scriptural instruction for the different Protestant denominations, but there should be no obligation to adopt it in every school'. As a safeguard for their interests the Presbyterians asked that an advisory council to the minister of education be established and that religious representatives be appointed to that body. As their final point the Presbyterian representatives singled out one particular subject in the primary school curriculum as pernicious: 'owing to the difficulty of having unbiased history taught in primary schools, the subject should be forbidden' (Ibid, pp 73-6)

48 The position of the representatives of the Church of Ireland's boards of education and school managerial committees

was that it would be in the best interest of education in Northern Ireland if all primary schools came under direct governmental control. As with the Presbyterian witnesses, the Anglican representatives were unclear about the precise arrangements necessary and seem to have desired varying degrees of central and local governmental control dependent upon how much money was received by each school from the central and local authorities. The Church of Ireland representatives were satisfied with the existing religious arrangements in the primary schools and the only change they asked was that the right of entry of clergymen or other religious teachers be extended to every primary school in Northern Ireland. The affirmation by both the Anglicans and the Presbyterians that the existing system of religious instruction was satisfactory should be noted, for when it later appeared to leaders of these two denominations that the Londonderry act altered the religious instruction arrangements they refused to cooperate fully with the ministry of education. When queried about the appointment of teachers in primary schools the Anglican witnesses stated that in schools built by public funds the teacher should be appointed in accordance with the religious composition of the pupils, and that in schools built by Church of Ireland funds, but later handed over to local authorities, the principal teacher should as a rule be a member of the Anglican Church. Clearly, in any future arrangements both the Anglicans and the Presbyterians would be most concerned to see that the introduction of rate aid and local control did not interfere either with religious teaching or with the denominational privileges of appointing teachers. (Ibid, pp 38-40)

49 When the Lynn committee was appointed, civic and education officials involved in technical education became apprehensive because it appeared that their interests had been slighted in the composition of the committee. The technical authorities were satisfied with the status quo. Thus, one finds the joint secretaries of the association of technical instruction committees of Northern Ireland, Messrs W. M. Clow and Cecil Webb, submitting a strong brief against any major change in the technical education arrangements. Their reasons were simple and compelling: the technical instruction system had been successful largely because of its system of local control which aroused local interest. They added that

the system of technical instruction had 'brought all creeds and classes into working harmony, alike as regards the membership of committees, staffing of schools, and pupils in schools . . .'. The representatives of the technical instruction committees were convinced that it was best to leave control of technical education in the hands of subcommittees of the local urban district councils, because these councils were also the local rating authorities. To interpose the county councils between the ministry of education and the urban district councils would, they felt, be inefficient and administratively unwieldy. (Ibid, p 44)

50 The message that control of technical education should remain in the hands of the existing local authorities was transmitted to the Lynn committee by the association of urban district councils of Northern Ireland. They went even farther, however, and recommended that the proper authorities for supervision of primary schools should be the urban district councils. 'On all the grounds then,' they urged, 'whether of administrative efficiency, of educational efficiency, or of local interest, we urge that urban districts be constituted educational units.' (Ibid, p 163)

51 The teachers of Northern Ireland presented their views through their unions and professional associations. Because of the centrality of Belfast in any scheme of educational reform, the opinions of the Belfast teachers' association were especially important. This association was a branch of the Irish national teachers' organisation, an all-Ireland primary teachers' union which remained intact after the partition of Ireland. In Northern Ireland as a whole the membership of the union was chiefly Roman Catholic (and was to become more so during the 1920s when it tacitly became recognised as the Catholic teachers' union). In Belfast, however, it appears to have been a non-sectarian body which, because of the Unionists' concern with improving education in Belfast, was willing to work closely with the Unionist politicians. The Belfast teachers were bluntly critical of the past regime. The administration of primary education in Ireland for the preceding twenty years had been decidedly unsatisfactory, especially in two respects: it had produced widespread discontent among the teachers and never had gained the sympathy, cooperation, and support of the public. The main cause of the teachers' discontent had been the unjust

treatment of Irish primary education by the British treasury and the incompetent administration of local authorities, by which the association meant the school managers. The remedy for these faults, the teachers' association declared, was to establish a very strong ministry of education in Belfast that would be both representative of the various local professional and religious interests and would be strong enough to compel local authorities to correct local inadequacies. The teachers were distrustful of local government bodies. While recommending that it be mandatory for each county and urban council to levy an education rate, they wished the rate to be fixed by the ministry of education and to be paid into a central fund which the ministry would disburse. Naturally the teachers were concerned with their own professional situation and therefore demanded a softening of the system of school inspection, the instigation of new appeal procedures for dismissed teachers, and the representation of teachers on all school management committees.

(For the fullest version of the views of the Belfast teachers' association see the ten typed pages, drawn up as a brief for the testimony of the association's president, John Harbison, in 'Minutes of the Belfast Teachers' Association', 15 February 1922. PRONI, D.O.D. 1285/1)

52 *Interim Report of the Departmental Committee on the Educational Services in Northern Ireland*, pp 27-9, 31-4, 38-42. For the evolution of the committee's recommendations of the categories of schools see 'Minutebook of the Departmental Committee on the Educational Services in Northern Ireland', pp 30-31, 139-41. Early in its deliberations the committee was inclined to be more generous to the class II schools than it was in the published interim report

53 Commons XIII: 1381-2, 6 May 1931

54 Commons III: 131, 14 March 1923

55 *Interim Report of the Departmental Committee on the Educational Services in Northern Ireland*, p 34

56 In drawing up these recommendations Lynn later stated, 'we had the unique advantage of having on the committee the bishop of Down and Connor, the moderator of the general assembly, and the vice-president of the Methodist conference.' In other words, the religious instruction recommendations represented an agreement between the powers of the three major Protestant denominations. (See Commons

III: 131, 14 March 1923.) That the meaning of the Lynn report's ambiguous religious recommendations is properly interpreted in the text is established by the attitudes and actions of the Protestant clerics as detailed in Chapter 4. The dissenting comment of Adam Duffin in the interim report of the Lynn committee (pp 87-8) is misleading because it states that the Protestant Churches wanted half an hour set aside each day for catechetical and dogmatic denominational instruction. Although the Lynn recommendations did not preclude the daily half hour being used in such a manner, the heads of the Protestant denominations clearly preferred that the time be used for agreed Bible reading, not denominational catechism(s)

57 The October 1922 draft bill, as well as subsequent versions, is found in the Londonderry papers in the possession of Lady Mairi Bury, Mount Stewart, Newtownards (hereafter 'Mount Stewart MSS'). On the referral to London see (copy) Lord Londonderry to E. F. L. Wood, 1 December 1922; L. C. Duke to Lord Londonderry, 11 December 1922; (copy) Lord Londonderry to E. F. L. Wood, 15 December 1922 (Mount Stewart MSS).

See also cabinet agendas for meeting of 12 December 1922 and 11 January 1923 (Mount Stewart MSS)

58 (Copy) [Montgomery Hyde] to Sir James Craig, 8 February 1923 (Mount Stewart MSS)

59 13 and 14 Geo. 5, C. 21, sections 7 and 19

60 Ibid, section 2 and schedule 4; Marquess of Londonderry, 'Public Education in Northern Ireland. The New System', *Nineteenth Century and After*, vol XCV, no 565 (March 1924), p 329. In point of law nothing kept the county council from declaring the county a single educational region and thus doing away with the intermediate committees. This was done from the beginning in Counties Armagh, Down, and Fermanagh (Senate XII: 192, 27 May 1930)

61 Senate III: 172, 4 June 1923. A complete list of the ways in which Londonderry's bill differed from the Lynn recommendation is found in the Mount Stewart MSS. Most differences were technical, not substantive

62 *Interim Report of the Departmental Committee on the Educational Services in Northern Ireland*, pp 84-5

63 See, for example, Commons III: 121, 14 March 1923, and Senate III: 151, 4 June 1923

64 See 13 and 14 Geo. 5, C. 21, sections 3, 8, 14-17, and schedules 2 and 3

65 Thus, there were actually three forms of nomenclature: (1) according to the degree of local civic control, whether controlled by local authority, four-and-two committees, or by independent management. Each of these classes of school received a different degree of financial support; (2) according to whether or not the local civic body controlled the school. Thus, local authority schools were distinguished from voluntary schools, the latter comprising both four-and-two schools and independently managed schools; (3) among the local authority schools a distinction was made between provided and transferred schools. This was a distinction according to who built the school. Doubtless the reader is becoming aware that the Londonderry act was very poorly drafted. The most lucid explication of the act is Lord Londonderry's article 'Public Education in Northern Ireland. The New System', cited above, note 60

66 13 and 14 Geo. 5, C. 21, sections 22-5, 73; Londonderry, 'Public Education in Northern Ireland. The New System', pp 331-2

67 13 and 14 Geo. 5, C. 21, sections 19, 21, and schedule 2

68 Ibid, sections 19, 69, and schedule 6; Londonderry, 'Public Education in Northern Ireland. The New System', pp 331-2; Ministry of Education, *Report of the Ministry of Education for the Year 1923-4* [H.C. 54] (Belfast: HMSO, 1924, pp 15-16

69 13 and 14 Geo. 5, C. 21, sections 10-12

70 Ibid, sections 30-46

71 Ibid, section 8

72 Commons III: 125-6, 14 March 1923

73 Commons III: 125

74 Senate III: 158, 4 June 1923

75 13 and 14 Geo. 5, C. 21

76 Ministry of Education, *Public Education in Northern Ireland* (Belfast: HMSO, 1970), p 8

77 The reader may well ask how the granting of hundreds of thousands of pounds each year to pay the salaries of teachers in schools which were managed in the usual case by a priest or a minister, and which were effectively denominational institutions, could be squared with the provisions of the 1920 government of Ireland act prohibiting the Ulster parliament

from directly or indirectly endowing any religion. The only explanation that is at all plausible would be to suggest that the teacher was not compelled by the government to give religious instruction; thereby the fiction was maintained that the religious instruction was an optional duty performed by the teacher voluntarily or in return for extra remuneration from the school manager, not the state

78 Commons III: 789-90, 9 May 1923

79 Londonderry, 'Public Education in Northern Ireland. The New System', pp 330-31

80 See especially *Belfast News-Letter*, 10 April 1923; *Church of Ireland Gazette*, 6 April 1923; *Irish News*, 7 April 1923 and 12 April 1923

81 Until the ministry of education opens its archives for historical research the precise dating of the compromise negotiations must be conjectural. The boundaries of the negotiating period can be set at 5 and 6 April, when the Protestant negotiating committee was formed, and 9 May when the compromise was announced in parliament

82 Commons IV: 362-3, 26 March 1924

83 Commons III: 791, 9 May 1923

84 Londonderry, 'Public Education in Northern Ireland. The New System', p 331

85 (Copy) Lord Londonderry to Charles T. P. Grierson, 26 April 1923 (Mount Stewart MSS).

Londonderry was correct here in his reference to the official regulations of the former commissioners of national education, but incorrect in his implication that the commissioners' rules separating religious and secular instruction were adhered to in practice. For evidence that by the later nineteenth century the rules were commonly breached see Donald H. Akenson, *The Irish Education Experiment: The National System of Education in the Nineteenth Century* (London: Routledge & Kegan Paul, and Toronto: University of Toronto Press, 1970), pp 351-2

86 A. N. Bonaparte Wyse, the most expert of the ministry's civil servants in matters of elementary education, had strongly criticised the religious clauses of the draft bill and stated, 'I believe the majority of the people of Northern Ireland desire to secure the regular giving of religious instruction in all public elementary schools as part of their ordinary daily work.' 'Education (Northern Ireland) Bill, 1923: Suggestions

for Amendment' (Mount Stewart MSS)

87 Presbyterian Church in Ireland, *Minutes of the General Assembly of the Presbyterian Church in Ireland, June 1923,* p 43

88 Ibid, pp 43-4

89 Commons III: 917, 16 May 1923

90 *Belfast News-Letter,* 9 April 1923; *Church of Ireland Gazette,* 13 April 1923

91 *Church of Ireland Gazette,* 8 June 1923

92 See Commons III: 926, 16 May 1923

93 Londonderry, 'Public Education in Northern Ireland. The New System', p 334

CHAPTER 4, pp 72-88

1 *Belfast Gazette,* 28 September 1923, 28 March 1924, 30 May 1924; Ministry of Education, *Report of the Ministry of Education for the Year 1925-6* [H.C. 107] (Belfast: HMSO, 1926), p 6; *Times Educational Supplement,* 22 March 1924, 10 January 1925

2 William Corkey, *Episode in the History of Protestant Ulster, 1923-47* (Belfast: privately printed, nd), pp 25-6; *Irish News,* 27 June 1923

3 'Minutebook of the Departmental Committee on the Educational Services in Northern Ireland', 2, p 74. PRONI, uncatalogued MS

4 Corkey's chronicle of the clerical agitation (cited above, note 2) is a valuable source of information if used properly. Whenever possible I have checked Corkey's statements against contemporary reports.

   On his clerical career see his autobiography, *Glad Did I Live: Memoirs of a Long Life* (Belfast: Belfast News-Letter Ltd, 1962).

   Hereafter, when Corkey's writings are cited, the reference is to the *Episode . . .* , not to the autobiography

5 Corkey, pp 21-2

6 *Church of Ireland Gazette,* 3 August 1923

7 Corkey, p 30

8 See Commons IV: 37, 11 March 1924

9 Commons IV: 37, 13 March 1924; 364-5, 26 March 1924

10 *Statutory Rules and Orders of Northern Ireland . . . 1924,* pp 126-30. The full text is found also in the *Belfast News-Letter,* 18 March 1924

11 Commons IV: 369-70, 26 March 1924
12 (Copy) Lord Londonderry to J. Mulhall, 17 March 1924, Durham County Record Office, D/Lo/C/232 (2)
13 Commons IV: 342-3, and 351-2, 26 March 1924
14 Commons IV: 343, 26 March 1924
15 J. J. Campbell, *Catholic Schools: A Survey of a Northern Ireland Problem* (Belfast: Fallons Educational Supply Co, *c* 1964), p 12
16 *Belfast News-Letter*, 20 March 1924
17 Ibid, 16 February 1925
18 *Times Educational Supplement*, 13 October 1923
19 *Belfast News-Letter*, 24 April 1924
20 Corkey, pp 30-34; Presbyterian Church in Ireland, *Minutes of the General Assembly of the Presbyterian Church in Ireland, June 1924*, pp 45 ff
21 Corkey, pp 34-5
22 Ibid, pp 36-7
23 *Belfast News-Letter*, 22 January 1925
24 Letter by Reverends Corkey, Smith, and Quinn, *Belfast News-Letter*, 29 January 1925
25 *Belfast News-Letter*, 31 January 1925; *Church of Ireland Gazette*, 6 February 1925
26 *Church of Ireland Gazette*, 6 March 1925. See also *Belfast News-Letter*, 11 February 1925
27 *Belfast News-Letter*, 21 February 1925
28 Corkey, p 39
29 Ibid, pp 40-44; *Belfast News-Letter*, 6 March 1925
30 *Belfast News-Letter*, 7 March 1924; Corkey, pp 44-5
31 Ibid, 4 March 1925
32 Lord Londonderry to J. Mulhall, 17 March 1924
33 *Belfast News-Letter*, 7 March, 9 March 1925; Corkey, pp 44-5
34 *Belfast News-Letter*, 11 March 1925; St John Ervine, *Craigavon: Ulsterman* (London: George Allen & Unwin Ltd, 1949), pp 495-6
35 15 Geo. 5, C. 1
36 Commons V: 87, 12 March 1925
37 *Belfast News-Letter*, 7 March 1925
38 Corkey, pp 47-8
39 Ibid, pp 52-6
40 *Report of the Ministry of Education for the Year 1925-6*, p 8
41 Senate XII: 56, 26 March 1930
42 See 5 Hansard Commons (UK) 949-50, 22 February 1945

CHAPTER 5, pp 89-118

1 On the required procedures for enforcing school attendance see *Statutory Rules and Orders of Northern Ireland ... 1924*, pp 131-8

2 *Times Educational Supplement*, 15 November 1930

3 Ibid, 10 November 1928

4 Ibid, 19 October 1929

5 Ibid, 15 November 1930

6 Ministry of Education, *Interim Report of the Departmental Committees on the Educational Services in Northern Ireland* [Cmd. 6] (Belfast: HMSO, 1922), p 38

7 County Borough of Belfast, Belfast Education Committee, *Annual Report for the Year 1924*, p 21

8 Ibid, p 22

9 County Borough of Belfast, Belfast Education Committee, *Report for the Year ending 31 March 1930*, p 26.
    The former management of the transferred schools was as follows: Church of Ireland clerical, 18; Presbyterian clerical, 26; Methodist clerical, 9; lay managers and other Protestant denominations, 21. There were approximately forty primary schools in Belfast under Roman Catholic management.
    The transfer of Protestant schools in Belfast contrasted to the situation in the county borough of Londonderry where, by 1930, there were as yet no schools transferred. See Ministry of Education, *Report of the Ministry of Education for the Year 1929-30* [H.C. 211] (Belfast: HMSO, 1930), p 29

10 Ministry of Education, *Report of the Ministry of Education for the Year 1927-8* [H.C. 154] (Belfast: HMSO, 1928), p 10

11 Ibid, p 10

12 Ministry of Education, *Report of the Ministry of Education for the Year 1928-9* [H.C. 180] (Belfast: HMSO, 1929), p 38

13 Ministry of Education, *Report of the Ministry of Education for the Year 1924-5* [H.C. 80] (Belfast: HMSO, 1925), p 7; *Statutory Rules and Orders of Northern Ireland ... 1929*, p 24

14 *Report of the Ministry of Education for the Year 1929-30*, p 11

15 Ministry of Education, *Public Education in Northern Ireland* (Belfast: HMSO, 1970), pp 9-10; *Report of the Ministry of*

Education for the Year 1924-5, pp 18-19

16 Ministry of Education, *Report of the Committee on the Scholarship System in Northern Ireland* [Cmd. 192] (Belfast: HMSO, 1938), pp 4-10

17 Ministry of Education, *Report of the Ministry of Education for the Year 1926-7* [H.C. 131] (Belfast: HMSO, 1927), p 62

18 Commons VIII: 1448, 17 May 1927

19 *Public Education in Northern Ireland*, p 10

20 Lord Londonderry to Sir James Craig, 6 January 1926, reproduced in St John Ervine, *Craigavon: Ulsterman* (London: George Allen & Unwin Ltd, 1949), p 509.

In her diary for 8 January 1926 Lady Craigavon wrote: 'Lord Londonderry resigns from the Cabinet. J.[ames Craig] was sorry in a way, but in some ways he said it was a relief, as he was very difficult, constantly taking offence at nothing, and having to be humoured all the time.' PRONI, D 1415/B/38

21 Londonderry was becoming increasingly rigid in his thinking about the coal dispute. He wrote to a close friend that 'I am coming to the conclusion which other owners have reached some time ago, that the miners are led by people who are thoroughly unpatriotic and that the sooner the struggle comes the better it will be for all the nation.' (Copy) Lord Londonderry to J. Mulhall, 15 April 1926, Durham County Record Office, D/Lo/C/236 (5). It is interesting to note that just prior to the period in which his mind hardened on the mines issue, Londonderry was flitting about the edges of British fascism. It appears that Lady Londonderry joined one of the fascists' women's units. See Cecil Battine to Lord Londonderry, 30 June 1925, Durham County Record Office, D/Lo/C/236 (4). Lady Londonderry initiated arrangements for her husband to meet with a representative of the fascist council, an invitation which Lord Londonderry accepted with alacrity. (Copy) Londonderry to Cecil Battine, 7 July 1925, Durham County Record Office, D/Lo/C/236 (4). I have been unable to trace further the extent of Londonderry's involvement, if any, in British fascism

22 Ervine, p 508

23 *Belfast Gazette*, 15 January 1926

24 Interviews with James Scott, esq.

25 Lord Charlemont to A. N. Bonaparte Wyse, 19 January 1929. National Library of Ireland (hereafter NLI), PC 647

26 For information on Wyse I have relied chiefly on a number

R

of untitled memoranda in the NLI, PC 647, and upon my interviews with James Scott, esq. Two additional points should be added. First, Wyse's Catholicism was of a liberal stripe, more English than Irish in character. 'It would be ridiculous that your religion should stand in your way as you are practically a free thinker,' his brother Lionel wrote to him (9 August 1927, NLI, PC 647). Secondly, Wyse would have preferred to have stayed in the south and it seems that only a confusion in the delivery of mail prevented his making satisfactory arrangements to stay. See Seamus Fenton, *It All Happened* (Dublin: M. H. Gill & Son Ltd, 1949), pp 263-4

27 *Belfast News-Letter*, 6 October 1927
28 Resolution quoted in A. N. Bonaparte Wyse to W. Dawson, 9 March 1928, in Government of Northern Ireland, *Correspondence between the Ministry of Education and the Armagh Regional Education Committee on the Subject of Bible Instruction in Transferred Schools* [Cmd. 84] (Belfast: HMSO, 1928), p 3
29 Ibid, p 5
30 W. Dawson to A. N. Bonaparte Wyse, 24 March 1928, and enclosures, reproduced in Ibid, pp 6-8
31 A. N. Bonaparte Wyse to W. Dawson, 30 March 1928, reproduced in Ibid, pp 10-11
32 W. Dawson to A. N. Bonaparte Wyse, 19 April 1928, and enclosures, reproduced in Ibid, pp 11-14
33 See William Corkey, *Episode in the History of Protestant Ulster 1923-47* (Belfast: privately printed, nd), pp 59-65
34 Presbyterian Church in England, *Minutes of the General Assembly of the Presbyterian Church in Ireland, June 1928*, p 45
35 Corkey, pp 59-60
36 For a crushing rebuttal to the assertion that the Catholics were treated preferentially see A. N. Bonaparte Wyse to C. H. Blackmore, 28 December 1928, NLI, PC 647
37 Commons IX: 811, 29 March 1928
38 Corkey, pp 68-70
39 *Times Educational Supplement*, 15 December 1928. The de-rating proposals were published in midsummer, 1929. See *Times Educational Supplement*, 15 June 1929
40 See *Belfast News-Letter*, 24 January 1929; 16 February 1929
41 For reports on the meeting see *Belfast News-Letter*, 26 February 1929; Corkey, pp 65-6; *Times Educational Supplement*, 2 March 1929

42 *Belfast News-Letter,* 22 March 1929

43 Ibid, 8 April 1929

44 Ibid, 3 April 1929, 4 April 1929. For the clerical committee's reply see Ibid, 6 April 1929

45 Ibid, 6 April 1929; Corkey, p 66

46 *Belfast News-Letter,* 10 April 1929; Corkey, pp 67-8

47 *Belfast News-Letter,* 9 April 1929

48 See Ibid, 23 March 1929; *Times Educational Supplement,* 6 April 1929

49 *Belfast News-Letter,* 30 March 1929

50 Senate X: 149-51, 10 April 1929

51 *Times Educational Supplement,* 4 May 1929

52 *Belfast News-Letter,* 17 April 1929

53 Ibid, 18 April 1929

54 *Times Educational Supplement,* 4 May 1929

55 Corkey, p 81

56 Ibid, p 82

57 An additional reason for preferring my account to Corkey's is that he ignores the fact that the clergymen and the Orange Order were divided upon education issues. By so doing he is able to imply that the concessions granted to the Order were in response to the combined actions of his committee and the Order

58 Roman Catholic Church, *Codex Juris Canonici* (Rome: Polyglot Press, 1907), p 379

59 Ibid, p 379

60 'Pastoral Address issued by the Archbishops and Bishops of Ireland to their Flock on the Occasion of the Plenary Synod held in Maynooth', *Irish Ecclesiastical Record,* 5 series, vol XXX, no 11 (November 1927), pp 536 ff

61 *Codex Juris Canonici,* pp 380-81

62 Commons VII: 1243, 13 May 1926

63 *Belfast News-Letter,* 18 May 1927; Commons VIII: 1445, 17 May 1927.

The Christian Brothers' schools had been part of the national system only from its founding until 1836, when the order severed the connection. One of the educational furors of the late nineteenth century had centred on the terms of the schools' re-admission to the national system, a controversy which was not settled until after Ireland was partitioned

64 *Belfast News-Letter,* 22 February 1930; *Irish News,* 22 February 1930; *Times Educational Supplement,* 1 March 1930

65 *Irish News*, 18 March 1930

66 *Times Educational Supplement,* 22 March 1930

67 Commons XII: 4-5, 11 March 1930

68 Commons XII: 497-8, 1 April 1930

69 Commons XII: 716-17, 9 April 1930; *Irish News*, 2 April 1930

70 Commons XII: 717

71 *Irish News*, 2 April 1930

72 *Belfast News-Letter*, 9 April 1930; *Irish News*, 8 April 1930

73 *Irish News*, 14 April 1930

74 Commons XII: 696-743, 767-855

75 *Belfast News-Letter*, 9 April 1930

76 *Times Educational Supplement,* 29 March 1930

77 Ibid, 3 May 1930

78 *Belfast News-Letter*, 25 April 1930, 29 April 1930, and 30 April 1930

79 Unfortunately the minutes of the Belfast corporation record only the resolutions passed and not the contents of the debate. See 'Belfast Corporation City Council Minute Book [1928-32]', pp 352-3

80 *Belfast News-Letter*, 24 April 1930; *Irish News*, 23 April 1930

81 See *Belfast News-Letter*, 25 April 1930; *Irish News*, 6 May 1930

82 *Belfast News-Letter*, 9 May 1930; *Irish News*, 9 May 1930; *Times Educational Supplement*, 17 May 1930

83 20 & 21 Geo. 5, C. 14. For school regulations framed under the act see *Statutory Rules and Orders of Northern Ireland ... 1930*, pp 104-26

84 I am here anticipating the fact that soon after the act's passage about half of the formerly Protestant voluntary schools came under local control

85 *Irish News*, 3 April 1930

86 Commons XII: 726, 9 April 1930

87 For illustrations of the impact of gerrymandering on the thinking of Catholic spokesmen, see the statements of Archdeacon Tierney (*Irish Times*, 5 April 1930) and of Cahir Healy (Commons XII: 783, 10 April 1930)

88 I am not establishing the fact in detail here because I have dealt with it at length in *The Irish Education Experiment: The National System of Education in the Nineteenth Century* (London: Routledge & Kegan Paul, and Toronto: University of Toronto Press, 1970)

89 Commons XII: 1166, 13 May 1930

90 Commons XII: 717, 9 April 1930
91 Commons XXVII: 2801, 24 January 1945; Commons XXVIII: 838, 16 May 1945; Senate XXX: 554, 4 February **1947**
92 *Northern Ireland Law Reports* (1929), 47, quoted in George I. Dent, 'The Law of Education in Northern Ireland and the Influence of English Law' (unpublished PhD thesis, University of London, 1965), p 342; also see Commons XXVII: 2842-8, 25 January 1945
93 Commons XXVII: 2844-55, 25 January 1945

CHAPTER 6, pp 119-33

1 Ministry of Education, *Report of the Committee on the Recruitment and Training of Teachers* [Cmd. 254] (Belfast: HMSO, 1947), pp 10-11
2 John W. Musson, 'The Training of Teachers in Ireland from 1811 to the Present Day' (unpublished PhD thesis, Queen's University, Belfast, 1955), p 179
3 Ministry of Education, *Final Report of the Departmental Committee on the Educational Services in Northern Ireland* [Cmd. 15] (Belfast: HMSO, 1923), p 13
4 *Times Educational Supplement*, 27 May 1922
5 Commons II: 525, 17 May 1922
6 Ministry of Education, *Report of the Ministry of Education for the Year 1923-4* [H.C. 54] (Belfast: HMSO, 1924), p 27; *Times Educational Supplement*, 7 October 1922
7 Presbyterian Church in Ireland, *Minutes of the Presbyterian Church in Ireland, June 1921*, p 44; *Times Educational Supplement*, 4 March 1922
8 The members of the committee were Messrs H. Garrett, senior chief inspector in the ministry of education; W. Haslett, headmaster of the Belfast Model School; R. M. Jones, headmaster of the Royal Belfast Academical Institution; A. N. Bonaparte Wyse, assistant secretary to the ministry of education; and Major Rupert Stanley, principal of the Municipal College of Technology, Belfast; Professor Gregg Wilson, nominated by the Queen's University senate and Rev W. A. Watson, also nominated by the Queen's senate (*Statutory Rules and Orders of Northern Ireland ... 1922*, p 35). Why

the minister of finance, rather than the minister of education, was chairman of the committee is unclear

9 Ministry of Education, *Report of the Ministry of Education for the Year 1922-3* [Cmd. 16] (Belfast: HMSO, 1923), pp 56-7. For details of the course of study see *Final Report of the Departmental Committee on the Educational Services in Northern Ireland*, pp 14-16. Roughly one third of the entering students had transferred from the Marlborough Street Training College in Dublin into the second year of the two-year Stranmillis course

10 Ministry of Education, *Report of the Ministry of Education for the Year 1930-31* [H.C. 242] (Belfast: HMSO, 1931), p 26

11 *Report of the Ministry of Education for the Year 1923-4*, p 27

12 *Times Educational Supplement*, 2 May 1925. The ministry's point about the small number of Catholic candidates was well founded. In 1928, for example, there were only forty Catholic men teachers in training; this included both first- and second-year students (Commons IX: 1351-2, 3 May 1928)

13 Commons XIII: 2701-2, 10 December 1931

14 Ministry of Education, *Report of the Ministry of Education for the Year 1925-6* [H.C. 107] (Belfast: HMSO, 1926), p 40

15 Government of Northern Ireland, *Higher Education in Northern Ireland* [Cmd. 475] (Belfast: HMSO, 1965), p 37

16 See Senate X: 108, 27 March 1929; Commons XI: 1060, 7 November 1929; Commons XXI: 872, 4 May 1938

17 Commons VIII: 1553, 18 May 1927; Commons XI: 1060, 7 November 1929; Commons XXI: 872, 4 May 1938

18 Senate XV: 360, 18 October 1933

19 One should credit the Northern Ireland ministry of education with its success in improving the quality of the entrants to the primary school teaching profession. The chief, but not the sole, source of candidates for entrance to the training colleges was the ranks of those who had held apprentice teacherships, usually called either 'monitorships' or 'teacher-pupilships'. Monitors were primary school pupils who at age fourteen (boys) or fifteen (girls), or later in some cases, began a three- or four-year period of service assisting in selected primary schools. During the monitors' service the teacher of the school in which they assisted were supposed to aid them in continuing their general education. At the end of their period of service they took the 'king's scholarship examination', and if they were successful were admitted to a training

college. While serving as monitors the apprentices received a minimum payment of £8 a year and when admitted to the training college received residence and tuition for a very low fee (£22 10s in 1927). Pupil-teachers, who outnumbered the monitors as entrants to the training colleges by a ratio of approximately four to one, were students in secondary schools who served usually for three years as part-time teachers in a selected primary school and simultaneously as part-time students in a secondary school. They sat for the king's scholarship examination, and entered the training colleges under the same scheme as the monitors. Sometimes students who had not been apprentice teachers entered the training college directly from secondary schools. Also, a very few university graduates became primary school teachers. (See Commons VIII: 2380-81, 27 October 1927; *Higher Education in Northern Ireland*, pp 184-5; Musson, pp 192-212.)

The flaws in this system of teacher apprenticeship were considerable. First, monitors entered the training colleges without having received any formal secondary education. They were at a particular disadvantage in the training colleges vis-à-vis the pupil-teachers because the latter had attended a secondary school, even if not full time. Secondly, as for the pupil-teachers, although they did receive a secondary school education, they received it under conditions which, compared to those students who were able to attend the schools full time, made them second-class citizens within the secondary schools. The Lynn committee's final report of 1923 recognised the first of these flaws and recommended that the monitorships be abolished and that two categories of pupil-teacherships be established. These would represent successive stages, the junior stage requiring two or three years of full-time secondary school up to the junior secondary examination level, the senior to consist of two years' advanced secondary education combined with one day a week in practice teaching. A student would follow these stages successively, or if he had already passed the junior certificate examination, could enter the senior stage directly. (*Final Report of the Departmental Committee on the Educational Services in Northern Ireland*, pp 11-12.)

These recommendations were accepted by the teacher training committee and by the minister of education. (See *Report of the Ministry of Education for the Year 1925-6*, pp 15-16.)

Gradually the monitorships were abolished, the last appointment being made in 1929. (The second flaw, the requirement that the pupil-teachers who advanced successfully along the path to training college be required to spend time while still in secondary school in practice teaching, was not corrected until 1939.) The effect of abolishing the monitorships was to improve during the 1920s the quality of entrants into the teaching profession quite markedly. (*Higher Education in Northern Ireland*, pp 186-8.) The training colleges, some complained, were full almost completely of the children of the poor, but this was their virtue, not their vice: the new system of junior and senior pupil-teacherships provided one of the few avenues to secondary and further education for the talented children of the working classes, who (unless they were one of the few winners of secondary school scholarships) were otherwise precluded by financial considerations from receiving anything but a primary schooling

20 William Corkey, *Episode in the History of Ulster, 1923-47* (Belfast: privately printed, nd), pp 61-2, 90-91

21 Ibid, p 69

22 Ibid, p 91

23 See *Belfast News-Letter*, 14 July 1931; also, 3 October 1931; *Irish News*, 14 July 1931

24 *Times Educational Supplement*, 13 June 1931. In a letter to Lord Craigavon Lord Charlemont later referred to 'the anti-clericalism of Mr Pollock (who has in this matter, at any rate, a certain sympathy with the rulers of Soviet Russia)'. See St John Ervine, *Craigavon: Ulsterman* (London: George Allen & Unwin Ltd, 1949), p 524

25 Ministry of Education, *Report of the Ministry of Education for the Year 1930-31*, pp 26-7. Ironically, in the actual event it was unnecessary for Charlemont to have dissolved the committee, for soon thereafter Pollock was taken seriously ill and Lord Craigavon had to assume Pollock's cabinet duties (Commons XIII: 1423-4, 6 May 1931)

26 See Charlemont's speech at the Armagh diocesan synod (*Belfast News-Letter*, 3 October 1931)

27 *Belfast News-Letter*, 14 July 1931

28 Corkey, p 95

29 *Belfast News-Letter*, 6 July 1931

30 Ibid, 1 August 1931

31 Ibid, 10 August 1931

32 Ibid, 13 August 1931; Corkey, p 98
33 *Belfast News-Letter*, 8 September 1931
34 Ibid, 8 September 1931. See also Commons XIV: 1080, 28 April 1932
35 See *Belfast News-Letter*, 8 September 1931, 6 October 1931
36 *Times Educational Supplement*, 2 April 1932
37 *Belfast News-Letter*, 6 July 1931
38 Ibid, 6 October 1931
39 *Times Educational Supplement*, 2 April 1932
40 *Belfast News-Letter*, 26 September 1931, 3 October 1931, 29 October 1931, and 4 November 1931
41 Ibid, 3 October 1931
42 Ibid, 23 March 1932
43 Ibid, 24 March 1932; Corkey, pp 99-100; Senate XV: 353-4, 18 October 1933
44 Corkey, p 99
45 Commons XIV: 1102-3, 28 April 1932
46 Lord Charlemont to William Corkey, 2 May 1932, quoted in Corkey, p 100
47 *Belfast News-Letter*, 1 April 1932; *Irish News*, 1 April 1932; Senate XV: 354, 18 October 1933
48 *Irish News*, 11 April 1932; Senate XV: 355, 18 October 1933
49 *Belfast Gazette*, 28 July 1933; *Statutory Rules and Orders of Northern Ireland ... 1933*, p 81
50 Of the clerical triumvirate, the Anglican Quinn's name was missing. Archbishop D'Arcy, it will be recalled, had disagreed with some of the principles of the clerical committee and, further, prior to the 1930 amending act had found it necessary to reprimand Quinn for an unnecessarily outspoken attack on the government. Thus, D'Arcy exercised his powers under the government's July 1931 proposal and appointed someone other than Quinn to be the Church of Ireland's representative. Quinn protested that this procedure was irregular (*Times Educational Supplement*, 4 June 1932). The matter was referred to the general synod in Dublin which decided that the appointment should be made by the members of the general synod who resided in Northern Ireland and the name chosen by this group to be presented by the lord primate to the ministry of education (*Times Educational Supplement*, 20 May 1933). Quinn was victorious, the northern synodsmen did not accept the archbishop's nominee but substituted the name of a United Education Committee man

CHAPTER 7, pp 134-61

1 K. S. Isles and Norman Cuthbert, *An Economic Survey of Northern Ireland* (Belfast: HMSO, 1957), p 37
2 Commons XIII: 26, 3 March 1931
3 Commons XIII: 506, 20 March 1931
4 Commons XIII: 1378-9, 6 May 1931
5 B. R. Mitchell with Phyllis Deane, *Abstract of British Historical Statistics* (Cambridge: Cambridge University Press, 1962), p 478
6 Commons XIII: 1412-13, 1428-30, 6 May 1931
7 Ministry of Education, *Report of the Ministry of Education for the Year 1931-2* [H.C. 269] (Belfast: HMSO, 1932), p 6
8 *Times Educational Supplement*, 27 April 1935
9 Ibid, 1 February 1936
10 Commons XVIII: 1574-6, 14 May 1936
11 Commons XVIII: 1933, 17 June 1936; *Times Educational Supplement*, 27 June 1936
12 Commons XVIII: 2044-88, 15 October 1936
13 *Times Educational Supplement*, 31 October 1936
14 Ministry of Education, *Report of the Ministry of Education for the Year 1937-8* [H.C. 440] (Belfast: HMSO, 1938), p 13
15 Commons XIV: 1075-6, 28 April 1932
16 *Times Educational Supplement*, 14 March 1936
17 Commons XVIII: 1189, 30 April 1936
18 *Times Educational Supplement*, 7 November 1931 and 12 December 1931
19 Ibid, 16 January 1937
20 Ibid, 11 October 1929
21 *Belfast Gazette*, 31 March 1933
22 *Times Educational Supplement*, 27 May 1933
23 Commons XXII: 1075-6, 25 April 1939
24 Ministry of Education, *Report of the Ministry of Education for the Year 1934-5* [H.C. 349] (Belfast: HMSO, 1935), p 9
25 Commons XXI: 637-8, 5 April 1938
26 *Report of the Ministry of Education for the Year 1937-8*, p 5
27 Ministry of Education, *Report of the Ministry of Education for the Year 1938-9* [H.C. 483] (Belfast: HMSO, 1965), p 14
28 Government of Northern Ireland, *Higher Education in Northern Ireland* [Cmd. 475] (Belfast: HMSO, 1965), p 188;

Times Educational Supplement, 6 May 1933

29 Ministry of Education, *Report of the Ministry of Education for the Year 1933-4* [H.C. 315] (Belfast: HMSO, 1934), p 10; *Times Educational Supplement,* 6 July 1935

30 Compare data in Appendix, Table III, to Commons XXI: 914, 5 May 1938

31 See Appendix, Table III and Government of Northern Ireland, *Educational Reconstruction in Northern Ireland* [Cmd. 226] (Belfast: HMSO, 1944), p 5

32 Commons XXV: 838, 24 March 1942

33 Commons XXI: 914-15, 5 May 1938

34 Commons XVI: 1008, 19 April 1934

35 *Irish News,* 18 December 1931

36 See Ministry of Education, *Report of the Departmental Committee of Enquiry on the Programme of Instruction in Public Elementary Schools* [Cmd. 136] (Belfast: HMSO, 1931), *passim*

37 Ibid, pp 9-10

38 Ministry of Education, *Report of the Primary Schools Programme Committee* (Belfast: HMSO, 1956), p 4

39 *Report of the Ministry of Education for the Year 1937-8,* p 12

40 25 & 26 Geo. 5, C. 8, section 6

41 *Times Educational Supplement,* 4 March 1939

42 Senate XVI: 598, 8 November 1934

43 Commons XVI: 2737, 13 November 1934

44 Commons XXI: 1094, 17 May 1938

45 Presbyterian Church in Ireland, *Minutes of the General Assembly of the Presbyterian Church in Ireland, June 1936,* p 46

46 *Times Educational Supplement,* 5 February 1938

47 2 Geo. 6, C. 20

48 Senate XXI: 23, 1 March 1938

49 Estimate by Rupert Stanley, Director of Education in Belfast, *Times Educational Supplement,* 15 April 1939

50 *Belfast Gazette,* 3 December 1937 and 23 May 1939; *Report of the Ministry of Education for the Year 1937-8,* p 5; *Report of the Ministry of Education for the Year 1938-9,* pp 12-13; *Times Educational Supplement,* 9 October 1937, 25 December 1937, and 27 May 1939; interviews with James Scott, esq

51 For an extremely thorough official history see John W. Blake, *Northern Ireland in the Second World War* (Belfast: HMSO, 1956)

52 Earl of Longford and Thomas P. O'Neill, *Eamon De Valera* (London: Hutchinson, 1970), pp 365-6
53 'Statement of the Northern Bishops on Conscription issued Sunday, 30 April', *Irish Ecclesiastical Record*, 5 series, vol LIII, no 6 (June 1939), p 665
54 *Times Educational Supplement*, 6 April 1940
55 *Report of the Ministry of Education for 1945-6* [H.C. 783] (Belfast: HMSO, 1948), p 5
56 Blake, pp 218-19
57 *Times Educational Supplement*, 13 May 1939
58 Ibid, 20 May 1939
59 Ibid, 8 July 1939
60 Ibid, 15 July 1939
61 Ibid, 12 August 1939
62 *Belfast News-Letter*, 1 September 1939, 2 September 1939, 7 September 1939
63 *Times Educational Supplement*, 23 September 1939
64 2 & 3 Geo. 6, C. 21
65 Blake, p 219
66 *Belfast News-Letter*, 8 February 1940; *Times Educational Supplement*, 27 January 1940 and 24 February 1940
67 *Belfast News-Letter*, 5 July 1940
68 Ibid, 16 February 1940 and 22 February 1940; Commons XXIII: 344-5, 27 February 1940
69 *Belfast News-Letter*, 4 July 1940, 5 July 1940 and 6 July 1940
70 Ibid, 8 July 1940
71 Ibid, 30 August 1940
72 Blake, pp 240-43
73 *Report of the Ministry of Education, 1945-6*, p 14
74 Blake, p 241
75 *Report of the Ministry of Education, 1945-6*, p 14
76 Commons XXIV: 999, 10 June 1941. See also Commons XXIV: 857-8, 20 May 1941
77 *Report of the Ministry of Education, 1945-6*, p 14. Officially, the evacuation did not end until 21 July 1948 (see *Belfast Gazette*, 9 July 1948)
78 For an evocative semi-fictionalised account of a happy evacuation experience see Robert Harbinson, *Song of Erne* (London: Faber & Faber Ltd, 1960)
79 *Times Educational Supplement*, 27 August 1938
80 *Report of the Ministry of Education, 1945-6*, pp 14, 42
81 Commons XXII: 2031, 19 September 1939

82 *Report of the Ministry of Education, 1945-6,* p 15
83 Church of Ireland, *Seventy-Third Report of Proceedings of the Representative Body laid before the General Synod of the Church of Ireland at its Seventy-Third Ordinary Session* (Dublin: APCK, 1943), pp 211-12; Presbyterian Church in Ireland, *Minutes of the General Assembly of the Presbyterian Church in Ireland, June 1943,* p 52
84 *Report of the Ministry of Education, 1945-6,* pp 15-27
85 Commons XXIII: 1291, 29 May 1940; Commons XXVI: 130, 3 March 1943
86 Commons XXVII: 303, 320, 29 February 1944
87 The displacement of the headquarters of the ministry of education served as the pretext for a comic, but thoroughly vicious, fight between the parliamentary secretary of the ministry of education and the minister. Here is the outline of events: Lord Craigavon died on 24 November 1940. John M. Andrews, previously minister of finance, became prime minister with John Hanna Robb staying on as minister of education and Mrs Dehra Parker as parliamentary secretary. In April 1943 Sir Basil Brooke led a coup which ousted Andrews from the prime ministership and led, on 1 May, to Brooke's being elected to the post. Mrs Parker remained as parliamentary secretary of the ministry of education. John Hanna Robb, however, left office and was replaced by the Reverend Professor Robert Corkey, professor of ethics at the Presbyterian College, Belfast, and brother of the Reverend William Corkey, the leading Protestant education agitator. Mrs Parker and the professor did not get along and in February 1944 she prevailed upon the prime minister to recall Corkey's portfolio. His place was taken in March 1944 by Lieutenant Colonel S. H. Hall-Thompson. Mrs Parker was induced to resign her parliamentary secretaryship in March 1944 and for the duration of the war that post remained vacant.

Until the ministry of education opens its archives the precise details of this wartime controversy will remain obscure, but several facts are clear. In the first place it is clear that Professor Corkey did not attend the headquarters at Portrush regularly, indeed he appeared there only three times during his tenure of office. Instead he frequented the Belfast office of the ministry. Mrs Parker attended Portrush headquarters regularly and supervised the ministry. Having said this, one should quickly add that in moving the ministry to Portrush the government had moved the headquarters near to Mrs Parker's home, a venue much less convenient for Corkey than for Parker. Next, it is clear Mrs Parker was the aggressor; she called the prime minister's attention to Corkey's non-attendance at Portrush and it was on these grounds that Sir Basil Brooke publicly explained his demanding Corkey's resignation. Whether there were additional reasons for Parker's attacking Corkey and for Brooke's cashiering him cannot be yet known. Mrs Parker was an extremely strong personality and a simple case of political in-fighting may have been involved in her attack on her superior.

Corkey argued that the reason he was fired was because he objected to the senior officials of the ministry of education and Mrs Parker's planning to repeal the agreed settlement of 1930 between the government and the Protestant Churches. Further, he stated that whenever he raised the possibility of following the English plan of securing a more definite place for religion in Northern Ireland's schools, he was baulked by the same individuals. Thus, Corkey claimed that the issue of his attendance at Portrush was merely an excuse to remove him, the real reason being his religious views. In any case, Corkey was out and Mrs Parker soon followed. Significantly, whatever the truth of Corkey's claim that he was fired for his religious views, it found credence among the Presbyterian populace who chose him moderator of the general assembly in June 1945 as a sign of their faith in his testimony. This last fact more than the actual veracity of his position was important for it predisposed large numbers of Presbyterians to distrust the motives and plans of the government in shaping post-war educational programmes. Sources: the chronology is from the prefatory pages of the Commons debates, vols XXIII-XXVI; *Belfast Gazette*, 7 May 1943 and 24 March 1944; and *Report of the Ministry of Education, 1945-6*, p 7. On the charges and counter-charges see Commons XXVII: 255-94, 22 February 1944; and 303-8, 318-22, 29 February 1944. See also William Corkey, *Episode in the History of Protestant Ulster, 1923-47* (Belfast: privately printed, nd), pp 105-6

88 *Report of the Ministry of Education, 1945-6*, p 6

89 County Borough of Belfast Education Committee, *Report for the Period 1st April 1939 to 31st March 1946*, pp 7-8

90 Ibid, p 7

91 *Report of the Ministry of Education, 1945-6*, pp 7-8, 19-22; *Times Educational Supplement*, 30 November 1940 and 15 February 1941
92 *Report of the Ministry of Education, 1945-6*, pp 6-7, 16-18; see also Appendix, Table VII
93 For a discussion of England's wartime problems plus documentation for statements of fact and interpretation made in this section see Donald H. Akenson, 'Patterns of English Educational Change: The Fisher and Butler Acts', *History of Education Quarterly*, vol XI, no 2 (summer 1971), pp 143-56
94 Presbyterian Church in Ireland, *Minutes of the General Assembly of the Presbyterian Church in Ireland, June 1944*, p 49
95 *Times Educational Supplement*, 4 September 1943
96 Commons XXVI: 1752-84, 19 October 1943
97 Presbyterian Church in Ireland, *Minutes of the General Assembly of the Presbyterian Church in Ireland, June 1942*, p 62
98 Commons XXV: 1705-6, 30 June 1942
99 Senate XXVII: 5-6, 1 February 1944
100 Commons XXVII: 2695-6, 5 December 1941
101 In order to avoid unnecessary duplication, only the outlines of the white paper are here mentioned. Most of its details were embodied in the final statute, the education act of 1947, whose contents will be discussed in the next chapter

CHAPTER 8, pp 162-92

1 Interviews with James Scott, esq, and with Dr George Dent. Dr Dent was private secretary to Hall-Thompson
2 Notably by Dr John Renshaw and Mr John Beattie during the debates on the white paper (Commons XXVII: 2760-61, and 2779, 23 January 1945), by the association of principals of technical institutions (*Belfast News-Letter*, 22 January 1945) and by the Down and Dromore Synod of the Church of Ireland (*Church of Ireland Gazette*, 2 November 1945)
3 See Beattie's comments (Commons XXVII: 2761, 23 January 1945), and the resolutions of a special meeting on educational reconstruction of the Ulster teachers' union (*Belfast News-Letter*, 15 January 1945)

4 *Belfast News-Letter*, 22 January 1945

5 Commons XXVII: 2968-9, 1 February 1945

6 Commons XXIII: 843-4, 17 April 1940

7 Commons XXIII: 1302-5, 29 May 1940

8 Church of Ireland, *Seventy-Second Report of Proceedings of the Representative Body laid before the General Synod of the Church of Ireland at its Seventy-Second Ordinary Session, 1942* (Dublin: Hodges, Figgis & Co, 1942), pp 221-2.

It is worth noting that the educational organisation of the Church of Ireland had been modified during the 1930s. Whereas previously there was no single institutional authority on educational matters in Ulster, in 1936 a Northern Ireland committee of the Church's board of education was appointed to supervise the Church's interests. It consisted of the archbishop of Armagh, the bishops of Derry, Clogher, Kilmore, and Down, of six northern clergymen and six northern laymen. This group had the power to co-opt up to ten additional members. See Church of Ireland, *Journal of the Third Session of the Twenty-Fourth General Synod of the Church of Ireland* (Dublin: Hodges, Figgis & Co, 1936), 13 May 1936

9 *Statutory Rules and Orders of Northern Ireland ... 1943*, p 43

10 Commons XXV: 2188-9, 21 July 1942

11 Commons XXV: 3046, 24 November 1942

12 Ibid

13 In mid-December the prime minister was still waiting for the Church leaders to set a time for the meeting (Commons XXV: 3206, 16 December 1942). The Protestant leaders postponed the talks with the government in order to initiate conversations with the representatives of the headmasters' association and the association of assistant masters. See Church of Ireland, *Seventy-Third Report of Proceedings of the Representative Body laid before the Church of Ireland at its Seventy-Third Ordinary Session 1943* (Dublin: APCK, 1943), p 219

14 Commons XXVI: 1752-84, 19 October 1943

15 Church of Ireland, *Seventy-Fourth Report of Proceedings of the Representative Body laid before the General Synod of the Church of Ireland at its Seventy-Fourth Ordinary Session, 1944* (Dublin: APCK, 1944), p 184

16 Church of Ireland, *Seventy-Fifth Report of Proceedings of*

the Representative Body laid before the General Synod of the Church of Ireland at its Seventy-Fifth Ordinary Session, 1945 (Dublin: APCK 1945), pp 185-6

17 Speech of the Reverend James Quinn, reported in *Belfast News-Letter*, 21 December 1944

18 *Belfast News-Letter*, 22 January 1945; Church of Ireland, *Seventy-Fifth Report of Proceedings of the Representative Body laid before the General Synod of the Church of Ireland at its Seventy-Fifth Ordinary Session, 1945*, pp 188-9; Presbyterian Church in Ireland, *Annual Reports, 1945*, p 43

19 Commons XXVII: 2844-55, 25 January 1945

20 *Belfast News-Letter*, 22 January 1945; Church of Ireland, *Seventy-Fifth Report of Proceedings of the Representative Body laid before the General Synod of the Church of Ireland at its Seventy-Fifth Ordinary Session, 1945*, pp 118-19; Presbyterian Church in Ireland, *Annual Reports, 1945*, p 43

21 Commons XXVII: 2816, 24 January 1945

22 William Corkey, *Episode in the History of Protestant Ulster, 1923-47* (Belfast: privately printed, nd), pp 112-13

23 Government of Northern Ireland, *Educational Reconstruction in Northern Ireland* [Cmd. 226] (Belfast: HMSO, 1944), pp 27-8

24 *Belfast News-Letter*, 22 January 1945; Church of Ireland, *Seventy-Fifth Report of Proceedings of the Representative Body laid before the General Synod of the Church of Ireland at its Seventy-Fifth Ordinary Session, 1945*, pp 118-19; Presbyterian Church in Ireland, *Annual Reports, 1945*, p 43

25 Commons XXVII: 2785, 23 January 1945

26 Commons XXVII: 2790-98, 24 January 1945

27 *Belfast News-Letter*, 12 February 1945; *Irish News*, 12 February 1945

28 *Belfast News-Letter*, 12 February 1945; *Irish News*, 12 February 1945

29 *Irish News*, 12 February 1945

30 Ibid

31 Ibid

32 'Statements of the Bishops on Educational Reconstruction in Northern Ireland', *Irish Ecclesiastical Record*, 5 series, vol LIX, no 5 (May 1945), p 347

33 Ibid, p 349

34 Ibid, p 350

35 Ibid, p 351

s

36 Commons XXVII: 2979-80, 1 February 1945
37 *Belfast News-Letter*, 24 January 1945; Church of Ireland, *Seventy-Sixth Report of Proceedings of the Representative Body laid before the General Synod of the Church of Ireland at its Seventy-Sixth Ordinary Session, 1946* (Dublin: APCK, 1946), p 193
38 Commons XXVIII: 219, 6 March 1945
39 Commons XXVIII: 359-60 (13 March 1945); 748 (15 May 1945). Church of Ireland, *Seventy-Sixth Report of Proceedings of the Representative Body laid before the General Synod of the Church of Ireland at its Seventy-Sixth Ordinary Session, 1946*, p 193
40 Corkey, p 119
41 *Belfast News-Letter*, 2 June 1945; Church of Ireland, *Seventy-Sixth Report of Proceedings of the Representative Body laid before the General Synod of the Church of Ireland at its Seventy-Sixth Ordinary Session, 1946*, p 194; Presbyterian Church in Ireland, *Minutes of the General Assembly of the Presbyterian Church in Ireland, June 1945*, p 28
42 Corkey, p 119
43 Protestant delegates to Archbishop Gregg, 11 January 1946, reproduced in Corkey, pp 124-7. See also pp 118-19
44 Commons XXIX: 240, 31 July 1945
45 Corkey, pp 122-6
46 Ibid, pp 121-2
47 Government of Northern Ireland, *Education Bill (Northern Ireland), 1946* (Belfast: HMSO, 1946), section 23 (3)
48 Commons XXX: 2002, 15 October 1946
49 Commons XXX: 2265, 23 October 1946
50 *Belfast News-Letter*, 9 November 1946; *Church of Ireland Gazette*, 15 November 1946; Corkey, pp 138-41
51 *Belfast News-Letter*, 12 November 1946, 13 November 1946, 14 November 1946, 19 November 1946, 21 November 1946, 28 November 1946, 3 December 1946; Corkey, pp 141-4
52 *Belfast News-Letter*, 11 November 1946
53 Commons XXX: 2775-7, 20 November 1946
54 Commons XXX: 3099-100, 8 December 1946
55 Commons XXX: 3107-8, 3 December 1946
56 Commons XXX: 3110-13, 3 December 1946
57 Commons XXX: 3585-7, 11 December 1946
58 10 & 11 Geo. 6, C. 3
59 Because the relevant government records for the period are

sealed, I can only speculate on why the government in this case was able to defend itself, when previous governments had not. Clearly, not because of any great change in the personnel leading the Protestant campaign. The Reverend William Corkey and the Reverend Chancellor Quinn were still in the vanguard of the clerical opposition, admittedly somewhat older, but still able to make fiery speeches and write denunciatory letters. Perhaps Sir Basil Brooke was a stronger character when it came to enduring hectoring clerics than was Lord Craigavon, but that is speculation.

What can be documented is that in 1945-7 the Protestant educational phalanx was weaker internally than it had been on previous occasions. Crucially, in October 1946 the leaders of the Orange Order stopped cooperating with the United Education Committee of the Protestant Churches on the grounds that the minister of education was trying to be accommodating and that the clergymen were being unreasonable about the conscience clause. (Senate XXX: 623-9, 5 February 1947.) The Orange Order took no official part in the anti-government meetings which flared in November and early December. Further, in mid-October the board of education of the Methodist Conference accepted the conscience clause and associated arrangements as proposed by the government and therefore dropped out of the campaign. (*Belfast News-Letter*, 15 November 1946.) These defections placed the Protestant clerics in a weaker position than they had been in any of their previous campaigns

60 Commons XXX: 2247, 23 October 1946
61 *Education Bill (Northern Ireland), 1946,* sections 81 and 106
62 *Belfast News-Letter,* 14 May 1945
63 Senate XXX: 661, 18 February 1947
64 Senate XXX: 582-3, 4 February 1947
65 Senate XXX: 718, 27 February 1947
66 Admittedly there were still large numbers of Protestant voluntary schools, but the concession was directed at conciliating the Catholics
67 *Belfast News-Letter,* 4 November 1946
68 *Times Educational Supplement,* 16 November 1946
69 Commons XXX: 2268, 2270, 23 October 1946
70 See, for example, Commons XXX: 2110-16, 16 October 1946
71 Commons XXX: 2692, 14 November 1946

72 10 & 11 Geo. 6, C. 3. The government's intentions in some of the more confusing passages are best explained in *Education Bill (Northern Ireland). Explanatory Memorandum by the Minister of Education* [Cmd. 242] (Belfast: HMSO, 1946). One must be aware, however, of the amendments made during the bill's passage.

I have not had space to discuss the degree to which the Northern Ireland law followed the template set by England's Butler act of 1944. For a thorough discussion see George I. Dent, 'The Law of Education in Northern Ireland and the Influence of English Law' (unpublished PhD thesis, University of London, 1965)

73 10 & 11 Geo. 6, C. 3, sections 4-6, and 14-17. The nursery schools and special schools for the handicapped were special cases which did not fit into the basic categories.

'Further education' was officially a stage of education beyond secondary school, but the development of this stage was more a pious hope than an administrative reality

74 Ibid, sections 2-3, and schedules 2-3

75 Ibid, sections 14 and 18

76 Ibid, sections 6-8, 15, 18, 28, and 33

77 Ibid, section 17

78 Ministry of Education, *Public Education in Northern Ireland* (Belfast: HMSO, 1970), p 10.

The figures do not include preparatory schools

79 10 & 11 Geo. 6, C. 3, sections 16-17, and 64

80 I am grateful to A. A. Dickson, esq, financial and administrative officer, Belfast Education Committee, for providing me with his illuminating unpublished paper 'Educational Finance' (c 1961), upon which this discussion of finance is based

81 See Ministry of Education, *Report of the Ministry of Education, 1946-7* [H.C. 822] (Belfast: HMSO, 1948), pp 5-8

82 Ministry of Education, *Educational Reconstruction in Northern Ireland: The First Ten Years* (Belfast: HMSO, 1959)

83 Ibid, pp 4-5

84 William R. Spence, 'The Growth and Development of the Secondary Intermediate School in Northern Ireland since the Education Act of 1947' (unpublished MA thesis, Queen's University, Belfast, 1959), pp 21-2

85 *Educational Reconstruction in Northern Ireland: The First Ten Years*, p 7

86 Ministry of Education, *Report of the Ministry of Education,*

1947-8 [H.C. 883] (Belfast: HMSO, 1949), pp 13-14

87 Ibid, pp 10-12; Ministry of Education, *Report of the Ministry of Education, 1948-9* [H.C. 970] (Belfast: HMSO, 1951), pp 14-16.

One set of activities ancilliary to the 1947 act bears notice, namely the emergency training scheme for elementary school teachers. In September 1945 the ministry of education decided to augment the number of students in training with a special course for training ex-servicemen and women who held promise but whose background and qualifications were not of the ordinary sort. In early 1946 the operation began and soon thereafter was moved into its own premises at Larkfield House in Dunmurry. By the time the scheme was brought to a close in November 1949, 405 ex-servicemen and women had been trained. (*Report of the Ministry of Education, 1945-6*, p 28; *Report of the Ministry of Education, 1946-7*, p 18; *Report of the Ministry of Education, 1947-8*, p 37; *Report of the Ministry of Education, 1949-50*, pp 20-21.)

The influx of new teachers from the emergency scheme facilitated two important improvements in the primary school arrangement: first, the ministry of education was able to introduce, on 1 January 1947, new staffing regulations which permitted a second teacher to be appointed to a primary school when there were more than forty pupils enrolled; this in contrast to the previous regulation that required an actual attendance of forty-five pupils before an assistant could be added. (*Report of the Ministry of Education, 1946-7*, p 9.) Further, the government was able to extend the teacher training course from two years to three years, effective with those students entering in 1948. Ministry of Education, *Report of the Ministry of Education, 1950-51* [Cmd. 313] (Belfast: HMSO, 1953), p 20.

This lengthening of the course was in accordance with the recommendations of a major study conducted under the chairmanship of Colonel W. D. Gibbon, headmaster of a Northern Ireland public school, and is noteworthy because it preceded by a dozen years the lengthening of the training course in England. See Ministry of Education, *Report of the Committee on the Recruitment and Training of Teachers* [Cmd. 254] (Belfast: HMSO, 1947). The report is valuable not only in its policy recommendations but in its survey of training policies of the past

88 Commons XXXIII: 934, 24 May 1949
89 *Journal of Education*, March 1950, p 150; Commons XXXIII: 1045-7, 7 June 1949
90 Commons XXXIII: 1045, 7 June 1949
91 Commons XXXIII: 1109, 14 June 1949
92 I am grateful to Dr George Dent, formerly private secretary to Hall-Thompson, for information and for analytic suggestions
93 Presbyterian Church in Ireland, *General Assembly of the Presbyterian Church in Ireland, Annual Reports, 1950*, pp 60-61
94 See *Belfast News-Letter*, 1 November 1949 and 14 November 1949. Eventually in 1953 Porter, running as an independent Unionist, unseated Hall-Thompson
95 *Belfast News-Letter*, 14 December 1949
96 Ibid, 15 December 1949
97 Precisely what occurred and why is impossible to say. Two unresolved questions are particularly intriguing. First, did Hall-Thompson resign in a gesture of noble sacrifice to maintain unity in the party (as suggested in the *Belfast News-Letter*, 15 December 1949), or was he forced to resign? Secondly, did John Andrews, imperial grand master of the Orange Order, use this occasion to wreak vengeance upon Sir Basil Brooke for Brooke's having overthrown Andrews's ministry during the war years?
98 For the resignation and subsequent debate on the bill see Commons XXXIII: 2275-92, 15 December 1949. The final statute is 13 & 14 Geo. 6, C. 1
99 *Report of the Ministry of Education, 1950-51*, p 6
100 See *Belfast Gazette*, 13 January 1950; *Belfast News-Letter*, 29 April 1930; County Borough of Belfast, Belfast Education Committee, *Report for the Period 1st April 1939 to 31st March 1946*, p 3; M. W. Dewar, John Brown, and S. E. Long, *Orangeism: A New Historical Appreciation* (Belfast: Grand Orange Lodge of Ireland, 1967), p 180
101 Commons XXXII: 949-64, 20 April 1948; 1952-3, 8 June 1948; 2799-800, 7 October 1948
102 For example, Commons XXXII: 1693-4, 26 May 1948; and comments of Hall-Thompson, Commons XXXIII: 711, 5 May 1949
103 Presbyterian Church in Ireland, *Minutes of the General Assembly of the Presbyterian Church in Ireland, 1949*, p 37

104 Commons XXXIII: 1227-35, 21 June 1949
105 Commons XXXIII: 2305, 20 December 1949
106 *Journal of Education*, October 1950, p 548; *Report of the Ministry of Education, 1950-51*, p 11
107 Commons XXXIV: 1293, 6 June 1950
108 See John Jamieson, *The History of the Royal Belfast Academical Institution, 1810-1960* (Belfast: for the Royal Belfast Academical Institution by William Mullan & Son, Ltd, 1959), pp 182-5
109 *Report of the Ministry of Education, 1950-51*, p 11; *Statutory Rules and Orders, Northern Ireland ... 1950*, pp 168-72, 175-7
110 *Report of the Ministry of Education, 1950-51*, p 11. One should emphasise that the split between group A and group B schools was not a division on religious lines

CHAPTER 9, pp 193-202

1 The structural prerequisite for bringing the 1947 act into substantially full operation was the establishment of a sufficient number of intermediate schools. The number of intermediate schools increased from 13 in 1953 to 55 in 1958 to 129 in 1964. Sources: Ministry of Education, *Educational Reconstruction in Northern Ireland: The First Ten Years* (Belfast: HMSO, 1959), p 5; Ministry of Education, *Educational Development in Northern Ireland, 1964* [Cmd. 470] (Belfast: HMSO, 1964), p 9. A valuable discussion of the intermediate schools is William R. Spence's 'The Growth and Development of the Secondary Intermediate School in Northern Ireland since the Education Act of 1947' (unpublished MA thesis, Queen's University, Belfast, 1959). The development of the intermediate schools in Belfast is discussed in Dorothy E. Eagleson's 'Employment and Training of Girls Leaving Belfast Primary, Secondary, Intermediate, and Grammar Schools in Relation to the Education System and the Employment Services' (unpublished PhD thesis, Queen's University, Belfast, 1958).

Concommitant with the development of intermediate schools, the primary schools had to be reorganised to take children only up to age 11-plus, instead of to age fourteen and fifteen as previously. At the end of the 1950s the majority of primary schools were still unreorganised: the proportion of unreorganised to reorganised schools was 840 to 705. By the end of the next decade only eighty-one primary schools remained unreorganised. Sources: Ministry of Education, *Report of the Ministry of Education, 1959-60* [Cmd. 423] (Belfast: HMSO, 1960), p 7; Ministry of Education, *Education in Northern Ireland in 1969* [Cmd. 542] (Belfast: HMSO, 1970), p 7.

Progress towards reorganisation made it possible for the ministry of education to raise the school leaving age to fifteen as of 1 April 1957. The raising of the leaving age was also facilitated by an increase of nearly one third in the total teaching force between 1947-8 and 1957-8. Source: *Educational Reconstruction in Northern Ireland: The First Ten Years*, pp 7 and 14.

As for the grammar schools, the number of pupils on their rolls rose from 17,178 in 1947-8 to 29,031 in 1957-8, and to 44,187 in January 1969. Sources: *Educational Reconstruction in Northern Ireland: The First Ten Years*, p 5; *Education in Northern Ireland in 1969*, p 9

2 R. J. Lawrence, *The Government of Northern Ireland: Public Finance and Public Services, 1921-64* (Oxford: Clarendon Press, 1965), p 125n

3 16 & 17 Eliz. 2, C. 2. Group A voluntary schools who agreed to have one third of their governors appointed by the ministry of education were to receive eighty per cent capital grants. This provision, unlike those dealing with primary and intermediate schools, should not be viewed as a response to religious factors.

Strictly speaking, the regulations for the maintained schools were not identical to those of the former four-and-two schools; whereas the number of governors under the old system was set at four representatives of the managers and two of the local authority, the stipulation for the maintained schools was simply that two thirds be nominated by the managers and one third by the authority, without limiting the number to six.

For a summary of events leading up to the passage of the act see Martin Wallace, *Northern Ireland: Fifty Years of Self-Government* (Newton Abbot: David & Charles, 1971), pp 108-11. See also the *Irish Catholic Directory* for 1968 and 1969 and the Ministry of Education's *Local Education*

Authorities and Voluntary Schools [Cmd. 513] (Belfast: HMSO, 1967)

4 Ministry of Education, *Education in Northern Ireland in 1969* [Cmd. 542] (Belfast: HMSO, 1970), p 7

5 Richard Rose, *Governing without Consensus. An Irish Perspective* (London: Faber & Faber Ltd, 1971), p 481

6 The present confused position of the government of Ireland act, 1920, makes it impossible to adjudge the relevance of one further possible argument against making one hundred per cent grants to Catholic maintained schools, namely that to do so would be illegal under the act. Section 5 (1) of that act prohibits the Northern Ireland parliament from making 'a law so as either directly or indirectly to establish or endow any religion. . . '. The judgement in the only case in law bearing on the interpretation of the word 'endow', the *Londonderry vs McClade* case of 1929, took the view that any disbursement of public funds resulting in a benefit either directly or indirectly to religion would constitute an endowment for the purpose of section 5 of the 1920 act. Further, that judgement held that if the Northern Ireland parliament enacted a law intending to pay for Roman Catholic religious instruction from public funds that this law would be void. See Harry Calvert, *Constitutional Law in Northern Ireland: A Study in Regional Government* (London: Stevens & Sons Ltd, and Belfast: Northern Ireland Legal Quarterly Inc, 1968), p 257.

Accepting this ruling brings us face to face with another point: the explicit statements of Roman Catholic canon law as well as the educational pronouncements of the northern bishops make it clear that religion pervades all aspects of the curriculum of the Catholic voluntary schools. (Similar pronouncements by individual managers of Protestant voluntary grammar schools also could be produced, but the issue at hand is the Catholic schools.) Now, if Catholic religious education cannot be separated from secular education, then it follows that the state is endowing the Catholic religion when it makes *any* grant for Catholic voluntary schools; and if it is prohibited to totally endow Catholic religious schools it is also prohibited to endow them at all. The argument that the general welfare is served by providing education for Catholic children does not obviate the fact that the promulgation of the tenets of a specific denomination already are being financed largely through public funds, and, therefore, that a religion is being endowed within the meaning of the 1920 act.

There is yet another way in which the existing system of aid to voluntary schools (as well as the separate-but-equal system I propose) violates the endowment clause of the 1920 act. This is through the delivery annually of hundreds of thousands of pounds of patronage to the clerical managers of voluntary schools, in teaching appointments and in custodial and maintenance places. Influence is also granted to religious authorities in the planning and development of capital projects, through which massive sums are allocated to architects, engineers, construction and equipment firms.

Also significant as an indirect endowment of religion is the strengthening of the local parochial religious structure which results from the government's underwriting the local parish schools. Here again the statements of the northern Catholic bishops and of canon law are explicit: the management of a parochial school is part of the religious duty of each priest and the state's carrying of most of the expenses of running the voluntary parish schools is a subvention towards the costs of one of the priest's most expensive religious activities.

Let us now throw the cart after the horse. If both the letter and the spirit of the 1920 government of Ireland act are violated by the state's aiding voluntary schools under religious jurisdiction, it can also be argued that the underwriting of the state schools ('county schools' in the vocabulary of the 1947 act) also violates the religious endowment clauses of the 1920 act. This occurs in three ways. First, as this book has demonstrated in detail, the educational system delivers into Protestant hands complete control of county (read ('state') primary, intermediate, and grammar schools which are allegedly non-denominational institutions. (I am not here discussing the Protestant voluntary grammar schools, which are explicitly denominational in the same sense that the Catholic schools are.) These Protestant-controlled schools appoint only Protestant teachers and their student bodies are composed almost entirely of Protestant children. Secondly, in the case of certain county schools, those which were transferred to the local authorities from the original Protestant voluntary managers, provisions have been made to perpetuate the control of the school by the former managers even though the entire expense of the schools now falls on public resources. This is accomplished by the provision that at least half of each school management committee be composed of the transferors of the original voluntary school which, it should be re-emphasised, in almost every case was a denominational religious institution. Thirdly, the requirement that in each county school a form of non-denominational religious worship and non-denominational religious instruction take place is, quite simply, a requirement that Protestantism be taught, and, like the requirement for 'simple Bible instruction' under the 1930 act (which in the mid-1940s was declared *ultra vires* by the attorney-general for Northern Ireland), is an endowment of Protestantism. *De facto* the state system of education is a Protestant system and the financing of that system is an endowment of Protestantism. And Northern Ireland's educational system is, therefore, not only separate and unequal, but probably illegal as well.

The most plausible defence of the legality of the present arrangements is to state that, indeed, the state school system does endow Protestantism, but that the 1920 government of Ireland act in prohibiting the endowment of 'any religion' means any specific denomination; to endow Protestantism is not to endow a specific denomination and is therefore legal. (For an elegant statement of this position see the speech of the Reverend Professor Corkey, Senate **XXX**: 558-63, 4 February 1947.) This, of course, is a rhetorical trick based on the confusion of religious typologies with societal realities. The very existence of Ireland's dual social system provides the best indication of the illusory nature of this argument by showing that the populace, as indicated by behaviour patterns which run through their entire social life, recognises that Protestantism and Catholicism are the two denominations which exist in Ulster; within the context of Ulster society Protestantism is a denomination in the same sense that Catholicism is a denomination, a fact which should not be obscured by the theological sub-categories of Protestant belief.

But why, if the legality of most existing educational provisions in Northern Ireland is open to question, have the arrangements not been challenged in court? It will be recalled that just before the 1930 education act was passed the Catholic Church threatened to take the *de facto* endowment of Protestantism in the state schools to the judicial committee of the United Kingdom privy council, but was dissuaded from doing so by Lord Craigavon's introducing a countervailing endowment for the Catholic schools, namely the fifty per cent grant for capital construction costs of voluntary primary schools. This transaction encapsulates the reasons why neither side has brought litigation against the endowment of religion under the present system; both religious denominations benefit greatly and could only suffer by raising the matter.

All this discussion of the legal aspects of the Northern Ireland educational situation has one important implication for future development: if an attempt is made to introduce a separate-but-equal scheme of education to replace the present separate-and-unequal arrangements, this change should be coupled with a modification of the government of Ireland act in order to prevent the system from being struck down at some future day as *ultra vires* under the terms of that fundamental statute

7 For an analytic discussion and a thorough bibliography of significant studies, see John Harding, Harold Proshansky, Bernard Kutner, and Isidor Chein, 'Prejudice and Ethnic Relations', in Gardner Lindzey and Elliott Aronson (eds), *The Handbook of Social Psychology* (Reading, Mass: Addison-Wesley Publishing Co, second edition, 1969), vol V, pp 1-76.

The reader may be familiar with *The Education of Catholic Americans* by Andrew M. Greeley and Peter H. Rossi (Garden City: Doubleday & Co, Inc, 1968), a questionnaire study produced in response to James B. Conant's charge that Catholic schools in America were 'divisive'. The Greeley and Rossi study produced many insights into the attitudes and behaviour of American Catholics, but it did not (despite the authors' claims) shed any conclusive light on the divisiveness issue. The reason for this failure was that the authors garnered information on Catholic attitudes and on the Catholic education system at one point in time, but did no longitudinal studies over time to determine the effect of the Catholic schools on individual children. Only by conducting carefully controlled longitudinal studies can the actual effect of

the schools (either Catholic or secular) be determined
8 Denis P. Barritt and Charles F. Carter, *The Northern Ireland Problem: A Study in Group Relations* (London: Oxford University Press, 1962), p 56
9 A useful recent article is John Magee's 'The Teaching of Irish History in Irish Schools', reprinted from *The Northern Teacher*, vol X, no 1 (winter 1970)
10 Alan Robinson, 'Education and Sectarian Conflict in Northern Ireland' (unpublished research study, Bishop Grosseteste College of Education, 1970), pp 1-9
11 Ibid, p 10
12 Bernadette Devlin, *The Price of My Soul* (London: Deutsch, 1969; New York: Alfred A. Knopf, 1969), pp 59-69
13 For a discussion of the attributes of belief systems and of their relation to the task of reducing inter-group tensions see Milton Rokeach, *The Open and Closed Mind: Investigations into the Nature of Belief Systems and Personality Systems* (New York: Basic Books Inc, 1960), pp 161-5
14 The results of surveys conducted before the recent disturbances implied that there would be no trouble in obtaining volunteers for integrated schools. The *Belfast Telegraph* commissioned the National Opinion Polls organisation to survey attitudes towards integrated education. These polls, conducted in 1967 and 1968, showed that 69 per cent of the Catholics approved of integrated education. Overall, 64 per cent of adults of both denominations and 65 per cent of youths of both faiths favoured educating Protestant and Catholic children together (Rose, pp 367, 543n). These results are heartening but they should not be overread. In the first place, the survey was taken near the apogee of the era of good feeling between the Ulster denominations and a great deal has happened since then to exacerbate community tensions. Secondly, asking if Protestant and Catholic children should be educated together is a loaded question unless one specifies to the respondent what the social cost of the new arrangements will be. These costs would include an abandonment of many practices previously sanctioned under Ulster's dual social system, plus a rewriting of the curriculum to a bland standard inoffensive to either side, and, most important, the banning of religion from the schools. Thirdly, it should be pointed out that in voicing approval for integrated schooling it was possible for a Protestant to mean

integrated schooling under the control of local government authorities; thus, in many cases the 'tolerant' response affirming the value of integration may actually have been an attack on the independent, denominational Catholic schools

15 It is clear that in the Catholic community there would be strong opposition on religious grounds from the clerical authorities. For a recent study of the Church's opposition to Catholic children attending a non-Catholic-controlled school, in this instance in the New Barnsley estate in Belfast, see articles on 'The Vere Foster Affair' in the *Irish Times*, 17 and 18 June 1971

16 Readers who are familiar with Richard Rose's pioneering work *Governing without Consensus* may conclude that despite all my caution, I am still too optimistic about the influence school integration could have: Rose's study (pp 336-7) revealed that people who had attended integrated schools had only slightly different views on basic political and social issues than did those who had attended segregated schools. Indeed, because there were no social controls in Rose's study for family background or place of geographic origin, it is not yet established that there is *any* difference in attitudes between persons of the same social background and geographic origin which would stem from one group having been to an integrated, the other to a segregated, school.

But given Rose's data there are two reasons for not being immobilised by it. The first is that Rose has made the same methodological error committed by Greeley and Rossi (see above, note 7) in attempting to draw conclusions about change over a period of time, while having collected data at only one point in time. It is one thing to note that there is only a very small correlation between integrated schooling and moderate political and social views and quite another to conclude that 'while attendance at mixed schools tends to reduce Ultra and rebel views, it does so only to a very limited extent'. Only if one has information on the children's attitude *before* they began schooling *and* on other influences upon their developing attitudes *and* upon their attitudes when they finish schooling can one claim to have established what the effects of integration are. Until such a study is conducted, it would be infinitely wiser for everyone concerned with the problem to walk humbly and admit that the question is a speculative one.

Secondly, even if Rose's conclusion were justified by his data (and it is not), it still would not be a compelling argument against experiments in integration. His data are essentially historical, having been produced by the chance mixing of Protestant and Catholic children in Ulster schools at unspecified and uncontrolled times in the past. What is advocated in the text is a set of conscious, well-planned experiments wherein children are integrated with those of the opposite faith in a highly supportive, controlled environment. This, unhappily, has yet to be tried in Northern Ireland

APPENDIX, pp 203-15

1 The figures do not include expenditure for superannuation for teachers and for civil servants.

Through the fiscal year 1924-5 the ministry's accounts included a substantial 'miscellaneous' category, most of whose items should have been allocated to the educational sub-heads. The accounts were regularised in 1925-6 and a precise annual analysis becomes available from then onward.

Although the ministry gave no reason for ceasing to provide a breakdown of expenditure from the parliamentary vote according to educational level after 1947-8, it seems clear that the restructuring of the educational system after the passage of the 1947 act made the old categories inappropriate.

Sources: 1937-8 (p 104), 1947-8 (p 125), 1950-51 (p 97)

2 In 1948-9 and thereafter the ministry's figures became untrustworthy: the figures began to include as local contributions the unspecified amounts local education authorities received from the ministry of health and local government, but did not include as local contributions the amounts payable from local rates under section 105 of the 1947 act.

Sources: 1926-7 (p 108), 1927-8 (p 94), 1928-9 (p 92), 1929-30 (p 82), 1930-31 (p 82), 1931-2 (p 98), 1932-3 (p 78), 1933-4 (p 94), 1934-5 (p 88), 1935-6 (p 85), 1936-7 (p 89), 1937-8 (p 86), 1938-9 (p 94), 1945-6 (p 88), 1946-7 (p 84),

1947-8 (p 107), 1948-9 (p 99), 1949-50 (p 97), 1950-51 (p 89)
3 The table does not include nursery schools but does include special schools.

For the years 1936-8 the average numbers on the rolls given in this table differ slightly from the figures given in Table IV. This is an artifact of the ministry's procedures, not a mistake of the present author's. Probably the difference arose because the ministry during those years ceased including the Haypark Special School in the data from which Table IV is derived but included it in the data from which the present table is derived. There is no way to make a correction because the ministry's files, in which the original data are contained, are under the fifty-year rule.

For 1950 the ministry did not calculate the average number on the rolls for the entire year, but did give a tabulation as of a specific date, namely 31 December. The number in state schools on that day was 98,047, in voluntary schools under statutory committees 8,208, in voluntary schools not under statutory committee 81,736, the total being 187,991.

Sources: 1922-3 (pp 5-6), 1923-4 (pp35, 38), 1924-5 (pp 51, 54), 1926-6 (pp 50-53), 1926-7 (p 69), 1927-8 (p 52), 1928-9 (p 47), 1929-30 (p 38), 1930-31 (p 38), 1931-2 (p 49), 1932-3 (p 28), 1933-4 (p 42), 1934-5 (p 36), 1935-6 (p 32), 1936-7 (p 36), 1937-8 (p 32), 1938-9 (p 38), 1945-6 (pp 28, 98), 1946-7 (p 28), 1947-8 (p 80), 1948-9 (p 40), 1949-50 (p 31), 1950-51 (p 35)
4 The table does not include nursery schools but includes special schools.

Sources: 1922-3 (p 6), 1923-4 (p 38), 1924-5 (p 54), 1925-6 (p 53), 1926-7 (p 126), 1927-8 (p 91), 1928-9 (p 87), 1929-30 (p 77), 1930-31 (p 77), 1931-2 (p 52), 1932-3 (p 31), 1933-4 (p 45), 1934-5 (p 39), 1935-6 (p 35), 1936-7 (p 39), 1937-8 (p 35), 1938-9 (p 41), 1945-6 (p 37), 1946-7 (pp 30, 98), 1947-8 (p 52), 1948-9 (p 42), 1949-50 (p 35), 1950-51 (pp 38, 94)
5 The table does not include nursery schools but includes special schools.

For the year 1935 the number of schools shown in this table is one less than that shown for the same year in Table III, because Haypark Special School was not included in the ministry's tabulation of size-distributions but was included in its summation of schools according to type of management.

Notes 273

Sources: 1923-4 (p 39), 1925-6 (p 54), 1930-31 (p 42), 1935-6 (p 36), 1938-9 (p 42), 1945-6 (p 38), 1950-51 (p 39)

6 The table does not include nursery schools but includes special schools.

Sources: 1922-3 (p 6), 1923-4 (p 41), 1924-5 (p 52), 1925-6 (p 56), 1927-8 (p 53), 1928-9 (p 48), 1929-30 (p 39), 1930-31 (p 39), 1931-2 (p 54), 1932-3 (p 33), 1933-4 (p 47), 1934-5 (p 41), 1935-6 (p 37), 1936-7 (p 41), 1937-8 (p 37), 1938-9 (p 43), 1945-6 (p 39), 1946-7 (p 32), 1947-8 (p 54), 1948-9 (p 44), 1949-50 (p 33), 1950-51 (p 36)

7 The figures are as of mid-November or early December each year.

The terminology of Northern Irish education changed bewilderingly between 1920 and 1950. To clarify the situation Table VII employs headings accurately indicating the kind of schooling involved and does not invoke the confusing titles 'secondary' and 'intermediate' whose meanings changed considerably during the period under study.

Sources: 1922-3 (p 16), 1923-4 (p 49), 1924-5 (p 67), 1925-6 (p 66), 1937-8 (p 103), 1947-8 (p 123)

8 Source: 1950-51 (p 95)

T

Bibliography

This bibliographic commentary is not intended to be a comprehensive listing but to highlight certain aspects of the literature relevant to this study. I hope its selectivity will not be a great inconvenience to the reader; the first time any work is mentioned in any given chapter, a full bibliographical citation is given in the footnotes.

The most striking thing about the historiography of Northern Ireland is how little historical writing of any real quality there is. Despite (or perhaps because of) the great number of recent books by scholars-cum-journalists trying to cash in on the interest stemming from Northern Ireland's civil disturbances, there is as yet no satisfactory general history of Northern Ireland since 1920. Further, there are no biographies of major political figures in Northern Ireland which would be rated as satisfactory by the standards of historical biography as practised elsewhere in the British Isles. The book which comes closest to being a major study, St John Ervine's *Craigavon: Ulsterman* (London: George Allen & Unwin Ltd, 1949) is marred by a lofty refusal to document statements of fact, much less statements of opinion. The absence of useful biographies is not entirely the fault of the professional historians, for the families of Northern Ireland's major figures have been reticent in the extreme about allowing access to their family papers.

Happily, attorneys, geographers, economists, political scientists, and anthropologists have made major studies which are of great value to the historian. A very helpful legal survey is Harry Calvert's, *Constitutional Law in Northern Ireland: A Study in Regional Government* (London: Stevens & Sons Ltd, and Belfast: Northern Ireland Legal Quarterly Inc, 1968). E. Estyn Evans's (ed) *Belfast in its Regional Setting: A Scientific Survey* (Belfast: British Association for the Advancement of Science, 1952) is a geographers' contribution, as is the invaluable *A Social Geog-*

raphy of Belfast by Emrys Jones (London: Oxford University Press, 1960). A lawyer with strong historical interests, Geoffrey J. Hand, has edited the *Report of the Irish Boundary Commission, 1925* (Shannon: Irish University Press, 1969) which contains information on the religious affiliation of the population unavailable elsewhere. *An Economic Survey of Northern Ireland* by K. S. Isles and Norman Cuthbert (Belfast: HMSO, 1957), is a definitive economic treatise. In *The Government of Northern Ireland: Public Finance and Public Services, 1921-64* (Oxford: Clarendon Press, 1965), R. J. Lawrence has used the tools of a political scientist and the instincts of a detective to unravel Northern Ireland's Byzantine financial patterns. Although marred by inaccuracies and inconsistencies, Nicholas Mansergh's *The Government of Northern Ireland: A Study in Devolution* (London: George Allen & Unwin Ltd, 1936) stands as a valuable piece of contemporary political observation. John M. Mogey's *Rural Life in Northern Ireland* (London: Oxford University Press, 1947) is a sophisticated anthropological study. Finally, the pioneering work of a political scientist, Richard Rose, *Governing without Consensus. An Irish Perspective* (London: Faber & Faber Ltd, 1971), bears special notice. It is controversial in the best sense, forcing one to question many of the accepted clichés regarding Ulster life.

Turning now to the educational matters which are the focus of this book, I should note that because of the fifty-year ban which pertains to all Northern Ireland's governmental papers, the manuscript material available for this study was severely limited. As indicated in the footnotes I have used some manuscript material found in the Public Record Office, Belfast, in the National Library of Ireland, Dublin, in the Durham County Record Office and in the Londonderry papers, 'Mount Stewart', Newtownards. In the Public Record Office, Belfast, is a descriptive hand-list of several hundred files which the ministry of education has weeded as irrelevant to its daily operation, but which, nevertheless, are inaccessible to the historian.

Fortunately, much of what the historian loses because of the Ulster government's fifty-year rule on manuscript material is compensated for by the information found in the debates of the Northern Ireland parliament, especially the House of Commons. Debate in the Commons often has reached a remarkably vituperative level and sooner or later most grievances and scandals are amply aired.

The daily newspapers on which I have relied are the *Irish News*, a Catholic paper, and the *Belfast News-Letter*, a Protestant paper, with appropriate caution in each case. The *Times Educational Supplement* and several educational journals also have been consulted in an effort to obtain reports less interwoven with political controversy than are those of Northern Ireland's daily press.

A number of unpublished theses deserve note: George I. Dent, 'The Law of Education in Northern Ireland and the Influence of English Law' (PhD, University of London, 1965); John F. Harbinson, 'A History of the Northern Ireland Labour Party, 1891-1949' (MSc, Queen's University, Belfast, 1966); Rosemary L. Harris, 'Social Relations and Attitudes in a N. Irish Rural Area—Ballygawley' (MA, University of London, 1954); Thomas Kirk, 'The Religious Distributions of Lurgan with Special Reference to Segregational Ecology' (MA, Queen's University, Belfast, 1967); Thomas J. McElligott, 'Intermediate Education and the Work of the Commissioners, 1870-1922' (MLitt, Trinity College, Dublin, 1969); Patrick F. McGill, 'The Senate in Northern Ireland, 1921-62' (PhD, Queen's University, Belfast, 1965); John W. Musson, 'The Training of Teachers in Ireland from 1811 to the Present Day' (PhD, Queen's University, Belfast, 1955); Alan Robinson, 'A Social Geography of the City of Londonderry' (MA, Queen's University, Belfast, 1967); William R. Spense, 'The Growth and Development of the Secondary Intermediate School in Northern Ireland since the Education Act of 1947' (MA, Queen's University, Belfast, 1959).

I am grateful to the authors of the following unpublished papers for generously providing me with copies: 'Educational Finance' (prepared for Belfast Education Authority, *c* 1961) by A. A. Dickson; 'Educational Reform and the Realities of Irish Politics in the Early Twentieth Century' (presented to the American Historical Association, 30 December 1969) by David W. Miller; 'Education and Sectarian Conflict in Northern Ireland' (research study, Bishop Grosseteste College of Education, 1970), by Alan Robinson.

Among studies in the public domain, the most useful general survey of Irish educational history is Norman Atkinson's *Irish Education: A History of Educational Institutions* (Dublin: Allen Figgis, 1969). I have discussed the Victorian background in *The Irish Education Experiment: The National System of Education in the Nineteenth Century* (London: Routledge &

Kegan Paul, and Toronto: University of Toronto Press, 1970), a précis of which, entitled 'National Education and the Realities of Irish Life, 1831-1900', is found in *Eire-Ireland*, vol IV, no 4 (winter 1969), pp 42-51.

Of the handful of works focused directly upon education in Northern Ireland, Robert Harbinson's semi-fictionalised account of his childhood experiences during the wartime evacuation, *Song of Erne* (London: Faber & Faber Ltd, 1960) is especially charming. *The History of the Royal Belfast Academical Institution, 1810-1960* (Belfast: for the Royal Belfast Academical Institution by William Mullan & Son Ltd, 1959) is a first-rate institutional history. An indispensable article for understanding the 1923 education act is 'Public Education in Northern Ireland. The New System', written by the Marquess of Londonderry, *Nineteenth Century and After*, vol XCV, no 565 (March 1924), pp 328-34. 'The Teaching of Irish History in Irish Schools', by John Magee, has recently been reprinted from *The Northern Teacher*, vol X, no 1 (winter 1970).

An excellent introduction to the Catholic view of Ulster's educational history is J. J. Campbell's *Catholic Schools: A Survey of a Northern Ireland Problem* (Belfast: Fallons Educational Supply Co, *c* 1964). Less discriminating is William Conway's *Catholic Schools* (Dublin: Catholic Communications Institute of Ireland, 1971). Of course, no study of the Catholic Church's attitudes would be possible without reference to the relevant edition of *Codex Juris Canonici*.

The most consistently useful periodical relating to Catholic attitudes is the *Irish Ecclesiastical Record*. The following *Record* articles are especially revealing: 'Pastoral Address issued by the Archbishops and Bishops of Ireland to their flocks on the occasions of the Plenary Synod held in Maynooth', 5 series, vol XXX, no 11 (November 1927), pp 526-44; 'Pastoral Address of the Irish Bishops on the Managership of Catholic Schools', 4 series, vol IV, no 367 (July 1898), pp 75-8; 'Pronouncement of the Irish Hierarchy at a General Meeting held at Maynooth on Tuesday, January 27th', 5 series, vol XV, no 2 (February 1920), pp 150-52; 'Statement of the Standing Committee of the Irish Bishops on the Proposed Education Bill for Ireland', 5 series, vol XIV, no 12 (December 1919), pp 504-7; 'Statements of the Bishops on Educational Reconstruction in Northern Ireland', 5 series, vol LIX, no 5 (May 1945), pp 347-53. The following articles from the *Irish Educational Review* are of value: 'Catholic Clerical Managers'

Association, Meeting of Central Council', vol II, no 10 (July 1909), pp 629-32; 'Control of Primary Education in Ireland', vol I, no 12 (September 1908), pp 729-36.

Fortunately for the historian the Protestant bodies have published regular journals of their proceedings. Each year during the period under study the Church of Ireland published the *Journal* of its General Synod, and also the *Annual Report of the Representative Church Body laid before the General Synod*. Similarly, each year the Presbyterian Church made public both the *Minutes of the General Assembly*, and the *Annual Reports to the General Assembly*. No mention of sources on Protestant activities would be complete without reference to William Corkey's extraordinary *Episode in the History of Protestant Ulster, 1923-47* (Belfast: privately printed, nd). At once a primary and a secondary source, this account has numerous defects, but blandness is not among them.

Many secondary works contain material on educational matters. Even the most selective list should include: Denis P. Barritt and Charles F. Carter, *The Northern Ireland Problem: A Study in Group Relations* (London: Oxford University Press, 1962); John W. Blake, *Northern Ireland in the Second World War* (Belfast: HMSO, 1956); Bernadette Devlin, *The Price of My Soul* (London: Deutsch, 1969; New York: Alfred A. Knopf, 1969); M. W. Dewar, John Brown, and S. E. Long, *Orangeism: A New Historical Appreciation* (Belfast: Grand Orange Lodge of Ireland, 1967); and Martin Wallace, *Northern Ireland. Fifty Years of Self-Government* (Newton Abbot: David & Charles, 1971).

Finally, I am listing below the official government publications which bear on education. In this case a list is more useful than a commentary because, unlike the official publications of the United Kingdom, those of Northern Ireland are not bound in standardised, indexed sets; I hope the list will be useful to others working in the field. For reasons of space the annual reports of the ministry of education and of the Belfast education committee are not listed individually.

OFFICIAL PUBLICATIONS OF NORTHERN IRELAND

County Borough of Belfast, *The Belfast Book: Local Government in the City and County Borough of Belfast* (Belfast: R. Carswell & Son Ltd, 1929)

County Borough of Belfast, Belfast Education Committee, *Annual Report for the Year 1924* and following

Government of Northern Ireland, *Correspondence Between the Ministry of Education and the Armagh Regional Education Committee on the Subject of Bible Instruction in Transferred Schools* [Cmd. 84] (Belfast: HMSO, 1928)

Government of Northern Ireland, *Disturbances in Northern Ireland* [Cmd. 532] (Belfast: HMSO, 1969)

Government of Northern Ireland, *Education Bill (Northern Ireland), 1946* (Belfast: HMSO, 1946)

Government of Northern Ireland, *Education Bill (Northern Ireland). Explanatory Memorandum by the Minister of Education* [Cmd. 242] (Belfast: HMSO, 1946)

Government of Northern Ireland, *Educational Reconstruction in Northern Ireland* [Cmd. 226] (Belfast: HMSO, 1944)

Government of Northern Ireland, *Higher Education in Northern Ireland* [Cmd. 475] (Belfast: HMSO, 1965)

Government of Northern Ireland, *Ulster Year Book, 1966-8* (Belfast: HMSO, 1967)

Government of Northern Ireland, Committee for Instruction of Unemployed Juveniles, *The Instruction of Unemployed Juveniles* [Cmd. 193] (Belfast: HMSO, 1938)

Ministry of Education, *Attendance of Pupils from Public Elementary Schools at Classes in Manual Instruction (Woodwork) and Domestic Economy (Cookery and Laundry Work) Specially Organised for Such Pupils in Centres of Technical Instruction* (Belfast: HMSO, 1926)

Ministry of Education, *Conditions of Service of Teachers* [Cmd. 243] (Belfast: HMSO, 1946)

Ministry of Education, *The Curriculum of the Secondary (Intermediate) Schools* (Belfast: HMSO, 1967)

Ministry of Education, *Educational Development in Northern Ireland, 1964* [Cmd. 470] (Belfast: HMSO, 1964)

Ministry of Education, *Educational Reconstruction in Northern Ireland: The First Ten Years* (Belfast: HMSO, 1959)

Ministry of Education, *Examinations for Secondary Intermediate (Including Technical Intermediate) Schools* [Cmd. 413] (Belfast: HMSO, 1960)

Ministry of Education, *Final Report of the Departmental Committee on the Educational Services in Northern Ireland* [Cmd. 15] (Belfast: HMSO, 1923)

Ministry of Education, *Final Report of the Departmental Com-*

mittee on the Salaries of Teachers in Public Elementary Schools [Cmd. 50] (Belfast: HMSO, 1925)

Ministry of Education, *First Report of the Committee on the Senior Certificate Examination in Grammar Schools* [Cmd. 297] (Belfast: HMSO, 1949)

Ministry of Education, *Interim Report of the Departmental Committee on the Educational Services in Northern Ireland* [Cmd. 6] (Belfast: HMSO, 1922)

Ministry of Education, *Interim Reports of the Departmental Committee on the Salaries of Teachers in Public Elementary Schools* [Cmd. 48] (Belfast: HMSO, 1925)

Ministry of Education, *List of Books in History, Citizenship and Economics, Approved for Use in Public Elementary Schools for the School Year 1936-7 and for the School Years Following* (Belfast: HMSO, 1936)

Ministry of Education, *Local Education Authorities and Voluntary Schools* [Cmd. 513] (Belfast: HMSO, 1967)

Ministry of Education, *Memorandum in Regard to the Transfer of Public Elementary Schools to Education Authorities under Section 14 of the Education Act (Northern Ireland), 1923* (Belfast: HMSO, 1923)

Ministry of Education, *Minute, Dated the 19th May 1922, Appointing and Constituting the Committee for the Training of Teachers for Northern Ireland* [Cmd. 4] (Belfast: HMSO, 1925)

Ministry of Education, *Primary Education in Northern Ireland: A Report of the Advisory Council for Education* (Belfast: HMSO, 1968)

Ministry of Education, *Public Education in Northern Ireland* (Belfast: HMSO, 1970)

Ministry of Education, *Report of the Committee on the Recruitment and Training of Teachers* [Cmd. 254] (Belfast: HMSO, 1947)

Ministry of Education, *Report of the Committee on the Scholarship System in Northern Ireland* [Cmd. 192] (Belfast: HMSO, 1938)

Ministry of Education, *Report of the Departmental Committee of Enquiry on the Programme of Instruction in Public Elementary Schools* [Cmd. 136] (Belfast: HMSO, 1931)

Ministry of Education, *Report of Inquiry into the Architects Department of the Down County Regional Education Committee* (Belfast: HMSO, 1935)

Ministry of Education, *Report of the Ministry of Education for the Year 1922-3*, and following

Ministry of Education, *Report of the Primary Schools Programme Committee* (Belfast: HMSO, 1956)

Ministry of Education, *Rules and Schedule Containing the Programme of Intermediate Examinations for 1923* [H.C. 18] (Belfast: HMSO, 1922)

Ministry of Education, *Rules with Regard to Grants and Advances to Secondary Schools and Awards to Students in Respect of the School Year, 1921-2, etc* [Cmd. 3] (Belfast: HMSO, 1922)

Ministry of Education, *Rural Education: A Report of the Advisory Council for Education in Northern Ireland* [Cmd. 300] (Belfast: HMSO, 1951)

Ministry of Education, *Salaries of Teachers in Primary and Secondary Schools* [Cmd. 230] (Belfast: HMSO, 1945)

Ministry of Education, *Salaries of Teachers in Technical Schools* [Cmd. 233] (Belfast: HMSO, 1945)

Ministry of Education, *Salaries of Teachers 1948* [Cmd. 257] (Belfast: HMSO, 1948)

Ministry of Education, *Secondary Schools. School Year 1922-3. Rules* [Cmd. 9] (Belfast: HMSO, 1923)

Ministry of Education, *Second Report of the Committee on the Senior Certificate Examination in Grammar Schools* [Cmd. 282] (Belfast: HMSO, 1950)

Ministry of Education, *Selection of Pupils for Secondary Schools: Third Report* [Cmd. 419] (Belfast: HMSO, 1960)

Index

For Product Safety Concerns and Information please contact our EU
representative GPSR@taylorandfrancis.com Taylor & Francis Verlag GmbH,
Kaufingerstraße 24, 80331 München, Germany

Printed and bound by CPI Group (UK) Ltd, Croydon, CR0 4YY
11/04/2025
01843992-0001